KESSLER

SHAPING
SOUTHERN
SOCIETY

SHAPING
SOUTHERN
SOCIETY
THE COLONIAL EXPERIENCE

edited by **T. H. BREEN**
Northwestern University

New York · **OXFORD UNIVERSITY PRESS** · 1976

for Susan, Sarah, and Bant

PREFACE

Shaping Southern Society brings together thirteen essays on the changing character of social relations in England's southern colonies in Mainland America. Survey courses in early American history have frequently slighted the experiences of southern colonists simply because there was no adequate paperback on this topic for the instructor to assign. This book meets that need. It would serve equally well, however, in courses dealing with the history of the South or the development of American race relations.

The editor elected to focus the book almost exclusively upon three major plantation societies, Maryland, South Carolina, and Virginia, and, within these societies, to examine first the processes by which men and women from Africa and Europe transferred fragments of their cultures to the New World and, second, the ways in which they then patterned social relations over the course of almost two centuries. By achieving an appreciation of these developments, the student will gain a richer understanding of the political institutions and economic practices described in textbooks and lectures.

Because of the need to keep this collection as short as possible, the footnotes have been eliminated. For the most part these references directed the reader to specific primary and secondary sources, and in those few cases in which a note deals with substantive matters, it has been incorporated in the text. Any student interested in pursuing particular topics covered in this book or discovering how historians handle different kinds of evidence should search out the journals and monographs from which these selections were taken.

I wish to thank the Northwestern University Research Committee for a grant to defray duplicating and clerical expenses. I am also indebted to Stephen Harper, a graduate student in economics at Northwestern, who served as my research assistant, and to Stephen Foster, George Fredrickson, and Stephen Innes. Professor Peter Wood of Duke University provided helpful suggestions at several stages of this project, and the entire experience was made much more enjoyable than it might otherwise have been by the enthusiastic cooperation of Nancy Lane, history editor for the college department of Oxford University Press. One of the greatest pleasures of putting this book together was working with the contributors, all of whom responded to my letters with alacrity and encouragement.

T. H. Breen

Evanston, Illinois
April 1976

CONTENTS

INTRODUCTION
Creating Cultural Interdependencies

The essays in this collection investigate the ways in which people of different racial and social backgrounds interacted in the New World, to create what anthropologists have termed cultural "interdependencies." In each plantation society discussed here—Maryland, South Carolina, and Virginia—large numbers of African and European migrants participated in the formation of complex new societies. Each group brought with it knowledge of a culture left behind, sets of values, beliefs, and norms that had patterned the ways in which men and women formed families, worked in the fields, and dealt with people who were physically or culturally different from themselves. Whenever possible these colonists, both black and white, drew upon their former experiences, to preserve what was familiar.

But the newcomers soon discovered that in the rich, expansive environment of these Southern colonies they would be forced to make cultural adjustments. In the rush to produce large profits from the land, some Europeans gained control over the lives and labors of other whites, many Indians, and most Africans. Within this exploitive agricultural system, the culture of both the Native Americans and the African-Americans suffered far greater strains than did that of the Europeans, but no group was free of the influence of the other two. However much they may have held each other in contempt, they were constantly brought together in work and commerce; and on the self-contained tobacco and rice plantations especially, blacks and whites came regularly into face-to-face contacts in which their cultural interdependencies were defined and tested.

Colonial historians are engaged in an effort to understand better the effects of migration upon the lives of the men and women who moved to America. The subject is extraordinarily complex. Even the English settlers came from strikingly diverse backgrounds. There simply was no uniform English heritage, no standard cultural baggage that English migrants inevitably brought to the colonies. A man's expectations about life in America were shaped by the specific region within the mother country from which he came and the social class to which he belonged, as well as by the timing of his departure from his homeland. The far-reaching social changes taking place within the mother country between the reigns of Elizabeth I and George III continually modified the system of values that people of their times carried to the New World. The culture of an emigrant heading for Virginia in 1607 was not the same as that of one going to South Carolina in 1680 or to Georgia in 1750.

It is considerably more difficult to ascertain the cultural backgrounds of African migrants. Historians who have tried to do so, however, have uncovered significant cultural variations within West Africa, and one day we may be able to discuss the relations between

African customs and behavior patterns among black colonists with far greater precision than is presently possible. Certainly, few people still believe that the trauma of enslavement or the terrors of the trans-Atlantic crossing stripped African-Americans of a meaningful cultural heritage.

The degree to which distinct Old World customs and beliefs, whether African or European, survived in the New World is only one of the concerns of the first group of readings in our collection. These essays not only examine assumptions about the social relations and work patterns that the settlers brought with them, but also raise questions as to how adequately these assumptions prepared the colonists to meet the demands placed upon them by their new environment.

Once the African and European migrants arrived in the Southern colonies, they were forced to interact with persons of other races and backgrounds. In so doing, they developed attitudes about men and women of other cultures, established patterns of race relations, and institutionalized certain forms of prejudice that still plague our society today. It is tempting to regard these processes as having been in some manner inevitable, to assume that once white adventurers armed with capital, eager for profits, and desperate for laborers came into contact with Africans and Native Americans, there was bound to be a struggle for mastery in which the Indians and blacks would lose out. We know that the English settlers invariably thrust the various local tribes aside, and whenever an Indian resisted, he was murdered or shipped out of the colonies as a slave. The steady degradation of black people, a process repeated in each of the mainland plantation settlements, is an equally well known and unhappy story.

To discuss the history of colonial race relations in this manner, however, misses the critical point that throughout the period the relations between races changed. Indeed, the development of racial attitudes was full of subtleties and contradictions, and in each colony a sorting-out process took place in which race relations were loosely defined. The enslavement of blacks and the extermination of Indians seems inevitable only to one who is armed with hindsight. The racial views of the dominant white planters were not simply the product of notions formed before migration and then carried whole into the New World. Equally important in this process of working out the character of cultural contacts were such diverse factors as the success of the Indians on the battlefield, the rate of African migration to the New World, and the discovery of a new staple crop such as rice. The second section of the book focuses upon these shifting patterns of race relations, paying close attention to the ways in which specific day-to-day experiences on the frontier and plantation shaped racial interdependencies. As a group these five articles underscore the fact that anyone who hopes to comprehend the complexities of cultural interaction in the Southern colonies must examine not only what the colonists said and wrote about race relations but also how members of the several races actually behaved in each other's presence.

In the final section we turn our attention to the attributes of the successful white planters of the Carolinas and the Chesapeake who dominate the pages of Southern colonial history. These men operated the great rice and tobacco plantations, controlled local politics, and determined the character of parish churches. The diaries, letters, and essays surviving from these years usually came from their pens; their homes still provide visitors with a sense of what plantation life was like for such families as the Byrds, Carters, and Lees. The rise of a few planters to the top of colonial society is a complex story. As the essays of this third section make clear, the road to social dominance was full of setbacks and uncertainties. A succession of poor crops, a hostile royal governor, or a run of unexpected deaths could retard a family's progress. Throughout most of the seventeenth century, membership in the planter elite changed regularly; new men suddenly achieved prominence, others dropped out of the mainstream. To maintain power over a long period of time required a concentrated combination of ambition, hard work, and good fortune.

The danger for the social historian is not in slighting the importance of these leading planters, but in crediting them with too great a part in the shaping of Southern societies. Their attainment of social and economic dominance must be analyzed in the context of the total society in which they lived. The center of their lives was the plantation, a self-contained, frequently isolated unit of commercial agricultural production. It was here that planters first learned and then practiced the social roles expected of men of their class. In regular face-to-face contacts with slaves and servants they had to demonstrate physical and mental toughness mixed with paternal compassion. The man who failed in plantation management never earned the full respect of other members of white society; and without this respect he might not win his neighbors' votes for the colonial legislature, or the patronage of more powerful planters.

The third section also examines the large number of colonial whites whose life-style was entirely different. Economically insecure, victims of an unusually high mortality rate, seldom able to purchase slaves, they viewed the great planters from afar at formal ceremonial occasions. When the local gentry filed into the parish church or provided treats at county elections, the poorer whites formed the audience. For the most part, they deferred to their social betters; yet, as time passed, some of these humbler planters developed distinct cultural patterns that were to challenge those of the colonial leaders. While the extent of such cultural diversity need not be exaggerated, the existence of obvious social strains, especially in Virginia on the eve of the American Revolution, should persuade us that Southern white society was not always the cohesive structure that it has sometimes been characterized.

One last point must be stressed. "The South" is a term often abused by colonial historians. The word suggests the existence of a monolithic culture, a unified society in which the great majority of the people accept the same values and customs. But such was obviously not the case during the colonial period. Before the American Revolution few English settlers south of Pennsylvania thought of themselves as "Southerners." Indeed, beyond a tenuous allegiance to Great Britain, they articulated no meaningful sense of common identity. They shared no cultural symbols, no myths about a common past. African-Americans and Native Americans, of course, followed their own cultural patterns. Because of this diversity, terms like "the South" and "Southern" must be employed with caution. In this collection of essays they refer not exclusively to European-American settlers or to the leading planters of colonial Virginia, but to everyone living in the region regardless of race, background, or class.

I
TRANSFERRING
CULTURES
TO THE
NEW WORLD
EXPECTATIONS and REALITIES

English men and women moved to the Southern colonies for a variety of personal reasons. Some, like Captain John Smith, were professional adventurers. Others sincerely hoped to convert the Indians to Christianity or, as in the case of Maryland, to establish a sanctuary in which Catholics could worship without fear of persecution. A small number simply wanted to escape from bad debts and ill-chosen spouses—the kind that one colonial official described as "unruly gallants packed thether [Virginia] by their friends to escape il destinies." But most people who crossed the Atlantic in the seventeenth century were no doubt lured by stories of economic opportunity. During the early years of settlement, official propagandists in every Southern colony painted glowing pictures of the possibilities for instant wealth that awaited immigrants to the New World. In his "True Relation of the State of Virginia" (1616), for example, John Rolfe rhetorically pitied England's hard-working farmers who barely managed to make ends meet when—if they would only move to Virginia—"they may have ground for nothing, more than they can manure, reap more fruits and profits with half the labours." And in 1622 another Virginian, ignoring a recent defeat at the hands of the Indians, announced confidently that "any laborious honest man may in a short time become rich in this Country."

The dream of riches easily obtained was a powerful magnet to the New World. Unfortunately for the early planters, the Southern colonies yielded no gold or silver, no precious stones, no short route to the Orient. Whatever wealth this sector of the New World offered came from the land in the form of tobacco and rice—and, as the colonists soon discovered, commercial agriculture in this fertile, well-watered region required large numbers of laborers who could perform the constant round of tedious tasks necessary to produce marketable crops.

Whatever the difficulties, the prospects of economic gain were generally sufficient to persuade some men with capital and connections to move to the colonies. Such "adventurers" obtained large tracts of land conveniently located on river frontage, and, through a mechanism of land distribution known as the headright system, they added from fifty to a hundred acres to their holdings every time they transported another person (usually a servant or slave) to the New World. After the mid-seventeenth century, the leading Chesapeake planters consisted increasingly of ambitious younger sons of prominent landed and merchant families in England, and the most successful of these used their contacts in the mother country to great personal advantage.

Such well-connected people were the exception, however. The majority of white migrants arrived in the Southern colonies as indentured servants. While still in the mother country these men and women signed contracts committing them to work for a stated number of years in return for the costs of transportation, food, clothing, and shelter in America. As historians of Maryland and Virginia have discovered, most of these people had been middling sorts, predominantly artisans and yeomen. They were certainly not recruited from England's lowest classes, for, contrary to popular myth, impoverished laborers and hardened criminals rarely took passage on ships bound for the colonial South. While we do not possess much information on their specific backgrounds—for example, from what parts of the mother country they were drawn—we know that the seventeenth-century servants tended disproportionately to be male and young, usually in their late teens or early twenties. Because mortality rates in the colonial South were high, far higher than in contemporary New England, many indentured servants died before attaining freedom. Moreover, in early Virginia some masters exploited their servants unmercifully and in at least one notorious case revealed their indifference to their servants' humanity by using them as stakes in games of chance. Despite such degrading experiences, a few white servants eventually became small planters, and a very few even rose to the highest ranks of colonial society.

What kind of culture did these people—the independent planters as well as the indentured servants—carry to the New World? What was their system of values? What do we know about their English background or about the way they viewed social relations, family structure, and governing institutions? Unfortunately these questions cannot be answered with certainty. No doubt, most of them subscribed to the dominant English values, a body of constitutional, familial, and religious beliefs that they translated into action whenever possible. Perry Miller, a leading intellectual historian, held that early seventeenth-century Virginians were recruited from those English who were "pious, hard-working, middle-class, accepting literally and solemnly the tenets of Puritanism—original sin, predestination, and election—who could conceive of the society they were erecting in America only within a religious framework." Other scholars, although not denying the importance of Calvinist Protestantism in the seventeenth-century South, have stressed the influence of English legal and political precedents in shaping institutional behavior. Wesley Frank Craven, who has written extensively on the development of this region, observes that Chesapeake migrants brought "their identification with the traditions of Common Law, a decentralized system of local administration, and parliamentary usages of government."

While such general beliefs certainly affected the character of

Southern societies, so too did the values of particular subcultures. The immigrants partook of the evolving dominant culture of the mother country, but they also carried specific ideas, norms, and assumptions formed in such places as rural Kent and urban London. Moreover, many of the white settlers pouring into the Southern colonies came not from England but from France, Ireland, and Switzerland, and thus became the transmitters of different systems of values.

Whatever their expectations, English colonists of all types quickly learned that the transfer of their traditional culture to the New World was bound to be imperfect. The Chesapeake region was not Kent, London, or Yorkshire. Life everywhere in the colonial South placed unexpected demands upon the migrants, forcing them to modify imported ideas, values, and norms, and to develop patterns of behavior that helped them first to survive and eventually to flourish in an unfamiliar environment.

In his essay "The Labor Problem at Jamestown, 1607–18," Edmund S. Morgan examines the ways in which a particularly famous—perhaps infamous—group of migrants attempted to transfer English culture to America. Using techniques sometimes employed by cultural anthropologists, Morgan asks why, contrary to what we would consider common sense, these first Virginians obstinately refused to work. Why were they apparently unwilling to plant the food necessary to ward off starvation? Earlier historians have suggested that these colonists were simply a bad lot. According to this interpretation, early Jamestown contained far too many gentlemen who because of an inflated sense of their social status refused to engage in menial physical labor.

Morgan, however, argues that the colonists' indolence can be traced to causes more complex than the earlier scholars imagined. Indeed, these settlers turn out not to have been inordinately lazy but, rather, men whose unspoken assumptions on the nature of work had been shaped by distinctive elements within Jacobean culture. Morgan analyzes such elements, pointing out that while the first Virginians were ill prepared to perform the kinds of work required of them in the New World, their values predisposed them to regard field work as something rightfully done by dependent laborers. Although at this time there were not enough of such workers available, it does not require a great effort of imagination to understand why later Virginians holding similar values enslaved masses of African immigrants without scruple or reflection.

We know a good deal about the social environment that produced some of seventeenth-century Virginia's most prominent families.

Many of these people had been members of distinct subcultures within the mother country before moving to America. Peter Laslett examines one of these subcultures in detail. He explains how the gentry of Kent, who sent many of its younger sons to the Chesapeake region, developed over a long period a set of assumptions about social relations within an area that Laslett calls the "county community." If English town and country dwellers of this period felt a sense of political loyalty toward anything beyond a few local institutions, it was probably to a county community rather than to the English nation as a whole.

Within each county community a network of interrelated gentry families usually stood between the king and his subjects. The gentry dominated local political affairs, drilled the militia, sat on the quarter courts, and served in Parliament. If the monarch alienated these powerful families, he lost effective contact with thousands of ordinary Englishmen. The gentry could not of course transfer the entire structure of their county community to the New World, but the experiences of migrating gentry sons in the mother country convinced them that they possessed the responsibility for political and social control over their humbler neighbors and an obligation to resist outside threats to the independence of the county community of Virginia.

In his contribution, "The English Sugar Islands and the Founding of South Carolina," Richard S. Dunn describes a different type of cultural transfer—the movement of a people from an established plantation colony to an unsettled frontier, specifically that of Barbadian settlers into the coastal region that became South Carolina. These men and women undoubtedly considered themselves representatives of a general English culture; and while their claim would have been in part correct, their system of values also reflected their unusual experiences on an overcrowded, multiracial Caribbean island, a social environment quite unlike any that the gentry of Kent would have known. By the 1660s the Barbadians had developed an elaborate plantation system based predominantly upon slave labor. As Dunn points out, although racial slavery would certainly have appeared in South Carolina without encouragement from the Barbadians, their presence may well have speeded up the process.

There are other aspects of cultural transfer you may want to consider. Beyond accelerating black enslavement, did the Caribbean background affect the character of South Carolina society? In what ways did the Kentish gentry differ from the Barbadian sugar planters? How long do you think the values of a particular subculture such as those brought to South Carolina by the Barbadians shaped general patterns of behavior with that colony? In other words, is the founding of a colony a process of experimentation having no significant relation to the subsequent history of that society, or do the actions and assumptions of the first settlers—the Jamestown group, for example—influence cultural patterns after the founders have died?

The difficulties in studying the cultural backgrounds of African migrants to the colonial South are immense. Perhaps it is to evade these difficulties that some historians have posited a general African background, a body of West African customs and beliefs supposedly common to the majority of black settlers. But such an approach works no more satisfactorily with the African background than it does with the European background. As is pointed out by Sidney W. Mintz, an anthropologist who has examined closely the transfer of cultures to the Caribbean islands, "An emphasis on common African traditions inevitably oversimplifies to some extent the unusual complexity of pre-slavery West African societies and cultures, and cannot but produce a synthetic, somewhat unconvincing vision of Africa itself." Moreover, most Africans arrived in the New World as slaves, and the arbitrary institutions that governed their lives restricted their opportunities of preserving a particular cultural heritage.

In his essay, "Acculturation among the Gullah Negroes," William R. Bascom recognizes the difficulties confronting anyone attempting to work out the relation between specific African customs and the behavior of African-Americans in the colonial South. Bascom, an anthropologist, selects as his subject the Gullah, an isolated group of blacks who settled along the Georgia and South Carolina coast. He rejects out of hand the idea that Gullah customs can be explained simply by reference to European culture. Although white institutions had an enormous impact upon the transmission of West African cultures to the Southern colonies and destroyed totally many elements of that heritage, Gullah work patterns and assumptions about friendship reveal clearly the survival of several distinctly African traditions. As you read this article, you may want to give further consideration to Bascom's statement, "It is now recognized that the differences in the general pattern of the cultures of Africa and Europe were not great." How would you compare the attitudes toward work found by Morgan in Jamestown to those of the Gullahs? How would you contrast elements of competition and cooperation in these different cultures?

EDMUND S. MORGAN
The Labor Problem at Jamestown, 1607-18

The story of Jamestown, the first permanent English settlement in America, has a familiar place in the history of the United States. We all know of the tribulations that kept the colony on the point of expiring: the shortage of supplies, the hostility of the Indians, the quarrels among the leaders, the reckless search for gold, the pathetic search for a passage to the Pacific, and the neglect of the crucial business of growing food to stay alive. Through the scene moves the figure of Captain John Smith, a little larger than life, trading for corn among the Indians and driving the feckless crew to work. His departure in October 1609 results in near disaster. The settlers fritter away their time and energy, squander their provisions, and starve. Sir Thomas Gates, arriving after the settlement's third winter, finds only sixty men out of six hundred still alive and those sixty scarcely able to walk.

In the summer of 1610 Gates and Lord La Warr get things moving again with a new supply of men and provisions, a new absolute form of government, and a new set of laws designed to keep everybody at work. But when Gates and La Warr leave for a time, the settlers fall to their old ways. Sir Thomas Dale, upon his arrival in May 1611, finds them at "their daily and usuall workes, bowling in the streetes." But Dale brings order out of chaos. By enlarging and enforcing the

Edmund S. Morgan, "The Labor Problem at Jamestown," *American Historical Review*, 76 (1971):595–611. Copyright © 1971 by Edmund S. Morgan; reprinted by permission.

colony's new law code (the famous *Lawes Divine, Morall and Martiall*) he starts the settlers working again and rescues them from starvation by making them plant corn. By 1618 the colony is getting on its feet and ready to carry on without the stern regimen of a Smith or a Dale. There are still evil days ahead, as the Virginia Company sends over men more rapidly than the infant colony can absorb them. But the settlers, having found in tobacco a valuable crop for export, have at last gone to work with a will, and Virginia's future is assured.

The story probably fits the facts insofar as they can be known. But it does not quite explain them. The colony's long period of starvation and failure may well be attributed to the idleness of the first settlers, but idleness is more an accusation than an explanation. Why did men spend their time bowling in the streets when their lives depended on work? Were they lunatics, preferring to play games rather than clear and plow and plant the crops that could have kept them alive?

The mystery only deepens if we look more closely at the efforts of Smith, Gates, La Warr, and Dale to set things right. In 1612 John Smith described his work program of 1608: "the company [being] divided into tennes, fifteenes, or as the businesse required, 4 hours each day was spent in worke, the rest in pastimes and merry exercise." Twelve years later Smith rewrote this passage and changed the figure of four hours to six hours. But even so, what are we to make of a six-hour day in a colony teetering on the verge of extinction?

The program of Gates and La Warr in the summer of 1610 was no more strenuous. William Strachey described it:

it is to be understood that such as labor are not yet so taxed but that easily they perform the same and ever by ten of the clock have done their morning's work: at what time they have their allowances [of food] set out ready for them, and until it be three of the clock again they take their own pleasure, and afterward, with the sunset, their day's labor is finished.

The Virginia Company offered much the same account of this period. According to a tract issued late in 1610, "the setled times of working (to effect all themselves, or the Adventurers neede desire) [requires] no more pains than from sixe of clocke in the morning untill ten, and from two of the clocke in the afternoone till foure." The long lunch period described for 1610 was also a feature of the *Lawes Divine, Morall and Martiall* as enforced by Dale. The total working hours prescribed in the *Lawes* amounted to roughly five to eight hours a day in summer and three to six hours in winter.

It is difficult, then, to escape the conclusion that there was a great deal of unemployment or underemployment at Jamestown, whether it was the idleness of the undisciplined in the absence of strong government or the idleness of the disciplined in the presence of strong government. How are we to account for this fact? By our standards the situation at Jamestown demanded hard and continuous work. Why was the response so feeble?

One answer, given by the leaders of the colony, is that the settlers included too many ne'er-do-wells and too many gentlemen who "never did know what a dayes work was." Hard work had to wait until harder men were sent. Another answer may be that the Jamestown settlers were debilitated by hunger and disease. The victims of scurvy, malaria, typhoid, and diphtheria may have been left without the will or the energy to work. Still another answer, which has echoed through the pages of our history books, attributed the difficulty to the fact that the settlement was conducted on a communal basis: everybody worked for the Virginia Company and everybody was fed (while supplies lasted) by the company, regardless of how much he worked or failed to work. Once land was distributed to individuals and men were allowed to work for themselves, they gained the familiar incentives of private enterprise and bent their shoulders to the wheel. These explanations are surely all valid—they are all supported by the testimony of contemporaries—and they go far toward explaining the lazy pioneers of Jamestown. But they do not reach to a dimension of the problem that contemporaries would have overlooked because they would have taken it for granted. They do not tell us what ideas and attitudes about work, carried from England, would have led the first English settlers to expect so little of themselves in a situation that demanded so much. The Jamestown settlers did not leave us the kind of private papers that would enable us to examine directly their ideas and attitudes, as we can those of the Puritans who settled New England a few years later. But in the absence of direct evidence we may discover among the ideas current in late sixteenth- and early seventeenth-century England some clues to the probable state of mind of the first Virginians, clues to the way they felt about work, whether in the Old World or the New, clues to habits of thinking that may have conditioned their perceptions of what confronted them at Jamestown, clues even to the tangled web of motives that made later Virginians masters of slaves.

Englishmen's ideas about the New World at the opening of the seventeenth century were based on a century of European exploration and settlement. The Spanish, whose exploits surpassed all others, had not attempted to keep their success a secret, and by the middle of the sixteenth century Englishmen interested in America had begun translating Spanish histories and memoirs in an effort to rouse their countrymen to emulation. The land that emerged from these writings was, except in the Arctic regions, an Eden, teeming with gentle and generous people who, before the Spanish conquest, had lived without labor, or with very little, from the fruits of a bountiful nature. There were admittedly some unfriendly exceptions who made a habit of eating their more attractive neighbors; but they were a minority, confined to a few localities, and in spite of their ferocity were scarcely a match for Europeans armed with guns. Englishmen who visited the New World confirmed the reports of natural abundance. Arthur Barlowe, for example, reconnoitering the North Carolina coast for Walter Raleigh, observed that "the earth bringeth foorth all things in aboundance, as in the first creation, without toile or labour," while the people were "most gentle, loving, and faithfull, void of all guile, and treason, and such as lived after the manner of the golden age. . . ."

English and European readers may have discounted the more extravagant reports of American abundance, for the same authors who praised the land often gave contradictory accounts of the hardships they had suffered in it. But anyone who doubted that riches were waiting to be plucked from Virginia's trees had reason to expect that a good deal might be plucked from the people of the land. Spanish experience had shown that Europeans could thrive in the New World without undue effort by exploiting the natives. With a mere handful of men the Spanish had conquered an enormous population of Indians in the Caribbean, Mexico, and Peru and had put them to work. In the chronicles of Peter Martyr Englishmen learned how it was done. Apart from the fact that the Indians were naturally gentle, their division into a multitude of kingdoms, frequently at odds with one another, made it easy to play off one against another. By aiding one group against its enemies the Spaniards had made themselves masters of both.

The story of English plans to imitate and improve on the Spanish strategy is a long one. It begins at least as early as Francis Drake's foray in Panama in 1572–73, when he allied with a band of runaway slaves to rob a Spanish mule train carrying treasure from Peru across the isthmus to Nombre de Dios on the Caribbean. The idea of joining with dissident natives or slaves either against their Spanish masters or against their wicked cannibalistic neighbors became an important ingredient in English plans for colonizing the New World.

Martin Frobisher's experiences with the Eskimos in Baffin Land and Ralph Lane's with the Indians at Roanoke should perhaps have disabused the English of their expectations; but they found it difficult to believe that any group of natives, and especially the noble savages of North America, would fail to welcome what they called with honest pride (and some myopia) the "gentle government" of the English. If the savages first encountered by a colonizing expedition proved unfriendly, the thing to do was to make contact with their milder neighbors and rescue them from the tyranny of the unfriendly tribe, who must be their enemies and were probably cannibals to boot.

The settlers at Jamestown tried to follow the strategy, locating their settlement as the plan called for, near the mouth of a navigable river, so that they would have access to the interior tribes if the coastal ones were hostile. But as luck would have it, they picked an area with a more powerful, more extensive, and more effective Indian government than existed anywhere else on the Atlantic Coast. King Powhatan had his enemies, the Monacans of the interior, but he felt no great need of English assistance against them, and he rightly suspected that the English constituted a larger threat to his hegemony than the Monacans did. He submitted with ill grace and no evident comprehension to the coronation ceremony that the Virginia Company arranged for him, and he kept his distance from Jamestown. Those of his warriors who visited the settlement showed no disposition to work for the English. The Monacans, on the other hand, lived too far inland (beyond the falls) to serve as substitute allies, and the English were thus deprived of their anticipated native labor.

They did not, however, give up their expectations of getting it eventually. In 1615 Ralph Hamor still thought the Indians would come around "as they are easily taught and may by lenitie and faire usage . . . be brought, being naturally though ingenious, yet idlely given, to be no lesse industrious, nay to exceed our English." Even after the massacre of 1622 Virginians continued to dream of an Indian labor supply, though there was no longer to be any gentleness in obtaining it. Captain John Martin thought it better to exploit than exterminate the Indians, if only because they could be made to work in the heat of the day, when Englishmen would not. And William Claiborne in 1626 invented a device (whether mechanical or political is not clear) that he claimed would make it possible to keep Indians safely in the settlements and put them to work. The governor and council gave him what looks like the first American patent or copyright, namely a three-year monopoly, to "have holde and enjoy all the benefitt use and profitt of this his project or inventione," and they also assigned him a recently captured Indian, "for his better experience and tryall of his inventione."

English expectations of the New World and its inhabitants died hard. America was supposed to be a land of abundance, peopled by natives who would not only share that abundance with the English but increase it under English direction. Englishmen simply did not envisage a need to work for the mere purpose of staying alive. The problem of survival as they saw it was at best political and at worst military.

Although Englishmen long remained under the illusion that the Indians would eventually become useful English subjects, it became apparent fairly early that Indian labor was not going to sustain the founders of Jamestown. The company in England was convinced by 1609 that the settlers would have to grow at least part of their own food. Yet the settlers themselves had to be driven to that life-saving task. To understand their ineffectiveness in coping with a situation that their pioneering descendants would take in stride, it may be helpful next to inquire into some of the attitudes toward work that these first English pioneers took for granted. How much work and what kind of work did Englishmen at the opening of the seventeenth century consider normal?

The laboring population of England, by law at least, was required to work much harder than the regimen at Jamestown might lead us to expect. The famous Statute of Artificers of 1563 (re-enacting similar provisions from the Statute of Laborers of 1495) required all laborers to work from five in the morning to seven or eight at night from mid-March to mid-September, and during the remaining months of the year from daybreak to night. Time out for eating, drinking, and rest was not to exceed two and a half hours a day. But these were injunctions not descriptions. The Statute of Laborers of 1495 is preceded by the complaint that laborers "waste much part of the day . . . in late coming unto their work, early departing therefrom, long sitting at their breakfast, at their dinner and noon-meat, and long time of sleeping after noon." Whether this statute or that of 1563 (still in effect when Jamestown was founded) corrected the situation is doubtful. The records of local courts show varying efforts to enforce other provisions of the statute of 1563, but they are almost wholly silent about this provision, in spite of the often-expressed despair of masters over their lazy and negligent laborers.

It may be said that complaints of the laziness and irresponsibility of workmen can be met with in any century. Were such complaints in fact justified in sixteenth- and early seventeenth-century England? There is some reason to believe that they were, that life during those years was characterized by a large amount of idleness or underemployment. The outstanding economic fact of the sixteenth and early seventeenth century in England was a rapid and more or less steady rise in prices, followed at some distance by a much smaller rise in wages, both in industry and in agriculture. The price of provisions used by a laborer's family rose faster than wages during the whole period from 1500 to 1640. The government made an effort to narrow the gap by requiring the justices in each county to readjust maximum wages at regular intervals. But the wages established by the justices reflected their own nostalgic notions of what a day's work ought to be worth in money, rather than a realistic estimate of what a man could buy with his wages. In those counties, at least, where records survive, the level of wages set by the justices crept upward very slowly before 1630.

Wages were so inadequate that productivity was probably impaired by malnutrition. From a quarter to a half of the population lived below the level recognized at the time to constitute poverty. Few of the poor could count on regular meals at home, and in years when the wheat crop failed, they were close to starvation. It is not surprising that men living under these conditions showed no great energy for work and that much of the population was, by modern standards, idle much of the time. The health manuals of the day recognized that people normally slept after eating, and the laws even prescribed a siesta for laborers in the summer time. If they slept longer and more often than the laws allowed or the physicians recommended, if they loafed on the job and took unauthorized holidays, if they worked slowly and ineffectively when they did work, it may have been due at least in part to undernourishment and to the variety of chronic diseases that undernourishment brings in its train.

Thus low wages may have begot low productivity that in turn justified low wages. The reaction of employers was to blame the trouble on deficiencies, not of diet or wages, but of character. A prosperous yeoman like Robert Loder, who kept close track of his expenses and profits, was always bemoaning the indolence of his servants. Men who had large amounts of land that they could either rent out or work with hired labor generally preferred to rent because labor was so inefficient and irresponsible.

Even the division of labor, which economists have customarily regarded as a means of increased productivity, could be a source of idleness. Plowing, for example, seems to have been a special skill—a plowman was paid at a higher rate than ordinary farm workers. But the ordinary laborer's work might have to be synchronized with the plowman's, and a whole crew of men might be kept idle by a plowman's failure to get his job done at the appropriate time. It is difficult to say whether this type of idleness, resulting from failure to synchronize the performance of related tasks, was rising or declining; but cheap, inefficient, irresponsible labor would be unlikely to generate pressures for the careful planning of time.

The government, while seeking to discourage idleness through laws requiring long hours of work, also passed laws that inadvertently discouraged industry. A policy that might be characterized as the conservation of employment frustrated those who wanted to do more work than others. English economic policy seems to have rested on the assumption that the total amount of work for which society could pay was strictly limited and must be rationed so that everyone could have a little, and those with family responsibilities could have a little more. It was against the law for a man to practice more than one trade or one craft. And although large numbers of farmers took up some handicraft on the side, this was to be discouraged, because "for one man to be both an husbandman and an Artificer is a gatheringe of divers mens livinges into one mans hand." So as not to take work away from his elders, a man could not independently practice most trades until he had become a master through seven years of apprenticeship. Even then, until he was thirty years old or married, he was supposed to serve some other master of the trade. A typical example is the case of John Pikeman of Barking, Essex, a tailor who was presented by the grand jury because he "being a singleman and not above 25 years of age, does take in work of tailoring and works by himself to the hindrance of other poor occupiers, contrary to the law."

These measures doubtless helped to maintain social stability in the face of a rapid population increase, from under three million in 1500 to a probable four and a half million in 1640 (an increase reflected in the gap between wages and prices). But in its efforts to spread employment so that every able-bodied person would have a means of support, the government in effect discouraged energetic labor and nurtured the workingman's low expectations of himself. By requiring masters to engage apprentices for seven-year terms and servants (in agriculture and in most trades) for the whole year rather than the day, it prevented employers from hiring labor only when there was work to be done and prevented the diligent and effective worker from replacing the ineffective. The intention to spread work is apparent in the observation of the Essex justices that labor by the day caused "the great depauperization of other labourers." But labor by the year meant that work could be strung out to occupy an unnecessary amount of time, because whether or not a master had enough work to occupy his servants they had to stay and he had to keep them. The records show many instances of masters attempting to turn away a servant or apprentice before the stipulated term was up, only to have him sent back by the courts with orders that the master "entertain" him for the full period. We even have the extraordinary spectacle of the runaway master, the man who illegally fled from his servants and thus evaded his responsibility to employ and support them.

In pursuit of its policy of full employment in the face of an expanding population, the government often had to create jobs in cases where society offered none. Sometimes men were obliged to take on a poor boy as a servant whether they needed him or not. The parish might lighten the burden by paying a fee, but it might also fine a man who refused to take a boy assigned to him. To provide for men and women who could not be foisted off on unwilling employers, the government established houses of correction in every county, where the inmates toiled at turning wool, flax, and hemp into thread or yarn, receiving nothing but their food and lodging for their efforts. By all these means the government probably did succeed in spreading employment. But in the long run its policy, insofar as it was effective, tended to depress wages and to diminish the amount of work expected from any one man.

Above and beyond the idleness and underemployment that we may blame on the lethargy and irresponsibility of underpaid labor, on the failure to synchronize the performance of related tasks, and on the policy of spreading work as thinly as possible, the very nature of the jobs to be done prevented the systematic use of time that characterizes modern industrialized economies. Men could seldom work steadily, because they could work only at the tasks that could be done at the moment; and in sixteenth- and seventeenth-century England the tasks to be done often depended on forces beyond human control: on the weather and the seasons, on the winds, on the tides, on the maturing of crops. In the countryside work from dawn to dusk with scarcely an intermission might be normal at harvest time, but there were bound to be times when there was very little to do. When it rained or snowed, most farming operations had to be stopped altogether (and so did some of the stages of cloth manufacture). As late as 1705 John Law, imagining a typical economy established on a newly discovered island, assumed that the persons engaged in agriculture would necessarily be idle, for one reason or another, half the time.

To be sure, side by side with idleness and inefficiency, England exhibited the first signs of a rationalized economy. Professor J. U. Nef has described the many large-scale industrial enterprises that were inaugurated in England in the late sixteenth and early seventeenth centuries. And if the development of systematic agricultural production was advancing less rapidly than historians once supposed, the very existence of men like Robert Loder, the very complaints of the idleness and irresponsibility of laborers, the very laws prescribing hours of work all testify to the beginnings of a rationalized economy. But these were beginnings only and not widely felt. The laborer who seemed idle or irresponsible to a Robert Loder probably did not seem so to himself or to his peers. His England was not a machine for producing wool or corn. His England included activities and pleasures and relationships that systematic-minded employers would resent and that modern economists would classify as uneconomic. At the opening of the seventeenth century, England was giving him fewer economic benefits than she had given his grandfathers so that he was often ready to pull up stakes and look for a better life in another county or another country. But a life devoted to more and harder work than he had known at home might not have been his idea of a better life.

Perhaps we may now view Jamestown with somewhat less surprise at the idle and hungry people occupying the place: idleness and hunger were the rule in much of England much of the time; they were facts of life to be taken for granted. And if we next ask what the settlers thought they had come to America to do, what they thought they were up to in Virginia, we can find several English enterprises comparable to their own that may have served as models and that would not have led them to think of hard, continuous disciplined work as a necessary ingredient in their undertaking.

If they thought of themselves as settling a wilderness, they could look for guidance to what was going on in the northern and western parts of England and in the high parts of the south and east. Here were the regions, mostly wooded, where wastelands still abounded, the goal of many in the large migrant population of England. Those who had settled down were scattered widely over the countryside in isolated hovels and hamlets and lived by pasture farming, that is, they cultivated only small plots of ground and ran a few sheep or cattle on the common land. Since the gardens required little attention and the cattle hardly any, they had most of their time to themselves. Some spent their spare hours on handicrafts. In fact, they supplied the labor for most of England's minor industries, which tended to locate in pasture-farming regions, where agriculture made fewer demands on the inhabitants, than in regions devoted to market crops. But the pasture farmers seem to have offered their labor sporadically and reluctantly. They had the reputation of being both idle and independent. They might travel to the richer arable farming regions to pick up a few shillings in field work at harvest time, but their own harvests were small. They did not even grow the wheat or rye for their own bread and made shift to live in hard times from the nuts and berries and herbs that they gathered in the woods.

Jamestown was mostly wooded, like the pasture-farming areas of England and Wales; and since Englishmen used the greater part of their own country for pasture farming, that was the obvious way to use the wasteland of the New World. If this was the Virginians' idea of what they were about, we should expect them to be idle much of the time and to get grain for bread by trading rather than planting (in this case not wheat or rye but maize from the Indians); we should even expect them to get a good deal of their food, as they did, by scouring the woods for nuts and berries.

As the colony developed, a pasture-farming population would have been quite in keeping with the company's expectation of profit from a variety of products. The Spaniards' phenomenal success with raising cattle in the West Indies was well known. And the proposed employment of the settlers of Virginia in a variety of industrial pursuits (iron works, silk works, glass works, shipbuilding) was entirely fitting for a pasture-farming community. The small gardens assigned for cultivation by Governor Dale in 1614 will also make sense: three acres would have been far too small a plot of land to occupy a farmer in the arable regions of England, where a single man could handle thirty acres without assistance. But it would be not at all inappropriate as the garden of a pasture farmer. In Virginia three acres would produce more than enough corn to sustain a man for a year and still leave him with time to make a profit for the company or himself at some other job—if he could be persuaded to work.

Apart from the movement of migrant workers into wastelands, the most obvious English analogy to the Jamestown settlement was that of a military expedition. The settlers may have had in mind not only the expeditions that subdued the Irish but also those dispatched to the European continent in England's wars. The Virginia Company itself seems at first to have envisaged the enterprise as partly military, and the *Lawes Divine, Morall and Martiall* were mostly martial. But the conception carried unfortunate implications for the company's expectations of profit. Military expeditions were staffed from top to bottom with men unlikely to work. The nucleus of sixteenth-century English armies was the nobility and the gangs of genteel ruffians they kept in their service, in wartime to accompany them into the field (or to go in their stead), in peacetime to follow them about as living insignia of their rank. Work was not for the nobility nor for those who wore their livery. According to the keenest student of the aristocracy in this period, "the rich and well-born were idle almost by definition." Moreover they kept "a huge labor force . . . absorbed in slothful and parasitic personal service." Aside from the gentlemen retainers of the nobility and their slothful servants the military expeditions that England sent abroad were filled out by misfits and thieves whom the local constables wished to be rid of. It was, in fact, government policy to keep the able-bodied and upright at home and to send the lame, the halt, the blind, and the criminal abroad.

The combination of gentlemen and ne'er-do-wells of which the leaders at Jamestown complained may well have been the result of the company's using a military model for guidance. The Virginia Company was loaded with noblemen (32 present or future earls, 4 countesses, 3 viscounts, and 19 barons). Is it possible that the large number of Jamestown settlers listed as gentlemen and captains came from among the retainers of these lordly stockholders and that the rest of the settlers included some of the gentlemen's personal servants as well as a group of hapless vagabonds or migratory farm laborers who had been either impressed or lured into the enterprise by tales of the New World's abundance? We are told, at least, that persons designated in the colony's roster as "laborers" were "for most part footmen, and such as they that were Adventurers brought to attend them, or such as they could perswade to goe with them, that never did know what a dayes work was."

If these men thought they were engaged in a military expedition, military precedent pointed to idleness, hunger, and death, not to the effective organization of labor. Soldiers on campaign were not expected to grow their own food. On the other hand they *were* expected to go hungry often and to die like flies even if they never saw an enemy. The casualty rates on European expeditions resembled those at Jamestown and probably from the same causes: disease and undernourishment.

But the highest conception of the enterprise, often expressed by the leaders, was that of a new commonwealth on the model of England itself. Yet this, too, while it touched the heart, was not likely to turn men toward hard, effective, and continuous work. The England that Englishmen were saddled with as a model for new commonwealths abroad was a highly complex society in which the governing consideration in accomplishing a particular piece of work was not how to do it efficiently but who had the right or the duty to do it, by custom, law, or privilege. We know that the labor shortage in the New World quickly diminished considerations of custom, privilege, and specialization in the organization of labor. But the English model the settlers carried with them made them think initially of a society like the one at home, in which each of them would perform his own special task and not encroach on the rights of other men to do other tasks. We may grasp some of the assumptions about labor that went into the most intelligent planning of a new commonwealth by considering Richard Hakluyt's recommendation that settlers include both carpenters and joiners, tallow chandlers and wax chandlers, bowyers and fletchers, men to rough-hew pike staffs and other men to finish them.

If Jamestown was not actually troubled by this great an excess of specialization, it was not the Virginia Company's fault. The company wanted to establish at once an economy more complex than England's, an economy that would include not only all the trades that catered to ordinary domestic needs of Englishmen but also industries that were unknown or uncommon in England: a list of artisans the company wanted for the colony in 1611 included such specialists as hemp planters and hemp dressers, gun makers and gunstock makers, spinners of pack thread and upholsterers of feathers. Whatever idleness arose from the specialization of labor in English society was multiplied in the New World by the presence of unneeded skills and the absence or shortage of essential skills. Jamestown had an oversupply of glassmakers and not enough carpenters or blacksmiths, an oversupply of gentlemen and not enough plowmen. These were Englishmen temporarily baffled by missing links in the economic structure of their primitive community. The later jack-of-all-trades American frontiersman was as yet unthought of. As late as 1618 Governor Argall complained that they lacked the men "to set their Ploughs on worke." Although they had the oxen to pull them, "they wanted men to bring them to labour, and Irons for the Ploughs, and harnesse for the Cattell." And the next year John Rolfe noted that they still needed "Carpenters to build and make Carts and Ploughs, and skilfull men that know how to use them, and traine up our cattell to draw them; which though we indeavour to effect, yet our want of experience brings but little to perfection but planting Tobacco."

Tobacco, as we know, was what they kept on planting. The first shipload of it, sent to England in 1617, brought such high prices that the Virginians stopped bowling in the streets and planted tobacco in them. They did it without benefit of plows, and somehow at the same time they managed to grow corn, probably also without plows. Seventeenth-century Englishmen, it turned out, could adapt themselves to hard and varied work if there was sufficient incentive.

But we may well ask whether the habits and attitudes we have been examining had suddenly expired altogether. Did tobacco really solve the labor problem in Virginia? Did the economy that developed after 1618 represent a totally new set of social and economic attitudes? Did greater opportunities for profit completely erase the old attitudes and furnish the incentives to labor that were needed to make Virginia a success? The study of labor in modern underdeveloped countries should make us pause before we say yes. The mere opportunity to earn high wages has not always proved adequate to recruit labor in underdeveloped countries. Something more in the way of expanded needs or political authority or national consciousness or ethical imperatives has been required. Surely Virginia, in some sense, became a success. But how did it succeed? What kind of success did it have? Without attempting to answer, I should like very diffidently to offer a suggestion, a way of looking ahead at what happened in the years after the settlement of Jamestown.

The founders of Virginia, having discovered in tobacco a substitute for the sugar of the West Indies and the silver of Peru, still felt the lack of a native labor force with which to exploit the new crop. At first they turned to their own overpopulated country for labor, but English indentured servants brought with them the same haphazard habits of work as their masters. Also like their masters, they were apt to be unruly if pressed. And when their terms of servitude expired— if they themselves had not expired in the "seasoning" that carried away most immigrants to Virginia—they could be persuaded to continue working for their betters only at exorbitant rates. Instead they struck out for themselves and joined the ranks of those demanding rather than supplying labor. But there was a way out. The Spanish and Portuguese had already demonstrated what could be done in the New World when a local labor force became inadequate: they brought in the natives of Africa.

For most of the seventeenth century Virginians were unable to compete for the limited supply of slaves hauled across the ocean to man the sugar plantations of the Americas. Sugar was a more profitable way to use slaves than tobacco. Moreover, the heavy mortality of newcomers to Virginia made an investment in Africans bound for a lifetime more risky than the same amount invested in a larger number of Englishmen, bound for a term that was likely to prove longer than a Virginia lifetime.

But Virginians continued to be Englishmen: the more enterprising continued to yearn for a cheaper, more docile, more stable supply of labor, while their servants loafed on the job, ran away, and claimed the traditional long lunch hour. As the century wore on, punctuated in Virginia by depression, discontent, and rebellion, Virginia's position in the market for men gradually improved: the price of sugar fell, making it less competitive with tobacco; the heavy mortality in the colony declined, making the initial outlay of capital on slaves less risky; and American and European traders expanded their infamous activities in Africa. The world supply of slaves, which had fallen off in the second quarter of the seventeenth century, rose sharply in the third quarter and continued to rise.

With these developments the Virginians at last were able to acquire substitute natives for their colony and begin, in their own English way, to Hispanize Virginia. By the middle of the eighteenth century Africans constituted the great majority of the colony's entire labor force. This is not to say that plantation slavery in Virginia or elsewhere can be understood simply as a result of inherited attitudes toward work confronting the economic opportunities of the New World. The forces that determined the character of plantation slavery were complex. But perhaps an institution so archaic and at the same time so modern as the plantation cannot be fully understood without taking into consideration the attitudes that helped to starve the first settlers of the colony where the southern plantation began.

PETER LASLETT
The Gentry of Kent in 1640

Students of history are liable to assume that the entity "England" has existed at all points in her past in roughly the same way as she exists in their present—not the same England of course, but the same sort of phenomenon, corresponding to a strictly similar social and political reality, apprehended in the same sort of way by contemporaries. When they read statements about any period, they tend to feel confident that the word "England" is one that can be taken for granted, as representing something self-evident or something which can easily be explained in terms of geography and political history.

It was pointed out by Maine in his *Ancient Law* in 1861 that "the principle of local contiguity is a first principle of developed political society." By this he meant that the higher political organizations are not simply logical categories, such as "all men descended from the same ancestor," or "all men accepting the same religious revelation," but are based on the acceptance of the fact of neighbourhood, the fact that all men live as part of a group of other men selected simply by the chance that they live in the same area. It is not necessary to accept Bosanquet's claim that "the neighbourhood is an ethical idea" in order to recognize that political scientists perpetually neglect this type of association because of their preoccupation with associations which do correspond to logical categories.

It is clear that "England" at any period is more than an association

Peter Laslett, "The Gentry of Kent in 1640," *Cambridge Historical Journal*, 9 (1948):148–74. Reprinted by permission of Peter Laslett.

of individuals in the same logical category. It must also be a "neighbourhood" covering the whole area of the country. It is more difficult to decide how this community of the whole country is related to the neighbourhood in the narrower sense, the sense in which it may be defined as that complex of associations which makes a man feel at home in his own locality. It is important to recognize, however, that the relationship between these two sorts of community, the community of the locality and the community of the country, must enter into any adequate definition of the word "England," though this relationship is very difficult to define. Which means that the definition of the word "England" for any particular historical present is a task of great complexity: it is not a "given" term and its apprehension is a final achievement of the historian's activity. Such a definition has to take into account every separable influence, local or national, transient or permanent, which mediates between the individual, the group and the society as a whole, and so helps to create political consciousness.

In the middle of the seventeenth century there existed in the form of the communities of county gentry an important intermediary institution of this kind. If the conclusions about the gentry of Kent which are presented here are correct, and if the other counties were generally similar, it is possible to draw the following picture of one of the ways in which the "England" of the historians was constructed in 1640.

Society was dominated by a series of groupings of county gentlemen, locally distinct but interconnected by numerous individual relationships. These county communities were important communities of locality, and mediated between the individual, or such closely knit groups of individuals as the family, and English society as a whole. They were, therefore, a medium of political consciousness: they were units through which political attitudes were formulated and spread about; also instruments through which pressure was brought to bear on government. It was through these organizations that the ruling groups exercised and retained their supremacy and English society at large, or even the English state, sometimes used them for purposes of administrative action. Their political possibilities and practical usefulness are aptly illustrated by what happened at the beginning of the Civil War. There was then both a failure of "governance" at the centre of society and a cleavage within the dominant minority over its whole area. The result was the establishment of County Committees. The administration, recruitment and financing of the hostilities were conducted on a county basis.

But the functions of the county community in 1640 were intellectual and social as well as political and administrative. It was not a mere whimsy which made Thomas Fuller arrange the "Worthies of England" under their counties of origin; this was the conventional method of presenting the intellectual activity of his generation. It was in the county community as well as in London that writer came into contact with writer: the individual thinker, when he was away from the centres of intellectual life, found in its social intercourse those things he would look for to-day in the literary reviews. In at least one instance its intellectual life took on the character of a dispersed university, a university whose professors were Deputy Lieutenants, whose faculty meetings took place at Quarter Sessions and whose research workers found their material in their own boxes of title deeds. For these reasons the intellectual life of the county community conditioned political speculation. This sort of function is normally ascribed exclusively to the universities and to London, especially to the court, the parliament and the Inns of Court. Though the functions of the universities have probably been exaggerated, the genuine source of most of the intellectual activity of the time was certainly in London. Nevertheless, it was the county community which ensured that the country as a whole shared in the intellectual life of the capital, and which interpreted it to individual members of the directive minority. It was here that political opinion, that is the set of beliefs which found expression in the Commonwealth and in the Revolution Settlement, was to be found "at the grassroots."

The county community was held together by blood as well as by class. The genealogical interrelationships between its members were extensive, complicated and meticulously observed by all of them: it is astonishing how distant a connexion qualified for the title "cozen." The reason for this excessive consciousness of kinship was patriarchalism. The unit of the county community at this time was the patriarchal household maintained by each recognized head of an individual family: indeed, full membership of the community tended to be restricted to such "prime and independent heads of families." Patriarchalism and the patriarchal family did more than hold together the county communities: they bound town to country and made possible emigration overseas. The identity of interest and the close integration of the ruling groups of the countryside with the merchant classes of the towns had been a distinguishing feature of English society for many generations before 1640 and it continued for many generations after. It is usually explained exclusively in terms of mutual economic advantage and the social ambition of the urban parvenu which could only be realized by the ownership of land. But it must not be forgotten that, in marrying into a landed family, the heir of a city merchant, whether daughter or son, was submitting to an authoritarian system and entering into a set of relationships which would inevitably involve all the descendants of the marriage. It made them all members of the same county community and submitted cousins and nephews in the cities to the family leadership, and even the domestic authority, of the head of the manorial household in the countryside. Emigration from such a group of interrelated patriarchal families occurred when a rising standard of living gave each of the younger sons an expectation of an establishment on the scale of his elder brother's. It could only take place when opportunities presented themselves and in areas where such opportunities became known. But it would have been less frequent without the inequalities of patriarchal economics.

The analysis of an English county community in 1640 may not tell us why a fighting war about political, social and religious differences became inevitable in 1642. But it can tell us something of how opinion and forces were mobilized and how the revolution was carried out: indeed, it can tell us how anything got done at all in England in the middle of the seventeenth century. Moreover, the evidence thrown up by such an inquiry can help us to explain other movements besides the Civil War. There are two characteristics of English society in this year which may prove to be more important to the world than the tensions which ended in fighting. One is that persistent preoccupation with political speculation which was a dominant trait of intellectual life in England in 1640 and for two generations thereafter. This finally gave us the theoretical presuppositions which now underlie our institutions and those of the whole English-speaking world. The other is that urge to create new societies in its own image, or in the image of its ideal self, which appeared in the self-confident years of Queen Elizabeth, though its first momentous consequences became apparent by about 1640—when the colony of Virginia was beginning to show the characteristics of American society in infancy.

For Noblemen, Knights, Gentlemen, Soldiers, Mariners; Virtuous and beauteous Ladies, and Women of meanest degrees, comely, pretty, proper, handsome, cleanly, neat and honest. Stored with all sorts of Artificers and inhabited with painefull and profitable husbandmen; famous for two most ancient cities (whereof one is the Chiefe Metropolitan seat of England). It hath many faire Market Townes, Impregnable Castles, secure and safe Havens and Harbours for Shipping, abundance of rich villages

and Hamlets: so that by the Almighties blessings and the peoples Industry this (Old Kingdom) County is for Fruit, Fowle, Flesh, Fish, Cloth,
Corne, Wood and Cattle, in all and anything that is for the use of man
to maintaine life and pleasure, Kent is and hath been renowned univer-
sally.

The county community of the gentry of Kent in 1640 was certainly
not of average size, wealth or importance. The briefest reference to
the geography and the history of the county will prove that the Kentish gentry were justified in thinking of themselves as the first in the
kingdom. Their county, to begin with, was for strategic purposes the
key area of the British Isles: it controlled the Thames Estuary, the approaches to London by water, the whole of the Narrow Seas and
the overland routes from the continent. Its rivers and roadways were
studded with castles and strongpoints; on its hilltops were the beacon
lights of the national system of military signals, warning the capital
of threats from abroad: on its coast were the Cinque Ports which
were the centre of the naval organization for the whole realm. It was
obvious that the attitude of the social, political and military leaders
of such a region would always affect the whole of the country. This
was to be clearly illustrated in the Civil War. On two occasions the
Kentish gentry intervened as a body on the side of the Crown. In
March 1642 they went *en masse* to Westminster and presented their
own county petition of grievances: this did much to bring about the
actual taking-up of arms. In May 1648 their sudden and unanimous
revolt in alliance with the Navy brought on the Second Civil War
and almost won it for the imprisoned King.

The gentry of Kent had always been peculiarly closely bound to
the city of London. There was, it is true, a knot of families directly
descended from the feudal magnates of this ancient British kingdom,
and intermarriage had brought the newer families into the same
stream of lineage. But in 1570 the first county historian [William
Lambard] wrote of the first of the English counties: "The gentlemen
be not heere (throughout) of so auncient stockes as else where, especially in the partes neerer to London, from which citie (as it were
from a certeine rich and wealthy seedplot) Courtiers, Lawyers and
Merchants be continually translated and do become new plants
amongst them." The religious, social and economic changes of the
sixteenth century had greatly extended the traditional interchange
between the gentry of Kent and the society of the capital. The monas-
tic lands were extensive, accessible and profitable—admirably suited
to the purpose of the merchant or the lawyer wishing to buy himself
into the landed classes. Kent was an ideal county for the improving

landlord of Tudor times. It had few open fields in the way of the new farming methods and the tradition of consolidated holdings enabled the landlords to fence in and capitalize at will. But the flow of capital and capitalists from London to Kent went parallel with the flow of sons of the manor house taking their portions from Kent to make their fortunes in London. It was the typically Kentish landed family which sent its younger brothers to become higher civil servants at the court in Whitehall, merchants in the City or lawyers in Westminster.

In 1640 the gentry of Kent could look back on two or three generations of increasing prosperity. Their wealth had grown primarily as a function of the expansion of London and the metropolitan area. The texture and fertility of Kentish soil made the county peculiarly fitted to profit from the food needs of a great city. Wheat and cereals of all sorts, fruits new and old, hops, hams and mutton could be supplied swiftly and easily from the rich valleys of the Medway and its tributaries, from the forest of the Weald and from the pastures of Romney Marsh. "Yet their revenues," continues Lambard,

are greater than anywhere else: which thing groweth not so much by the quantitie of their possessions, or by the fertilitie of their soyle, as by the benefitt of the situation of the contrie itself, which hath all that good neighbourhood, that Marc Cato and other olde authors in husbandrie require to a wel placed *graunge,* that is to say the *Sea,* the *River,* a populous *citie,* and a wel traded *highway* by the comodities whereof the superfluous fruites of the grounde be dearly sold, and consequently the land may yield a greater rent.

But their rents were not the only source of their recent access of prosperity. During late Tudor times the Weald, that wide central tract of forest-land which Kent shared with Sussex, began to earn them money on an industrial rather than an agricultural scale. Its timber was wanted for the navy, for the houses of London, for all the many purposes which made timber the basic industry of the Elizabethan economy. Wealden timber was of the right sort and it was accessible to the right sort of buyer, but it was also found in association with the most important deposits of iron ore known to the technology of that age. So rent rolls were reinforced by cash payments for the products of the woodlands and the forges: the floating assets of the gentry grew along with their income from real estate. Everyone in the county felt the warmth of the wealth as it burgeoned. The great lords were richer and the minor gentry more substantial: a yeoman of Kent worth as much as a squire of a northern or a western county.

The strategic and economic importance of the Kentish gentry combined to make of them a classic example of our conventional picture of the squirearchy of Elizabethan and early Stuart England. Their military responsibilities were heavy and during the crises of the sixteenth century it was in Kent that the Tudor system of mobilization for defence had operated most conspicuously. It had kept them in close contact with the Crown, which supervised these activities very carefully. The personal connexion of the royal court with the county community was maintained by residence at the royal palaces of Eltham and Greenwich, by visits to the large and important royal manors and by royal progresses through the county. The expense of these visitations—the elaborate meals, the dramatic entertainments and the sumptuous parting gifts—fell frequently and heavily on the Kentish gentry: so also did their compensations, the knighthoods and the minor places in the royal households. Such characteristics, heavy responsibilities as magistrates, a connexion with the city, the courts of law and the court of the sovereign, have come to be regarded as normal for the English gentry before the Civil War. But it was in the area of the home counties—Hertfordshire, Middlesex, Essex, Kent, Surrey and Sussex—that they were really widespread, and it may be significant that London already dominated the whole region. Kent was associated with all the other five of these counties, but her closest contact was with Essex across the Thames. The understanding between the gentry of Kent and the gentry of Essex made the Second Civil War a serious danger to the victorious Parliament in 1648.

There were features of the Kentish county community, however, which were by no means so conventional. They inherited a cosmopolitan culture from medieval times. The gateway to England with its archiepiscopal see had always been the area first influenced by the continent of Europe, and its gentry the most likely to travel abroad. The nearness of France is quite obvious from the family papers of the time. The English metropolitan see retained some of its international character even in the seventeenth century, and James I preferred the international Protestant scholars Isaac and Meric Casaubon to stalls in Canterbury Cathedral. The passage of ambassadors and of royalty to and from the Channel in itself kept Kentishmen aware of the world outside England, whilst in Canterbury and Sandwich there were communities of Walloons and Huguenots. But it was the nearness of London which made them conscious of events all over England and across the Channel. Many even of the minor families maintained a house in London both for business and for pleasure:

sometimes they described themselves indifferently as of Kent, or as of London, Westminster or Middlesex—wherever their town house happened to be. If there were no family house in the city, a relative amongst the merchants or the lawyers would be there to maintain contacts and to entertain the family. The country houses of Kent knew of what happened in Westminster Hall, in St Stephen's Chapel and at the Court of St James just as soon as it was known in South-wark or Lambeth. Their correspondence is full of letters from their business or professional relatives giving the news of the town: their bookshelves were stuffed with the pamphlets of the time. The great world was no far-off mystery to be talked of, criticized and visited only occasionally. They were in it and of it.

"These gentlemen be also (for the most part) acquainted with good letters," continues Lambard, "and especially trained in the knowledge of the lawes." He was writing at the beginning of a hundred years of striking intellectual activity amongst these county clans. As bevy after bevy of children succeeded each other in their manor houses there sprang up from amongst them a continuous series of authors, not only poets and pamphleteers, but also theologians, mathematicians, geographers, classicists, archaeologists and historians. Some of the more eminent of these literary lines were already active in Lambard's day, the Derings of Surrenden Dering, the Digges of Chilham, the Culpepers of Wigsell and later of Leeds Castle, the Scotts of Scotts Hall. By 1640 we have an impression of a large and flourishing school of gentlemen scholars. It had its own traditions, intellectual and genealogical. Sometimes the intellectual influence followed the succession of son to father or nephew to uncle, but often it passed from manor house to manor house by propinquity and recruited the newly established families as it spread. The intellectual disturbance which followed on the Civil War much intensified this activity, and by 1660 nearly every family in the county community had its own writer. Many of the earlier literary households still persisted, but there were added to them many other surnames. There were the Sandys of Northbourne, the Twysdens of East Peckham, the Knatchbulls of Mersham Hatch, the Weldons of Swanscombe, the Floods, the Marshams, Lovelaces, Wallers, Sedleys, Spensers, Sidneys, Evelyns and Wottons.

The county's representatives in the two parliaments of 1640 were typical. Sir Edward Dering, who was returned for the Long Parliament, was the latest holder of one of the oldest names in the county. There was no one better fitted to represent its numerous antiquarians. He was by nature, social connexion and personal experience a collector of manuscripts and a student of antiquities, but his supporters saw nothing extraordinary in his also being an important administrative and military official, a political and a religious controversialist. He had assembled at his family seat at Surrenden a collection of manuscripts which was one of the most important in the country and comparable with that of his friend Sir Robert Cotton. It was he who, whilst Warden of Dover Castle, had made the ultimate antiquarian's discovery in finding an original copy of Magna Carta. It was he who had joined in 1638 with Sir Christopher Hatton, Sir Thomas Shirley and the great Dugdale a sort of exchange agreement in historical discoveries in the counties of Kent, Northampton and Warwick. Sir Norton Knatchbull, one of those elected for the Short Parliament, represented very aptly another persistent preoccupation of his constituents. He was a lay theologian. Son of a father commended "for his pen and love to learning and antiquities," he was popular for a hundred years for his *Animadversions on the New Testament*. A competent Hebraist, he was typical of a good proportion of his neighbours who formulated their own theological positions independently of the clergy and the Universities. In Parliament Sir Edward Dering displayed the sort of vacillation which a later generation has come to associate with academic politicians, but in this he was decidedly atypical.

Knatchbull's companion as knight of the shire of Kent in the Short Parliament was certainly never guilty of vacillation. Sir Roger Twysden was perhaps the greatest scholar, the acutest thinker and the strongest character of them all, and he certainly showed the most consistent independence and individualism. His achievements as one of the earlier students of English legal and constitutional history have only recently come to be recognized. Sir Roger was in every respect the type of the seventeenth-century scholarly squire. He succeeded a father who had combined his strenuous activity as a county administrator and family politician with wide and miscellaneous private studies: his brother was a Hebraist, he himself the author of a whole series of treatises on theology, English government and constitutional law. He had only to be imprisoned, and this happened often, to write another work—a point which was typical of the mid-seventeenth century. All his life, nevertheless, he was primarily a county administrator and country gentleman.

But the intellectual activity of the county community was not entirely independent of the recognized institutions of education and learning. It owed something to the penetration of a graduate clergy throughout society and it must be remembered that the Dean of

Canterbury was also a member of the magistrates bench at Maidstone. It already owed a great deal more to that peculiar institution of the English church—a married clergy rich enough to educate its children as gentlefolk. The family of Sandys is an apt illustration of both these things, and also of the way in which families from outside the county quickly became established within it. The Sandys already had connexions in the county in Lambard's day, and its first great luminary, Edwin Sandys, Archbishop of York, married a wife from Kent. The Archbishop's own literary reputation came from the important part he took in the translation of the Bishops' Bible and above all from the encouragement he gave to Richard Hooker in his *Ecclesiastical Polity*. He made Hooker the tutor of his two sons, Edwin and George. It was whilst he was training them and writing the last books of his great work that Hooker held the rectory of Bishopsbourne, Kent, where he died. Both these sons were travellers. Edwin inherited his father's position as patron to Hooker, went all over Europe and wrote the much read *Europae Speculum*. George went even further, to Turkey, Palestine and Egypt. All this was published in his *Relation of a Journey* in 1615, but he has a much more important claim to fame as the translator of Ovid. Both brothers, as we shall see, went much further afield in the course of the part they played as Kentish gentlemen. By 1620 the family had acquired the manor of Northborne and were regular members of the county community.

But more notable even than the cosmopolitanism and versatility of the newly established family of Sandys was the persistent succession of writers which came from the ancient stocks of Culpeper and Digges. The Digges hierarchy began with Leonard, the head of his house, who wrote on mathematics, architecture and optics. When he died in 1571 he was recognized as one of the most eminent mathematicians of his day, and his heir Thomas "spent his youngest years, even from the cradle, in the study of liberal sciences." Thomas's mathematical capacities earned him the commendation of Tycho Brahé himself, and his successor in 1595, another Leonard, gained a high reputation as a poet and translator, who wrote in praise of Shakespeare. The succession continued unbroken through Sir Dudley Digges (succeeded in 1635) notable amongst many other things for his *Four Paradoxes of Politiques* and in 1643 it was represented by his son and collaborator, a second Dudley, author of the notorious *Unlawfulnesse of Taking up Armes*. In the same period the Culpepers produced John, noted by Lambard as an author, the well-known Nicholas, astrologer and medical writer, and the two Sir Thomases, father and son, writers on Usury. A member of another of the ancient families, Reginald Scott, wrote a truly remarkable work in 1584 in his *Discoverie of Witchcraft,* the earliest instance of a rational scepticism on this critical subject, and he wrote it because of his experience as a Kentish justice. In 1640 Sir Anthony Weldon was writing his biting records of recent Court History at Swanscombe, whilst at Otham Robert Fludd, the Rosicrucian, was but three years dead. Though their interests were varied, it is clear that it was the subject of the history of their own institutions and their own class which was most seriously studied by the Kentish scholar gentlemen.

The career and influence of William Lambard himself are proof of this. He himself only settled in Kent in the year in which he wrote his *Perambulation* but he founded a county family which has persisted until the present day. His entrance into the community was the occasion of his writing this book, in the same way as later changes of occupation and surroundings occasioned his other works. It was not only the earliest of the County Histories, it was, and is still, in many ways the most valuable. For it is the only volume in the whole series of studies of the English county gentries which includes in the chapter called "The Estate of Kent" a general, comparative analysis of the ruling group as such, its origins, occupations, income and interests. The gentry of Kent, to whom it was dedicated, read it critically, and since they were possessed already of a sense of historical identity, were inspired by it to continue with their own studies. Its popularity is obvious from the fact that it was re-edited in 1596, and from the numerous references to it by Kentish and other antiquaries.

Of even greater importance to them and to the county gentry all over England for two hundred years was Lambard's next work *Eirenarcha,* treating of the office of justice of the peace: it cannot be without significance that it was for the Kentish magistrates that this remarkable standard work of reference on their responsibilities was prepared. Before 1660 the *Perambulation* had been printed again and two further works on Kentish history had appeared, whilst the only other county which had inspired a treatise comparable with Lambard's was Warwickshire (Dugdale, 1656). It is no serious exaggeration to say that English local history was born in Kent in the late sixteenth century, was nurtured by its gentry in the early seventeenth century and nurtured in such a way as to become the point of departure for the whole modern movement in British institutional history.

The personal achievement of Lambard may have had a great deal to do with the fact that the county of Kent became the *locus classicus* for the first historians of British political institutions. Camden—who himself settled in Kent and became one of its gentry—Spelman and Selden, even Prynne and Fuller, all relied heavily on him. But the existence of a whole body of gentry capable of appreciating work such as his and of continuing it by their own independent researches, gave historical scholarship its political importance, and made it a source of constitutional principle and political theory. These men came to the study of "antiquities" with no conception of a "special interest" in some way divorced from their activities as magistrates, as electors and as members of the House of Commons. The study of history was not a "subject," it was a direct response to their situation and grew out of an understandable interest in the rights they had to possess their own land and their concern for the complexion of the government of the day. All their discussions of the rights and wrongs of the constitutional controversy which ended in Civil War were conditioned by their knowledge of the past development not only of the English state but of their own social order, even of their own field boundaries. As the issues grew critical, so the discussion grew hotter and the protagonists went from persuasion by word of mouth to controversy by written treatise. Such treatises had been circulating from hand to hand and manor house to manor house for many years: in 1640 it seems to have been a recognized way of publishing works addressed to those within the community. It was seldom that these manuscripts were printed except after many years of copying and recopying, and then the object was as much to preserve them in durable form as to make them available to a larger public. It was in this way that Sir Robert Filmer made his debut as an author in about 1630 and it was for this purpose that he wrote *Patriarcha*. To be born into one of these families between the years 1570 and 1640 was to be guaranteed the opportunity of developing cosmopolitan and academic interests. But it brought each new son of these houses not only into a circle of historians and authors but also into touch with a world of seafaring adventure, colonial enterprise and the first English-speaking society overseas.

By 1640 all the families we have been talking about were related to each other and to many other families, like the Codds, St Legers, Wyatts, Fleets, Horsemondens, Kemps, Fairfaxes, Dukes, Randolphs and Barhams. In their letters every one is "cosen." Though many of them were comparative newcomers, there had been ample opportunity to form the most complicated interrelationships. By 1660 this group of interrelationships existed in two places in the world; in middle eastern Kent and in Virginia in the area of the James River.

This process, by which an English county society reproduced its names, its attitudes, its literary interests, even its field sports, in the swamps of the Virginia creeks, had begun with the foundation of the Virginia Company of London in 1606. The city relatives of the Essex and Kent gentry—and indeed the gentry themselves in their business capacities—were interested in all the Elizabethan monopolist Adventure Companies. The Virginia Company was just one more opportunity for them to speculate with their floating capital and it opened another arena for their quasi-commercial-and-explorative, quasi-diplomatic activities. The Virginia project was, however, more than a question of the export of goods and services and the creation of a foreign market. It had to begin by the export and settling of men, men who would set up in the tidewater lands of Virginia not simply a "factory," but a new society. The most prominent of the entrepreneurs was the same Sir Edwin Sandys, who had befriended Hooker; his brother George the poet became treasurer of the company and wrote his translation of Ovid in the wilds of Virginia. The chief of the seamen who led the early expeditions, conquered the territory and rooted out Dutch and French competition was of both Essex and Kentish extraction, Admiral Sir Samuel Argall, a type of the Elizabethan seafaring rough. Piratical as he might have been, however, he was closely related to Sir Thomas Wyatt of Allington Castle in the county of Kent, who was the ruling head of the great family of Wyatts, poets, statesmen and rebels, and the colony's first important governor. Prominent also in these early days of desperate casualties and commercial failure was the family of another Kentish poet, Richard Lovelace.

At a meeting of the shareholders of the London Virginia Company in 1619 "it was agreed . . . about a Pattent to be graunted unto sundry Kentishmen, who would seate and plant themselves in Virginia, that they should have as Large priviledges and imunities as is graunted to any other in that kinde." So far as is known, no other group of settlers went out in this way as a county detachment to assist in the struggle against malaria, the Indians and starvation on the banks of the James River. When they arrived they regarded their membership of the county community of Kent as quite unaltered. They were still gentlemen and expected to be treated as such, though they showed no squeamishness about doing the dirty jobs.

The first contribution of the gentry of Kent to the foundation of Virginia was the provision of capital and of pioneers: it was not long, however, before they began to provide settlers. The men who actually carried out the tough task of founding the colony did not always regard themselves as colonists and many of them returned to their manor houses. As time went on, however, and as the colony began to establish itself in the 1620's and the 1630's, the holders of the Company's shares, whether active members or not, began to be attracted by the openings in the landowning profession in the colony. By 1640 settlement in Virginia had begun to be regarded as another opening for the younger son who failed to stay at the university, or for whom there was not enough capital to set up in the city or at the bar. The political and religious struggle which was to come, strengthened the motives for sending them off on this 3000-mile journey. The sons of dispossessed clergy, like the Washingtons, or of families ruined by the Civil War, like the Randolphs, set out to start a new life in the colony very much as did the sons of the Victorian middle classes bound for South Africa or New Zealand. When the King had lost the war a group of his soldiers themselves responded to "Sir William Berkely, the Governor there, who had industriously invited many gentlemen and others thither as to a place of security . . . where they might live plentifully," amongst whom were several Kentishmen, Culpepers, Honeywoods, Brodnaxes.

The analogy of nineteenth-century emigration must not be pressed too far. The young gentleman who set off for Virginia in early Stuart times was no penniless seeker after a fresh start in a freer world. He went complete with capital to stock his plantation and introductions to the important people in the colony, many of whom were his relatives and had been his father's neighbours. He does not seem to have expected to stay in America all his life and his career in the colony was nearly always punctuated by quite lengthy visits home, even though the journey was so lengthy and hazardous. At the family seat he was regarded as much as one of the family as those who had never left. The most interesting feature of the records at this period is that the facts of a man's being abroad was often not mentioned in wills and indentures: it has to be discovered from later documents, often in the colony itself. During his visits home the settler would attend to the business of his patrimony in the county. If he made a will, he could, like other younger sons and even cousins, settle the reversion of his Virginian estate on the head of the family and his heirs. If he married, he would be as likely to choose a member of one of the county families in the neighbourhood of his father's seat in England as would his brothers who remained at home. His bride could come, of course, from the Kentish manor house or its Virginian satellite. The story of the early Virginian planters' families illustrates the most important feature of the English gentry of the time—the immense strength of the family bond and the extraordinary cohesion of the grouping of families by locality. There could be no more vivid illustration of patriarchalism at work. It is quite impossible to single out one strand of surnames from the network of affiliations which grew up as generation succeeded generation. It so happens that the bloc of families in which we are interested became involved in Virginian colonization at the outset. It followed as a simple consequence that the whole network, not an individual strand, should reproduce itself in the colony within a generation.

Such then were the gentry of Kent in 1640. The most characteristic thing they produced was the political thinking of Sir Robert Filmer and the most surprising was the society of the Old South in the United States. There are two further questions which require an answer. One is the extent of the county community geographically. How far did the nexus of families respect the county boundaries? The other is the extent to which the life of the gentry can be said to subsume the other social groupings within the area, the yeomen, for example, or the growing urban proletariat in Canterbury and Maidstone: how far was the community of the gentry *the* community of locality?

The answers to both these questions, in so far as they can be given, tend to destroy the clarity of the picture which has been drawn. It cannot be pretended that there was a decisive line round the county families of Kent, distinguishing them from the rest of their class elsewhere. We have seen how easily newcomers established themselves and how closely the county was bound to the others near London. Intermarriage with people from far more distant parts of the country took place just as often as the restricted opportunities of meeting them would allow. It might be suggested that the useful unit of locality was in fact the home counties and that, through London, they had a far greater unity with each other than each had within itself. Though there is no doubt that such a distinction is historically valuable, it cannot be used to explain away all that is known of the distinctive characteristics of the gentry of Kent. Even if they cannot be defined in logic as a class of individuals, they did comprise at any one time both a series of patriarchal families in their patriarchal households and a series of distinctive intellectual traditions. The names of the families and the content of the traditions, the shape, the size and the texture of the community might vary from year to year. But Kentish letter-writers meant something when they said "the country," meaning their own county, and the Grand Jurymen of gentlemen at the Assizes at Maidstone in 1642 also meant something when they drew up a petition in the name of "the Gentry, Ministers and Commonalty of the County of Kent."

The very phrase used by this Grand Jury raises the question of how the Kentish gentlemen could suppose that they represented all the inhabitants of their county. Once more it cannot be pretended that other sorts of association may not have existed in the county, apart from the association of its social and political leaders. There were Levellers in Kent and there were religious radicals as extreme as anywhere in the kingdom. The men who met on the bench of justices could not claim to take them into account when they talked for the county. Nevertheless it is difficult to see how any other grouping could have made much of a contribution to the political consciousness within this area. The exceptions included the higher urban bourgeoisie, and we have seen that they cannot be regarded as distinct in origin from the country squires. It is possible that the yeomen, those who were not illiterate, might have had a sense of solidarity apart from their economic superiors, but if so there was very little evidence of it. The lower urban bourgeoisie certainly possessed a common consciousness when they found themselves all together in Cromwell's army, but at other times they seem to have acquiesced, or even played their part, in the leadership of the County Committees. The other elements in the community of locality seem to have lacked almost all of the coherence possessed by the community of the gentry.

It would be easier to envisage England in 1640 as an assemblage of county communities like the community of the gentry of Kent if we could be sure that Kent was truly typical of the whole country. Almost all that has been said here seems to point to the fact that it was not. Before statements such as these can be applied with confidence to the whole area of England in that year, something ought to be known of the texture of social life in every one of the English counties. The most obvious of the problems is to establish the real difference in atmosphere between the home counties and the rest of the country.

RICHARD S. DUNN
The English Sugar Islands and the Founding of South Carolina

Everyone who has examined the founding of South Carolina agrees that planters from the West Indies played a major role—some would say a decisive role—in shaping the new colony. The most recent historian of colonial South Carolina, Eugene Sirmans, argues that settlers from Barbados, congregating at Goose Creek a few miles above Charleston, formed the dominant political faction in the first generation of settlement. Sirmans labels the opening section of his book, spanning the years from 1670 to 1712, the age of the Goose Creek men.

Sirmans may exaggerate the prominence of West Indians in early Carolina, but not by much. Agnes Baldwin has just published a list of 684 settlers who came to Carolina between 1670 and 1680. In this list, half the settlers whose place of origin she can identify came from the West Indies. And if we examine the backgrounds of the governors of South Carolina between 1669 and 1737, it turns out that nearly half—eleven out of twenty-three—had lived in the islands or were sons of islanders. Seven of the early Carolina governors had Barbados backgrounds. Hence the Goose Creek men are indeed crucial to our understanding of early South Carolina.

Who were these Goose Creek men? Why did they leave the Caribbean islands at a time when the sugar industry was booming there, in order to face unknown challenges in the Carolina wilderness? What

Richard S. Dunn, "The English Sugar Islands and the Founding of South Carolina," *South Carolina Historical Magazine*, 72 (1971):81–93. Reprinted by permission of Richard S. Dunn and the South Carolina Historical Society.

sort of colonizing expertise did they bring with them from the island colonies? And what social habits did they introduce to Carolina? Such questions have hitherto gone unasked and unanswered, because no one has examined the social structure of the English sugar islands in the late seventeenth century. Now a number of scholars are exploring aspects of Caribbean history which bear directly upon the founding of South Carolina. Many puzzles remain. But I believe that a social analysis of Barbados and Jamaica, circa 1670, does tell us something about the Goose Creek men and the thrust they imparted to South Carolina.

In 1670, the several English island colonies were at quite different stages of development. Barbados was the richest, most highly developed, most populous, and most congested English colony in America, with a thriving sugar industry and 50,000 inhabitants, including 30,000 Negroes. The Leeward Islands of St. Kitts, Nevis, Antigua and Montserrat were considerably less prosperous and well settled than Barbados, though by mainland standards they were very crowded and intensively cultivated. In these four islands the sugar industry was not yet fully developed; most of the Leeward planters were still small farmers with few or no slaves. Jamaica, a far larger place than Barbados or the Leewards, and potentially the most valuable English sugar producer, was in 1670 a raw and boisterous frontier outpost, best known as a buccaneer's lair. The Jamaican sugar industry was growing fast, but most of the land on the island was still untamed jungle. In Bermuda and the Bahamas, by contrast, there was little potential for further growth. Both of these island groups were economically stunted, for they lay too far north for sugar production. Bermuda—the oldest and smallest English colony— was an overcrowded, isolated, bucolic community of small tobacco farmers and fishermen. The Bahaman archipelago sheltered a few squatters who cut braziletto wood and gathered ambergris.

Settlers were drawn to South Carolina from all of these islands during the late seventeenth century. The tie with the Bahamas was especially close, since the Carolina proprietors also governed these islands, or tried to. The Earl of Shaftesbury ordered the ragged island squatters to adopt his pet institutional scheme, the Fundamental Constitutions, but his effort to staff the Bahaman Grand Council with titled manor lords failed even more spectacularly than in South Carolina. Jamaica was of course some distance removed from Carolina, but it sent a number of settlers, including Thomas Pinckney, founder of a famous family, who arrived in 1692 on a Jamaican privateer. Mrs. Baldwin has not been able to uncover many recruits from the Leeward Islands, but I suspect there were a good number. The most notable early arrival from these islands was Sir Nathaniel Johnson, the Jacobite governor of the Leeward Islands, who fled to Carolina after the Glorious Revolution with his gang of 100 slaves and later became governor of South Carolina. But the principal Caribbean migration came from the most distant English island—Barbados.

It was a Barbados planter, Sir John Colleton, who first organized the proprietary group which received a royal charter from Charles II in 1663. Three boatloads of colonists from Barbados tried to plant at Cape Fear from 1665 to 1667, and about twenty Barbadians joined the first permanent South Carolina settlement on the Ashley River in 1670. During the decade of the 1670's, some 175 Barbadians can be identified as coming to the new colony. They brought with them at least 150 servants and slaves. This migration to Carolina was part of a general exodus from the overcrowded little island. One historian [Alfred D. Chandler] reckons that 30,000 white persons moved from Barbados to the other English mainland and island colonies in the thirty years between 1650 and 1680. Such an estimate is certainly inflated. The total out-migration from Barbados during the entire seventeenth century was more likely 10,000—which is still sizable enough! South Carolina was by no means the chief destination for these migrants. In 1679, for instance, at the height of the Carolina migration, 593 white persons obtained tickets to leave Barbados; Only thirty-eight of these people sailed to the Carolinas, many fewer than went to New England or Virginia. But the migration to Carolina was important, nonetheless, because many of the Barbados recruits were people of exceptional energy, experience and wealth.

It is often said that the people who quit Barbados and the other sugar islands were misfits and failures, poor whites who had not done well in the Caribbean, small planters squeezed off their farms by the aggressive big planters, and wage workers unable to compete with black slave labor. I think this picture is distorted at best. In Agnes Baldwin's list, we find a medley of rich and poor colonists moving from the islands to Carolina, a cross section of big and middling sugar planters, merchants, artisans, small farmers, sailors, servants and slaves. To me, the most striking thing is the number of persons of wealth and position who chose to come. And it is also striking to find how many poor whites did *not* leave. Here, the Barbados census of 1680 is an extraordinarily illuminating document. It shows that many thousand poor whites still hung on in Barbados, despite thirty years of out-migration. The great majority of Barbados landholders in 1680 were very small farmers who held a few acres of inferior land and a few slaves apiece. These people were as repressed and voiceless as the submerged laboring class in England. Richard Ligon has a vivid description of the miserable way they lived in Barbados back around 1650, toiling in the sun all day, eating a meager diet of cassava bread, corn meal mush, and salt meat, and cooped up in low-roofed and windowless little houses "like Stoves, or heated Ovens." The Barbados poor whites, he says, were so depressed and sluggish that they lacked the enterprise to open their houses to the refreshing breeze and make themselves comfortable. Such people cannot have been much better off in 1680. They had every reason to leave. But evidently many did not have the gumption to pick up and move to Carolina.

In mid-century Barbados, one of the most progressive-minded planters was a gentleman named Captain Benjamin Middleton. Richard Ligon designed an airy, shady home for him. Two of the Captain's sons, Edward and Arthur, moved to South Carolina in the 1670's and launched a great Carolina dynasty. The Middletons were members of the Barbados ruling caste, the inner circle of some 175 big sugar planters with 60 or more slaves apiece, who held the best land, sold the most sugar, and monopolized the chief offices on the island. Big planters like the Middletons enjoyed privileges in Barbados more tangible than the aristocratic trappings dreamed up by Shaftesbury and Locke in the Fundamental Constitutions of Carolina. Yet we find that representatives from at least eighteen of these preeminent families obtained extensive land grants in South Carolina between 1672 and 1692. Additional Carolina grants went to members of the lesser Barbados gentry, sugar planters with 20 to 60 slaves. Why should these people, who were making more money in the Indies than any North American planters or merchants, be willing to invest in an untracked wilderness 1,500 miles away? After all, the chief Virginia tobacco planters in 1670 took little or no interest in South Carolina.

The explanation, I think, is that the Barbados sugar planters needed fresh avenues for their younger children. They had no expansion room on Barbados. All of the choice land on the island was already partitioned into efficiently sized plantations by 1670, and the marginal land—which they did not want in any case—was all held by the poor whites. In the case of the Middletons, they tried to start new sugar estates in Antigua, and lost heart when the French plundered this island in the 1660's. So Edward and Arthur came to Carolina. These brothers were younger sons. Their elder brother Benjamin stayed in Barbados and operated the main family estate with its 379 acres and 130 slaves, which doubtless remained more valuable for many years than Edward's new plantation called "The Oaks" on Goose Creek.

Not all of the leading Barbados families prospered in South Carolina. Take, for example, the Colletons. Like the Middletons, the Colletons were big Barbados planters who developed extensive interests in South Carolina. Sir John Colleton had been the prime organizer of the Carolina proprietorship. In the 1670's and 1680's, his eldest son Sir Peter became head of the family. Sir Peter Colleton was one of the eight proprietors of Carolina, a member of the Barbados Council, and owner of a large Barbados sugar plantation manned by 180 slaves. Sir Peter could afford the luxury of living in England, leaving the management of his Barbados property to his younger brother Thomas. Though over-shadowed by Sir Peter, Thomas Colleton was a leading figure on the island also; he sat on the assembly, was a colonel of the militia, and a judge on the Barbados bench. A third brother, James Colleton, had no fruitful role in Barbados, and could rise to no office higher than vestryman for the local parish. So he came to Carolina, took out extensive land grants, and served as governor of the colony from 1686 to 1690. But the rambunctious Carolinians rose up in rebellion against James Colleton in 1690 and banished him from the colony. Poor James retreated back to Barbados. At this juncture brother Thomas conveniently died or retired to England, which opened a slot at last for James in Barbados. In 1692 he assumed management of Colleton plantation, and soon took his brother's seat in the Barbados Assembly, doubtless delighted at having escaped so well from South Carolina.

People like the Colletons and Middletons were drawn to Carolina because of its semi-tropical setting, which seemed to combine the advantages of Caribbean agriculture with the wholesome environment of the North American mainland. These island planters must have been convinced, after two generations of experience, that the West Indies were unhealthy for white men. The English islands in the West Indies had an appallingly high mortality rate in the late seventeenth century. Every index confirms this fact. For example, baptismal and burial registers for Barbados in 1678–1679 show that nearly twice as many whites were buried as were baptized on this island during an eighteen month period. Vital statistics are very spotty for Barbados during the seventeenth century, but there is a broken series of baptismal and burial registers for the parish which embraces Bridgetown, the chief port, from 1648 onwards. These

registers corroborate the evidence in the census of 1680 that Bridgetown was an exceptionally sickly community. In good years, three
persons were buried for every one baptized; in bad years, five persons were buried for every one baptized. Out in the Barbados countryside, the birth-death ratio seems to have been more evenly bal-
anced. But the vital statistics we have for two rural parishes in
Jamaica suggest that the white population in these districts became
increasingly unhealthy as the century wore on. At first, in the 1660's
and 1670's, births outnumbered deaths in both parishes, but after
1680 the burials always outnumbered the baptisms, generally by two
to one.

Another—and perhaps rather eccentric—method I have employed
for judging the West Indian mortality rate is to examine the inscrip-
tions on ancient tombstones, to see how old the colonists were when
they died. More than 350 Jamaica and Barbados tombstones for the
years 1670–1750 record the person's age at death. Tomb-counting has
obvious statistical defects. A grave marker in the West Indies was a
status symbol at this time, and the people memorialized were mostly
from the planter or merchant classes. The young and the old were
inadequately represented, the young because their parents generally
did not bother to set up stones for them, the old because they frequently retired to England. Nevertheless, for what it is worth, my
sample shows that these island people died very young. White males
who survived to age twenty, which was half the total number born
at best, died at a median age of forty-five. Females who survived to
age twenty died at a median age of thirty-six. The nine year sex dif-
ferential is grim testimony to the ravages of child-bearing in the
tropics, but the overall sample shows low life expectancy for both
sexes, with scarcely anyone lasting past age seventy.

Because of this crippling death rate, Englishmen in the sugar islands found it difficult to establish a healthy family structure in the
late seventeenth century. The Barbados and Jamaica parish registers
are unfortunately too incomplete to permit the "family reconstitu-
tion" which European demographers practice. It is evident from
these registers that West Indian couples could produce up to a dozen
children, but that they often lost all of their offspring in infancy and
childhood. The Barbados census of 1680 gives a devastating demographic profile of the population of Bridgetown at this date. Family
life in this port town was severely stunted in 1680. One third of the
householders were unmarried or widowed, the majority of householders were childless, and few married couples had more than one
or two living children. I doubt, however, that traditional domestic

patterns were ever so ruptured in the Barbados countryside. We have no solid evidence on this point, however, until 1715, when another census was taken which listed the age and sex of every white person on the island. According to this census, Barbados in 1715 had a very young white population; the median age was nineteen, and only three per cent of the inhabitants had passed their sixtieth birthday. But it was not a growing population, because only half the adults were married, and married couples had small families. There were many widows, widowers, and orphans; also many mulattos, demonstrating widespread miscegenation. On the whole, conditions in Barbados do seem to have improved demographically between 1680 and 1715. The average Barbados family in 1715 had two living children, double the figure for Bridgetown in 1680. But this was still well below the norm for the mainland colonies at this date. It would be interesting to see whether the Barbadians who migrated to South Carolina did in fact live longer, produce more children, and develop a healthier family structure than the colonists who stayed in the sugar islands.

The sugar planters naturally blamed the Caribbean environment for the debilitating diseases and early deaths they suffered. White men, so the argument ran, could not tolerate tropical heat, humidity, and insect life. But the sugar planters might well have blamed themselves. Englishmen who settled in the West Indies during the seventeenth century were not very successful in accommodating themselves to an alien environment. They retained English habits ill-suited to the tropical climate and developed new habits ill-suited to any climate.

It is not altogether easy to reconstruct the life style of the island colonists at the time South Carolina was founded. The sugar planters kept no diaries and left few personal papers. Fortunately, a number of visitors to the islands wrote graphic descriptions of what they saw. A few seventeenth-century houses and bits of furniture survive in Barbados and Jamaica, and the archeological work now in progress at Port Royal, Jamaica, is of capital importance; it will likely uncover a great slice of social data as of 1692 when an earthquake swamped this Jamaican town.

Another approach, which I have attempted, is to examine inventories of estates, compiled for probate purposes. Only scattered early inventories have survived in Barbados and the Leeward Islands. But there are some 800 Jamaican inventories in the Spanish Town archives, spanning the years from 1674 to 1701, which tell a lot about how the typical big planter, small planter, merchant, shopkeeper and artisan lived during these years. Some of these inventoried Jamaican estates are valued at less than £10, others at more than £10,000. Collectively, they differ markedly from late seventeenth-century inventories I have seen or read about in Massachusetts, Pennsylvania and Maryland. In Jamaica, more rich merchants and planters are represented than in the mainland colonies, and they parade their wealth more gorgeously. The Jamaica inventories exhibit a wide contrast between the living habits of the richest and poorest members of the community. Some colonists had a great deal of money and displayed it ostentatiously. Others had none and lived in grinding poverty.

For example, Samuel Long, one of the richest sugar planters in Jamaica, owned 11,000 acres and 288 slaves when he died at age 45. He had two expensively furnished houses, one at his chief plantation and the other at Port Royal. In this town house, the hall was sizable enough to hold sixty chairs and seven tables. In his dining room, Long had a dozen table cloths, twelve dozen napkins, and £76 worth of silver to dress his table. His wardrobe contained garments which cost more individually than the entire household furnishings of a typical small Jamaican farmer. At the opposite extreme, Ebenezer Hicks was a schoolmaster who owned a horse worth £2, furniture worth £1, and a parcel of books worth £1 when he died. He left no clothes, for he was buried in them. The parish owed him two years' back salary.

In most Jamaican inventories, large and small, Negro slaves were the chief asset. Five per cent of the people in the sample owned sixty or more slaves; these were the big sugar planters. But on the other hand, seventy per cent held at least one slave. Almost all the Jamaican farmers whose estates were inventoried, many of them very poor men, owned Negroes. The rich Jamaicans kept some Negroes for show rather than work, dressing them up in livery and assigning them ceremonial tasks. A Port Royal clergyman complained in 1687 that "a cooper's wife shall go forth in the best flowered silk and richest silver and gold lace that England can afford, with a couple of Negroes at her tail." Nearly ten per cent of these Jamaicans owned Indian slaves, used for hunting wild game and fishing. This helps explain why the Caribbean colonists, when they moved to Carolina, quickly developed an active Indian slave trade. South Carolina has the distinction of enslaving many more Indians than any other mainland colony.

The contrast between the eating habits of the upper and lower classes in the sugar islands was tremendous. The black slaves and white servants ate a monotonous and meager diet of corn, plantains, cassava bread, and—if they were lucky—salt fish and salt meat. They got drunk on rum every weekend. Members of the master class dined richly and drank copiously every day of the week. The main repast was mid-day dinner as in England, though this is a very hot time of day for heavy eating in the tropics. Dinner and after-dinner drinking lasted four or five hours if company was present. Roast meats, pies and custards, the diet of the upper class back home in England, dominated the planter's menu. In the cool of the evening at Port Royal, the merchants gathered at the taverns to eat cheese cake, tarts, creams, custards and sillabub, made as precisely as possible after the recipes of London pastry cooks. Nearly every planter kept a lusty bowl of cold rum punch ready on his table to accommodate friends and visitors, but since rum was considered a common and coarse drink, the island elite preferred to drink madeira and brandy. Around 1700 a Barbados planter described the annual Cockney feast, celebrated by all the island gentry born within the sound of Bow Bell in London. The company breakfasted on plum broth, marched to church for a sermon, and repaired to an elaborately decorated hall where they were summoned to dinner by twelve trumpeters. Each course of the banquet was punctuated by a toast and a volley of twenty-five guns! The more tenacious members of the party were still toasting and firing guns at midnight.

In short, the sugar planters ate too much heavy food for their own good, their servants and slaves ate too little, and everyone drank too much.

In clothing style as in dietary habits, the English refused to accept tropical realities. The late seventeenth century was a period when extremely elaborate costume was fashionable at home, and island ladies with money spent it on wired headdresses, corsets, bustles, layers of petticoats, and luxuriously textured skirts which trailed the ground. The island gentlemen sported periwigs, full-skirted coats, embroidered waistcoats and sleeves, flowing cravats, and beribboned knee breeches. The Jamaica inventories show that the shops of Port Royal were amply stocked with cases of flowered silk, boxes of lace, white kid gloves, beaver hats, silk hose, laced pumps, and leather fans. The islanders favored clothing made of linen, silk or calico, but many of their suits and cloaks were made of wool. Little of this clothing was given to the slaves, who went almost naked. Male Negroes generally wore drawers, and females wore skirts. The white servants wore much the same costume as agricultural laborers at home, including Monmouth caps, which being brimless, cannot have provided much protection from the sun. The wealthy planters and their wives wished to keep their complexions as white as possible, in contrast to their black-skinned slaves and red-necked servants. Consequently, they wore hoods or broad-brimmed hats, neckcloths, stockings and gloves. With all this ostentatious overdressing, the island elite probably suffered more from the humid heat than did their servants and slaves.

As with food and clothing, so with housing. Nearly all of the early buildings in the English islands have been obliterated by storms and fires, but we can tell from descriptions and inventories that the rich sugar planters built elaborate dwellings, sumptuously furnished. Visitors late in the century always described them as constructed "in the English style" or "after the English manner." This meant using brick or stone in preference to wood and plaster, building multi-storied houses in preference to wide, low bungalows, and using glazed windows rather than louvres or shutters. About 1695, Samuel Copen drew a panoramic "Prospect of Bridgetown in Barbados" which makes this Caribbean port look indistinguishable from a commercial town in England or Holland. The houses press close to the wharves, leaving no room for gardens or shade trees. They are tall and narrow structures, three to five stories in height, without balconies or verandahs. This architectural style was better geared to Northern Europe than to the Caribbean. As Sir Hans Sloane observed when he visited Jamaica in 1687, the old Spanish houses on the island were designed for maximum coolness and to withstand tropical storms, whereas the new English houses "are neither cool, nor able to endure the shocks of Earthquakes." No wonder the English found it necessary to install great fans in their parlors and lounged half-prostrate much of the time in hammocks. No wonder Sloane found that the planters liked to sit up half the night drinking, for when they went to bed they almost suffocated inside four-poster beds, enveloped by curtains, to keep out the bad night air. We learn from the inventory of his household goods that Sir Henry Morgan, the buccaneer king, slept in a silken nightgown on a costly bed equipped with mohair curtains, persian lining, and a "musketo nett." His servants, who slept in hammocks, and even his slaves, who slept on the ground, were very likely more comfortable.

Perhaps the sugar planters insisted so strenuously on English styles and English standards because they felt imperiled by the volatile Caribbean atmosphere. Nothing seemed permanent in the West Indies. A hurricane or an epidemic disease or a slave revolt or a French invasion could wipe out the most flourishing plantation overnight. It was a boom-and-bust way of life. The whites felt swamped by their black slaves, yet enjoyed lording it over them. For all their nouveau riche pursuit of English genteel standards, the sugar planters lived like no Englishmen at home. Their milieu was hectic, frantic. They grew rich fast, spent recklessly, played desperately, and died young. At the time South Carolina was founded, they had made their beautiful islands almost uninhabitable. Those who moved to Carolina may have sought escape from this style of life, yet surely they carried much of it with them.

Most basically, the islanders introduced Negro slavery to South Carolina. The institution of chattel slavery would have developed in colonial Carolina in any case, but certainly the island immigrants gave it an early boost. Starting with Sir John Yeamans in 1671, members of the big sugar planting families brought gangs of Negroes with them to South Carolina. I suspect that many of the poor whites who came from the islands also brought a slave or two. In the 1680's and 1690's, before the introduction of rice as a staple crop, the colony already had a sizable Negro labor force. Lowland Carolina would soon have a population ratio of four blacks to every white, not far different from the ratio in Barbados.

Carolina rice planters of the eighteenth century had more in common with Barbados sugar planters of the seventeenth century than large gangs of slaves. They too grew rich overnight. They too developed a proud and mettlesome school of politics. They too fashioned an aristocratic elite in which wealth, privilege and power were closely correlated. To be sure, the Carolinians adjusted more successfully to their semi-tropical environment than had Englishmen in the Caribbean. But Charles Town's brittle, gay and showy style of life echoed the Barbados milieu of a century before. Both societies displayed a remarkable compound of old world elegance and frontier boisterousness. In 1773 the *South Carolina Gazette* commented wryly on the aggressive habits of the Carolina gentry: "Their whole Lives are one continued Race: in which everyone is endeavoring to distance all behind him; and to overtake or pass by, all before him. . . . Every Tradesman is a Merchant, every Merchant is a Gentleman, and every Gentleman one of the Noblesse. We are a Country of Gentry. . . . We have no such thing as a common People among us: Between Vanity and Fashion the species is utterly destroyed." One hundred years before, the Barbados gentry had been caught up in the same sort of continual race, sustained by vanity and fashion. And when some of them moved to Carolina, they kept on running. So it was that these Caribbean pioneers helped to create on the North American coast a slave-based plantation society closer in temper to the islands they fled from than to any other mainland English settlement.

WILLIAM R. BASCOM
Acculturation Among the Gullah Negroes

The analysis of the accommodation of African and European customs in the New World presents a particularly difficult problem in the United States because the processes of acculturation have gone much farther here than in other regions. In dealing with the Negro cultures in South America and the West Indies, the African traits that have been retained are specific enough and numerous enough to make possible the identification of the tribes whose cultures have been involved. But even among the Gullah in the coastal regions of South Carolina and Georgia, where the Negroes have been as isolated as anywhere in the United States, resemblances to specific African tribes are very rare. For the most part the similarities are to those elements which are common to West Africa as a whole—to the common denominators of West African culture—and not to those aspects of culture which are distinctive of the tribes within that area. It is therefore extremely difficult to determine what particular West African cultures have contributed to the present situation.

It is now recognized that the differences in the general pattern of the cultures of Africa and Europe were not great; in fact their fundamental similarity justifies the concept of an Old World Area which includes both Europe and Africa. There were a number of institutions common to both regions, including a complex economic system

William R. Bascom, "Acculturation Among the Gullah Negroes," reproduced by permission of the American Anthropological Association from the *American Anthropologist*, 43(1), 1941.

based on money, markets, and middle-men, as well as a large number of crafts among which iron-working was important; a well developed system of government based on kings, and courts of law in which cases were tried by specialists (lawyers) and in which ordeals were employed to decide certain cases; a religious system with a complex hierarchy of priests and deities; a common stock of folklore and a common emphasis on moralizing elements and proverbs. Aside from writing, the wheel, the plow, and Christianity, most of the distinctive traits of Western civilization seem to have followed the industrial revolution.

This similarity between the fundamental patterns of Europe and Africa has further complicated the problem of assessing the relative influences of these areas in the culture of the Gullahs. Since most African traits of a specific nature have disappeared, what is to be found is, for the most part, a series of institutions which differ from the European forms only in their African flavor. To a person who is not familiar with West African cultures, it might seem possible to explain Gullah customs entirely in terms of European influence. The resemblances that are to be found might well be rejected as too general and too indefinite to prove diffusion from Africa to the Sea Islands, if taken by themselves. But we have the historical record of contact with Africa through the importation of African slaves into this region, so that the problem becomes not one of proving that there has been contact, but of assessing the importance of a known factor.

The result of the contact of the Negroes with the whites, both in slavery and in the period of freedom, seems to have been that in those cases where there was a difference or a conflict between African and European customs, the African customs have for the most part disappeared. But those institutions which were present in similar forms in both Africa and Europe, while manifesting a great many specifically European details, have retained an African stamp and have had a place in Gullah life the importance of which cannot be explained in terms of European forms alone. In these cases the two streams of tradition have reinforced one another.

An excellent example of the operation of this process is to be found in the institution of cooperative work among the Gullahs. In West Africa, cooperative work is a widespread and important institution, which among the Yoruba, for example, takes two forms. There is first of all the *aro*, which is a simple labor exchange between two or three farmers who have small families and are too poor to own slaves or "pawns." Such men work a certain amount of time on the farm of one, and then the same amount on the farms of the second and third. The other form of cooperative work is the more spectacular social event, *owe*, in which a man calls upon his friends, relatives, or society members to help him with the work he is required to do for his father-in-law: hoe the fields, thatch the house, build its mud walls, or whatever may be required. On such occasions a large number of men work together while the host directs the activities. Meanwhile the wife, who has called her friends and society together to help her, prepares a large feast for the men with palmwine or gin, if her husband can afford it. In this case there is no attempt to keep track of the amount of work accomplished or time spent, as is done for *aro*.

In Dahomey, besides the cooperative work done by members of the same guild, there is the *dokpwe* which is the equivalent of the Yoruba *owe* or working bee. The *dokpwe* is apparently even more closely associated with the society, however, and it differs in that the host hires a drummer to set the pace for the men working in the field, so that all the workers keep step and finish their rows at the same time. The Yoruba work in a line, so that each man hoes his own row, but they do not work in unison to music, although they are familiar with this procedure from contact with the Hausa. This Dahomean form of cooperative work, complete with hoeing in unison to a drummer, is a pattern which has been retained among other New World Negro cultures. It has been observed by [Melville J.] Herskovits in Haiti, by J. C. Trevor in the Virgin Islands, and by Miss Katherine Dunham in Jamaica.

Cooperative work, on the other hand, is not foreign to the European pattern. Certainly it played an important part in American colonial life in the form of house-raisings, quilting bees, log-rollings, husking bees, and the general pattern of neighborliness. According to informants, the white masters frequently loaned their slaves to one another for occasions of this sort, so that the Gullah had first hand contact with the European forms. Memories of the house-raisings, log-rollings, quilting bees, and even the associated candy pulls which the Negroes held on their own accord after freedom are still vivid in the minds of the older individuals. But at the same time certain forms of cooperative work show a closer correspondence to the West African pattern, especially with regard to hoeing side by side, hoeing in unison to music, and the association between cooperative work and the societies.

On Sapeloe Island in Georgia informants remember large groups, apparently of between 30 and 50 persons, hoeing side by side in the fields. This in itself is significant, since, during the period of slavery, work was assigned by the task in this region so that each slave worked out a separate area by himself. Furthermore, after freedom when a man got behind in his work, he would call on his neighbors or his society for help; and even today, on Sapeloe, people will still "jump right into the field and help you out." In the old days the man would give a big dinner on a long table under a tree, but nowadays people are invited into the house. In hoeing each person takes his own row, and while the host did not hire a drum for use in the fields, the people frequently sang church songs and worked in unison, finishing their rows at the same time. When they worked without singing, couples talked and fell behind so that they did not all finish together. As in Africa, working together is said to make the work more pleasant and to make it go faster; as one informant put it, "You're really cuttin' grass then."

Similarly, if a man needed help, he might call upon a neighbor, and this favor would be returned when requested. This resembles the Yoruba *aro* except that no strict account was kept of the amount of work done. The person called upon might be a relative, or a good friend, or just a neighbor. Significantly, these arrangements were more or less permanent, so that a man would always call upon the same person to help him out. Usually the host gave the helper a meal; but if he were alone and ill, this was omitted.

On the island of Hilton Head, South Carolina, cooperative work has disappeared, but shortly after slavery it existed in two forms. In the first place neighbors might help each other even when they were not ill, working first in the fields of one family and then in the fields of the other. In the second place, the societies such as Mutual Friendly Aid would come without being asked to help a member who fell behind in his work. In this case they did not take note of the amount of work done, but just went in and "hoed him out," while the host provided a dinner for his helpers, serving whatever he could afford. When several people hoed the fields together, each took his own row, and when they sang their hoeing was in unison and was said to go faster and with less effort. In recent times the Hilton Head societies have been primarily "policy clubs" of the type so common in the South, and the function of working in the fields has been abandoned.

African elements are not so evident in other parts of the coastal regions as they are in Hilton Head and Sapeloe. On St. Simons Island, Georgia, neither neighbors nor societies helped in the fields; and while several members of the same family might hoe side by side, each taking his own row, even when they did sing they did not work in unison. On St. Helena, South Carolina, it is said that neighbors never worked each other's fields, but on this island the society called Knights of Wise helped members who were not well and fined those who did not show up to work. Members of the Sisters of Zion were likewise expected, but not forced, to turn out to work the fields of a sick member; if the man proved to be lazy instead of ill, he was given a mock whipping. There was no singing while farming on St. Helena, where they say they had to "sing with the hoe." About Darien and on Harris Neck, on the Georgia mainland, the pattern of co-operative work was once strong, but the forms it took were mainly European, with log-rollings, quiltings, and the like. People would come to hoe the fields of a neighbor who was not well, but the work was not done in unison to music, and while societies were important shortly after slavery, they did not help their members with their work.

It is difficult to explain these local variations in terms of the information at hand, but explanations are probably to be sought in differentials in isolation, the rules laid down by individual slave owners, and perhaps the African sources of the slaves and the dates at which slaves were last imported directly from Africa. While cooperative work persisted in these localities for a long time, it has disappeared in all of them except Sapeloe Island. In all these places except St. Simons, informants respond with conviction to the suggestion that people were more neighborly in the old days than they are now.

Friendship is another institution which is common to both the European and African tradition, but in West Africa it takes a slightly different form and is considerably more formalized than it is in our society. Among the Yoruba there is a distinct emphasis on the best friend (korikosun) with whom every contemplated undertaking is discussed, and whose advice in financial matters, or affairs with women, or any matter whatsoever is very seldom disregarded. The best friend is told how a man wants his property to be divided and is called in by the family to see that these wishes are carried out when his partner dies. There are folktales which show that a man's best friend is more to be trusted than his own mother; and the best friend is told things which a man does not confide to his wife. A man's wife or members of his family would attempt—supposedly always without success—to find out a man's plans by "pumping" his best friend.

The affection between best friends is legendary. A man speaks of loving his best friend "like a woman," and there are stories of men dying of grief at the passing of their friends. The Yoruba belief is that women's mouths are "too big" to keep a secret; they do not remain faithful to any friend, but go through life with a series of them. In Dahomey the same general pattern holds but the institution is itself more elaborate in form. Each man has a first best friend in whom he confides everything; a second best friend to whom he tells slightly less; and a third best friend who receives only a part of his confidence.

In the Sea Islands the European practice of writing wills has been accepted completely so that an important and distinctively African function of friendship has disappeared. At most a man asks his friend's advice about the way his property should be divided. A few informants in their discussion of friendship, did, however, give an emphasis to the institution which seems characteristically African.

On Hilton Head men used to have one or two "sworn friends" upon whom they could depend and to whom they told all their secrets. These friends interpreted each other's dreams, gave advice on financial ventures, and criticized each other's behavior, for instance, in such matters as having "affairs" with women. A man's wife or even his parents might go to his sworn friend in an attempt to find out what plans he had in mind, and in some cases a wife's persistence in this led to a gradual breaking up of the friendship, since the man would stay away from the house rather than be forced to betray his confidence.

Such friendship had a special importance in the time of slavery when slaves banded together against the master. They continued for a time after slavery, but in succeeding generations people came to confide in too many individuals—having too many sworn friends—so that secrets soon spread. The inability of women to keep a secret was blamed in part for the disappearance of the institution, for "as soon as you tell a girl, your secret is gone."

An African influence can be seen in the present form of a number of other institutions which will simply be enumerated. It is apparent in the functions of the local clubs or societies such as the Mutual Friendly Aid, the Jolly Boys, the Golden Link, the Seaside Branch, and the Union Gospel Travellers on Hilton Head. In most other regions these local societies were followed by the well-known, national, chartered lodges, which in turn have almost disappeared. In the structure of the Gullah family there seems to be a certain matrilineal emphasis for which there are counterparts in West Africa. For example, there is the feeling that an individual is somehow more closely related to his mother than to his father. There are several rationalizations for this, but one is the same as that offered in Africa, namely that a person is fed on his mother's milk.

The emphasis on special circumstances of birth is characteristically African. [E. C.] Parsons has already pointed out how children born with a caul, children born "foot fo'mos'," twins, and the seventh child are all believed to have special qualities or abilities. The Gullah, like the West Africans, bury the navel cord in the yard, and frequently nursed their children for one, two, or three years in the old days. One woman was said to have nursed her child after it was old enough to help her in the fields. And people today remember women who carried their children on their backs, in some cases when working the fields. Certain Gullah beliefs are obviously comparable to the taboos of the West Africans; for example, the idea that a nursing mother should not eat beans, green corn, crabs, prawns, or net fish (channel fish caught with hook and line are all right), because it is not good for the baby's stomach.

The interpretation of dreams in order to predict the future is important in West African as well as in European tradition and it is widespread in the Sea Islands. Magic likewise is not foreign to the European tradition, but certain details of the practice are specifically African; the importance of "grave-yard dirt," of "foot track dust," and of hair and nails in working conjure; and the importance of "frizzled chickens" as a means of detecting charms buried in the earth.

The belief in multiple souls, the very vivid belief in ghosts, the special burial rites for persons who die by drowning, lightning, smallpox, and suicide, all resemble African beliefs more closely than they do European. A baby that is taken to a funeral must be passed across the coffin so that its soul will not accompany that of the deceased. When a mother starts home after a visit she takes her baby in her arms, and then calls its name so that its soul will not be left behind. As in Africa, a distinction is made between ghosts and witches, who take off their skins and can be caught either by sprinkling pepper and salt about the room in good African tradition, or by the distinctly European method of putting a Bible under the pillow.

Turning once more to agriculture, we find that a specifically West African form of motor behavior has been retained widely in this region. In the planting of several crops, and especially of rice in the old days, the hole into which the seed was dropped was first made with the heel and then covered over with the foot. Moving pictures taken in West Africa and in Haiti by Herskovits show very plainly this West African procedure which, as far as can be ascertained, was entirely foreign to European tradition.

Gullah speech, which has long been recognized as distinctive among Negro dialects in the United States, has a number of African idioms and grammatical peculiarities. A detailed analysis may show African influences in the phonetic system as well. Dr. Turner of Fisk University has listed several thousand words which he believes to be of West African origin. These are mainly in the form of nicknames and words for plants and animals, and are used only within the family circle so that they would not be noticed unless someone set out to look for them. Lastly there are the very specific correspondences between the animal tales of the Gullah and those of West Africa, the first aspects of Gullah culture to be recognized as having an African origin.

In conclusion then, while it is impossible in the case of the Sea Island Negroes to assign African influences to particular tribes, and while we are dealing with the problem of the relative influence of European and African culture on institutions common to both traditions, rather than with African origins of non-European institutions, these influences can be recognized in many aspects of present-day Gullah life. It would thus seem historically incorrect as well as methodologically unsound to explain Gullah customs by reference only to European culture. It is quite true that, as elsewhere in the United States, the European elements outnumber by far the African elements which have been retained, yet that Africanisms can be traced indicates the importance of the study of this society as an aid in the analysis of acculturation.

II

CULTURE, RACE,
AND LABOR
IN THE
COLONIAL SOUTH
SHIFTING PATTERNS

Race relations in the Southern colonies developed out of a continuing interplay between cultural assumptions and economic needs. Throughout the colonial period it was primarily the demand for labor that brought men and women of different races into regular contact, creating what we earlier called cultural interdependencies. The leading Southern planters could always obtain sufficient land to produce sizable harvests and, although they were sometimes hurt by periodic depressions in the world market, they usually found ways to turn a profit. What was missing, of course, was a large, dependable, and relatively inexpensive supply of laborers.

From the vantage point of the nineteenth century it appeared that the importation of thousands of Africans alone could have effectively met the planters' labor needs. By then it was forgotten that there had once been alternatives and that, given a slightly different set of conditions, Native Americans and indentured whites might have become the backbone of the plantation labor force. It is certain that, in 1619, the year that blacks were first sold as slaves in the South, it was by no means clear to the Chesapeake planters what the composition of the work force would become. In fact, in each of the major plantation colonies there was a period of experimentation, a sorting-out time during which Africans, Europeans, and Indians toiled side by side in the fields. The length of this period varied from colony to colony, but in all colonies the planters eventually developed a preference for black laborers. This change did not result from conscious decision or systematic planning, but came about because of complex economic, demographic, and social factors that the authors in this section undertake to explain.

To understand developing race relations in the Southern colonies, we should turn our attention first to the Indians. Unfortunately, our knowledge of Native American culture before the settlement of Virginia is limited. Since the Indians of this period produced no written records, we must rely for information solely upon archaeological findings and accounts left by European explorers. These sources reveal that Native Americans in this region had developed a complex culture long before the white man arrived. They possessed elaborate religious systems, sophisticated forms of government, and trade networks that extended as far west and north as the Great Lakes. We know also that these people comprised many different tribal groups. In coastal North Carolina and Virginia, English settlers encountered Algonkian Indians; farther south they met Catawbas, Cherokees, Creeks, and a host of smaller tribes. Most of these Indians were hunters, gatherers, and primitive cultivators. Their dealings with neighboring tribes were severely restricted not only by the hazards of travel but also by communications problems posed by the diversity of Indian languages.

The attitude of the Native Americans toward the first European settlers remains obscure. What little we know indicates that they in no way regarded their culture as inferior to that of the white man. English efforts to assimilate the Indians were generally unsuccessful. The indigenous peoples showed no genuine desire to take up the colonists' religion, wear their clothes, or live in their homes, but in a few other areas they did approve of intercultural contact. Thus, they saw immediately the importance of trade as a means of obtaining metal goods that they themselves could not produce; and because the English possessed firearms, the Indians sought their support in the wars waged constantly between coastal and inland tribes. One of Virginia's most powerful Indian leaders, Powhatan, hoped to form an alliance with the Jamestown settlers in his campaign to subdue the lesser tidewater tribes. Only when it became clear that the newcomers posed an even greater threat to Indian security did Opechancanough (Powhatan's cousin), resolve to exterminate the white invaders. This attempt failed, as did all subsequent attempts; but even when confronted with death or removal, Native Americans stubbornly refused to surrender their cultural independence.

In his essay, "The Image of the Indian in the Southern Colonial Mind," Gary B. Nash recounts the other side of this story. The European settlers had arrived in the New World possessing conflicting notions about Indians and their culture. Some expected to encounter a docile, edenic people; others feared that the forests were filled with wild men, perhaps even cannibals. Actual contact between the two cultures brought the white image of the Indian into sharper focus, and the English had to abandon their dream of recruiting a large Indian labor force similar to what the Spanish had so successfully exploited in Mexico. For one thing, Indian servants and slaves easily slipped away from their masters. And in any case, the number of Indians in this region was never sufficient to meet the expanding need for agricultural workers.

Thus it was that over the course of the seventeenth century, changing social and demographic conditions caused colonists to modify their opinion of the Indians. Nash traces this evolution. As you read his account, you should consider the kinds of experiences that were most influential in shaping racial attitudes. Did the shifting racial images really influence white-Indian relations? Indeed, why should you study these intellectual changes at all, if the European settlers invariably thrust the Indian aside? What group of people does Nash help us better to understand? Then, as you read the other articles in this section, you should contrast the whites' shifting image of the Indian with that of the black.

Over the long run, white indentured servants proved an equally unsatisfactory labor source, since their contracts expired after a relatively short period, so that the planters had to search continuously for replacement—a time-consuming and expensive process. Perhaps the greatest difficulty with indentured servants, ironically, was the fact that they came from the same culture as did their masters. The servants were aware of their rights as Englishmen; they had expectations of upward mobility. Indeed, one such servant defiantly exclaimed to the justices of the Accomack County court, "Wherefore should we stay here and bee slaves . . . [when we] may goe to another place and live like gentlemen!" The planters never knew when their servants would join with poor and landless white freemen in open rebellion. Even obedient servants posed a problem, for once they completed the period of indenture they became small planters producing staple crops in competition with their former masters.

The relations developing between blacks and whites throughout the colonial South reveal graphically the complexities of cultural interaction. The planters' attitudes about blacks evolved slowly, especially in the Chesapeake region, and for many years following the introduction of blacks into Virginia, no one bothered to define their precise legal status. During the early decades some African migrants unquestionably were slaves for life. But others appear to have been indentured servants, and a very small number even seem to have become full freemen, acquiring slaves of their own. Before the 1680s the number of black men and women in Virginia remained quite small, probably no more than 4,000; and despite a growing body of statutes restricting their rights, the African-Americans do not appear to have been significantly worse off than many of the colony's white servants. By the end of the century, however, this situation had changed dramatically. The Chesapeake tobacco planters imported Africans by the thousand, and it was clear that whites now regarded blacks not only as chattel but also as members of an inferior race.

How can we explain this curious process? Why did it take so long for race slavery to take root? One wonders why the earliest Virginians did not immediately enslave all Africans simply because they were black. Exactly how did the white image of the black man change over the seventeenth century? These are some of the questions that Winthrop D. Jordan wrestles with in his now classic study, *White Over Black: American Attitudes Toward the Negro 1550–*

1812. Jordan frankly admits, in the section of his book reproduced here, that the task is not easy. Few records dealing with colonial race relations have survived, and many of these are either ambiguous or incomplete. Jordan handles these difficulties imaginatively and provides us with the most comprehensive analysis available of colonial ideas about race.

In his book Jordan undertakes to discover the origins of race prejudice in this country. Before he launched his investigation, historians had attempted to identify the connection between slavery and racial discrimination, on the assumption that there was a causal relation between the two and that one element necessarily preceded the other. But when Jordan analyzes what he calls the "cycle of degradation" during the seventeenth century, he finds that slavery and discrimination developed together, and indeed reinforced each other. Before mid-century, white Virginians stressed the cultural differences between them and the blacks; and when planters were compelled to justify the enslavement of African migrants, they pointed to the black man's heathenism, or more specifically, to his ignorance of Christianity. But as more and more blacks entered the colony as slaves, the rationalization for slavery began to shift and, by the year 1700, planters defended the enslavement of another people on racial grounds alone. A man was a slave because he was black; all blacks were by definition potential slaves. No one planned that race relations should work out in this way. It just happened, the result of an "unthinking decision."

Jordan examines closely the process of debasement, and grounds his conclusions for the most part upon contemporaneous statutes, pamphlets, and sermons. As you read this essay, you should ask yourself who made this "unthinking decision." Was it all the whites or only some of them? Moreover, you should consider the wisdom of using laws as an index to changing cultural relations. Do legal sources necessarily reveal the ways different racial groups interacted?

Like Jordan's article, mine analyzes changing seventeenth-century race relations. In my article reprinted here, I seek to identify subtle currents of racial interaction. For the white community simply did not adopt a monolithic stance toward people of African background. Indeed, for a great part of the century, many Virginians apparently ignored colonial laws regulating race behavior. Black slaves and poor whites defied the planter elite in a number of ways, but the most dramatic was in their fighting side by side during Bacon's Rebellion (1676) in an effort to overthrow the colony's royal governor, William Berkeley.

These instances of interracial cooperation, of course, do not signify the absence of race prejudice in Virginia. The poor white servants and freemen may well have held the blacks in very low regard, and we have no knowledge of how the blacks viewed those whites with whom they ran away and rebelled. These activities do indicate, however, that some Virginians temporarily overcame racial and cultural differences and united to relieve their common economic grievances. By 1700 such joint actions had virtually ceased, and I discuss the several social and economic factors that I believe are responsible for this change. What are they? What role did demographic trends play? How would you contrast Jordan's account of this period with the account in my article? How would you now explain the development of race prejudice in colonial Virginia?

Although black slavery took root in South Carolina more quickly than in Virginia, in both colonies the process of working out patterns of race relations was strikingly similar. Our next collaborator, Peter H. Wood, examines the alternative sources of labor available to the founders of South Carolina. Like their Virginia counterparts, the Carolina planters experimented with both Indian and white servants, but both groups proved unsatisfactory for reasons that Wood describes in "Black Labor—White Rice," originally published as a chapter in his book, *Black Majority: Negroes in Colonial South Carolina from 1670 through the Stono Rebellion.*

Although some of the first planters in South Carolina brought black slaves with them from the Caribbean sugar islands, they did not envision the establishment of a massive, overwhelmingly black labor force. They certainly did not foresee that persons of African origin would soon outnumber whites by a sizable majority. But that is exactly what occurred, and in this essay Wood explains how the transformation came about. As he reasons, the treatment of black men and women in South Carolina makes little sense unless one understands the intricate interplay between the planters' need for a profitable staple crop and the Africans' unique cultural heritage. Without the cultivation of rice, there would surely have been no reason to import tens of thousands of Africans into the colony. But once the rice crop was flourishing, it seemed only logical to white Carolinians that the blacks should be the ones to cultivate it. Rice had been part of the blacks' culture. They had grown it in West Africa under climatic conditions similar to those prevailing in South Carolina. Wood's point—and it is an extremely significant one—is that historians cannot account for the predominance of blacks in the colony's labor force simply by reference to the planters' familiarity with Caribbean slavery or by pointing out that a large supply of black workers could easily be obtained. These elements were certainly important, but it was only when they were combined with cultural factors that a black majority developed in South Carolina. After you have completed Wood's study, you should compare race relations in Virginia and South Carolina. What conditions were common to the two colonies? What conditions were unique to each of them?

This section concludes with a chapter from Gerald W. Mullin's *Flight and Rebellion: Slave Resistance in Eighteenth-Century Virginia.* In this piece the author provides us with a detailed account of the day-to-day operations of a large-scale tobacco plantation. He describes this economic unit of production as the focus of intensive interracial contact. It was in this setting, full of contradictions and tensions, that a majority of the face-to-face encounters between blacks and whites probably took place. And it was here also that masters and slaves learned the social roles that each was expected to play.

The great tobacco planters of this period longed for nothing so much as to be totally independent, to direct the lives of everyone on the plantation exactly as they saw fit without interference. But their reliance on other people was made painfully evident at every turn. Most galling perhaps was their dependence upon their own slaves. According to Mullin, the plantation system by its very nature forced the planter to play the patriarch, a taxing social role requiring him to manage, judge, punish, and care for the black workers on whom his economic well-being depended. Because of these complex relations, Mullin concludes that the white planter, no less than the black laborer, was a "product of slave society." As you read this essay, you should consider how cultural interdependencies were formed on the plantation. What did the planters expect of their slaves? What did the slaves in turn demand of their masters? And last, you should ask yourself, what effect would the failure to perform the patriarchal role have had on the planter's life beyond the confines of his own plantation?

One additional point should be stressed. Unless you understand the workings of the plantation—an exploitive, self-contained, often physically isolated institution—you will never fully grasp the social forces that shaped the colonial South.

GARY B. NASH
The Image of the Indian in the Southern Colonial Mind

The changing image of the native inhabitants of North America provides a penetrating glimpse into the fears, desires, and intentions of Englishmen in colonial America. From the guileless primitive of certain sixteenth-century writers, to the savage beast of colonial frontiersmen, to the "noble savage" of eighteenth-century social critics, the Indian has furnished the social, intellectual, and cultural historian with an important analytical tool. Just as Europeans saw in Africa and Africans not what actually existed but what their prior experience and present needs dictated, so in America the image of the Indian was molded by the nature of colonization and the inner requirements of adventuring Englishmen.

Understanding the English image of the Indian not only reveals the conscious and unconscious workings of the Anglo-American mind, but also gives meaning to English relations with the Indian and to English policies directed at controlling, "civilizing," and exterminating him. Images of the Indian were indicators of attitudes toward him. Attitudes, in turn, were closely linked to intentions and desires. These intentions and desires, acted out systematically over a period of time and often provoking responses from the natives which tended to confirm and reinforce first impressions, became the basis of an "Indian policy." Thus, images of the Indians in colonial America

Gary B. Nash, "The Image of the Indian in the Southern Colonial Mind," *William and Mary Quarterly*, 3rd ser., 29 (1972):197–230. Copyright © 1972 by Gary B. Nash; reprinted by permission.

are of both explanatory and causative importance. They help us penetrate the innermost thoughts and psychic needs of Englishmen confronting a distant, unknown, and terrifying land, and they provide a
basis for understanding English interaction with the native inhabitants over a period of close but abrasive contact which lasted for more
than one hundred fifty years.

The early 1580s mark a convenient point to begin a study of the
images of the Indian refracted through the prism of the English
mind. It was then that Elizabethan England, already a century behind Spain and Portugal in exploiting the potentialities of the New
World, took the first significant steps toward extending her power
across the Atlantic. Two attempts at settlement in North America in
1583 and 1584, one by Sir Humphrey Gilbert, among the most active
promoters of English colonization, and the other by his half brother,
Walter Raleigh, the best known and most romantic of the early adventurers, were undertaken. Gilbert sailed the northern route, and
made a landfall in Newfoundland with five ships and 260 men. He
then turned west and disappeared at sea, leaving the other ships to
return to England. Raleigh, plying the familiar southern route,
touched land on the upper Carolina coast, left a small contingent
on what was to be called Roanoke Island, located at the mouth of Albemarle Sound, and returned to England with two natives of the region. Thus began an era of English participation in the great race for
colonial possessions that was to occupy—at times preoccupy—Europe
for the next two centuries.

What images of the Indians were lodged in the minds of men like
Gilbert and Raleigh as they approached the forbidding coast of North
America? One can be sure that they experienced the uncertainty and
apprehension that regardless of time or place fill the minds of men
who are attempting to penetrate the unknown. But in all likelihood
they also had well-formed ideas about the indigenous people of the
New World. Legends concerning other worlds beyond the sunset had
reverberated in the European mind for centuries. And, beginning
with Columbus's report on the New World, published in several
European capitals in 1493 and 1494, a mass of reports and stories had
been circulating among sailors, merchants, and geographers who were
participating in voyages of discovery, trade, and settlement.

From this considerable literature, men like Gilbert and Raleigh
were likely to derive a split image of the natives of North America.
On the one hand they had reason to believe that the Indians were
savage, hostile, beastlike men, whose proximity in appearance and behavior was closer to the animal kingdom than the kingdom of men,

as western Europeans employed that term to describe themselves. As early as the first decade of the sixteenth century Sebastian Cabot had paraded in England three Eskimos taken captive on his voyage to the Arctic in 1502. A contemporary described the natives as flesh eating, primitive specimens who "spake such speech that no man coulde understand them, and in their demeanour like to bruite beasts." In 1556, curious Englishmen could read an account of Giovanni da Verrazano's voyage of 1524 to North America, including descriptions of the natives which could have been little cause for optimism concerning the reception Europeans would receive in the New World. Other accounts were filtering back to England from fishermen operating off the Newfoundland Banks or from explorers such as Martin Frobisher, whose three attempts to find the Northwest Passage in the 1570s led to the publication of a number of descriptions of the northern reaches of the lands across the Atlantic. The accounts from the Frobisher voyages were filled with descriptions of crafty, brutal, loathsome half-men whose cannibalistic instincts were revealed, as Dionyse Settle wrote in 1578, by the fact that "there is no flesh or fishe, which they finde dead, (smell it never so filthily) but they will eate it, as they finde it, without any other dressing."

Other unsettling accounts also became available through the translation of Spanish and Portuguese writers. Sebastian Munster's *A Treatyse of the newe India* . . . was published in English in 1553; Peter Martyr's *The Decades of the newe worlds or west India* two years later; Jean Ribault's *The whole and true discoverye of Terra Florida* . . . in 1563; Nicolas Le Challeux's *A true and perfect description, of the last voyage or Navigation attempted by Capitaine John Rybaut* . . . *into Terra Florida* . . . in 1566; and André Thevet's *The New found worlde, or Antarcticke,* . . . in 1568. In all of these works Englishmen of the day could read accounts which suggested that the people of the New World were not only primitive—simply by not being English one was that—but bestial, cannibalistic, sexually abandoned, and, in general, moved entirely by passion rather than reason.

But another vision of the native was simultaneously entering the English consciousness. Columbus had written of the "great amity towards us" which he encountered in San Salvador in 1492 and described a generous, pastoral people living in childlike innocence. Thenceforth, the accounts which Englishmen read were tinged with a romantic image of the New World, as if, Howard Mumford Jones has written, to fill some psychic need of a dreary, tired Europe. Just a few years before the Gilbert and Raleigh voyages, Englishmen could read in translation Nicholas Monardes's *Joyfull Newes out of the Newe Founde Worlde,* . . . which limned America as a horn of plenty, an earthly paradise where nature's bounty allowed men to live for centuries in sensual leisure. To some extent this positive side of the image of the New World was based on the friendly reception which Europeans had apparently received in Newfoundland, parts of Florida, and elsewhere on the continent. Gilbert, for example, was familiar with the testimony of David Ingram, one of about a hundred sailors set ashore on the northern coast of the Gulf of Mexico by John Hawkins in 1568. Upon his return to England, Ingram wrote of the tractable and generous nature of the natives who provided food and were "Naturally very courteous, if you do not abuse them." Other accounts confirmed the notion that the natives as well as the climate in some parts of the New World would be hospitable.

Three books published in the early 1580s, as the Roanoke voyages were being launched, provide a clearer insight into this split vision of English writers as they pondered the nature of the people inhabiting the lands of the New World. Two were written by the Richard Hakluyts, uncle and nephew—the greatest colonial publicizers and promoters of their age. With pen rather than sword the Hakluyts inspired Elizabethan courtiers, adventurous sons of the lesser nobility, and merchants with venture capital to enter the colonial sweepstakes before Spain and Portugal, already firmly established in South America and the West Indies, laid claim to the whole of the New World. The third was penned by Sir George Peckham, who had accompanied Sir Humphrey Gilbert on the Newfoundland voyage of 1583 and left his impressions, *A True Reporte, of the late discoveries,* . . . *of the Newfound Landes* . . . , as the latest guide for Englishmen eager to unravel the mysteries of North America.

In all of these tracts the ambivalence and confusion in the English mind is readily apparent. Hakluyt the elder could write of the New World as "a Country no less fruitful and pleasant in al respects than is England, Fraunce or Germany, the people, though simple and rude in manners, and destitute of the knowledge of God or any good lawes, yet of nature gentle and tractable, and most apt to receive the Christian Religion, and to subject themselves to some good government." In the same vein, the younger Hakluyt wrote in 1584 of a "goodd clymate, healthfull, and of goodd temperature, marvelous pleasaunte, the people goodd and of a gentle and amyable nature, which willingly will obey, yea be contented to serve those that shall with gentlenes and humanitie goo aboute to allure them." These were useful promotional statements. And yet the Hakluyts could not banish the thought that planting English civilization in the New World would not be all gentleness and amiability. Festering in their minds was knowledge of the Spanish experience in America. They had read carefully every account of the Spanish conquest of Mexico, especially Bartholome de las Casas's *The Spanish Colonie, or Briefe Chronicle of the acts and gestes of the Spaniardes in the West Indies,* translated in 1583. Las Casas deplored the reign of death and terror which the Spanish had brought to aboriginal culture in the name of Christianity. In his own propaganda for colonization Hakluyt felt moved to quote several Spanish authors who labeled their countrymen "helhoundes and wolves"—men who claimed they had conquered and pacified the Indians, but who in reality had engaged in a policy bordering on genocide. The Indians, according to Hakluyt's source, "not havinge studied Logicke concluded very pertinently and categorically that the Spainardes which spoiled their Contrie, were more dangerous then wilde beastes, more furious then Lyons, more fearefull and terrible then fire and water."

Did the same experience await the English? Few doubted that they enjoyed the same technological superiority as the Spanish. If they desired, they could thus lay waste to the country they were entering. Moreover, the English experience with the Irish, in whose country military officers like Gilbert and Raleigh had been gaining experience in the subjugation of "lesser breeds" for several decades, suggested that the English were fully capable of every cruelty contrived by the Spanish. Thus, as the elder Hakluyt pointed out, if the English were not well received, they might be obliged to employ force to show the Indians the advantages of participating in the benefits of English civilization. "If we finde the countrey populous," he wrote in 1584, "and desirous to expel us, and injuriously to offend us, that seeke but just and lawfull trafficke, then by reason that we are lords of navigation, and they not so, we are the better able to defend our selves by reason of those great rivers, and to annoy them in many places." Hakluyt concluded that the English might find it necessary to "proceed with extremetie, conquer, fortifie, and plant in soiles most sweet, most pleasant, most strong, and most fertile, and in the end bring them all in subjection and to civilitie." So the bitter would be mixed with the sweet.

George Peckham, writing contemporaneously with the Hakluyts, gave an even clearer expression of the emerging formula for colonization: exterior expressions of goodwill and explanations of mutual benefits to be derived from the contact of two cultures, but lurking beneath the surface the anticipation of violence. In his promotional

pamphlet, *A True Reporte, . . . of the Newfound Landes,* Peckham began with elaborate defenses of the rights of maritime nations
to "trade and traficke" with "savage" nations and assured Englishmen
that such enterprises would be "profitable to the adventurers in per-
ticuler, beneficial to the Savages, and a matter to be attained without
any great daunger or difficultie." Some of the natives, Peckham allowed, would be "fearefull by nature" and disquieted by the "straunge
apparrell, Armour, and weapon" of the English, but "courtesie and
myldnes" along with a generous bounty of "prittie merchaundizes and
trifles: As looking Glasses, Bells, Beades, Braceletts, Chaines, or Col-
lers of Bewgle, Christall, Amber, Jett, or Glasse" would soon win
them over and "induce theyr Barbarous natures to a likeing and a
mutuall society with us."

Having explained how he hoped the English *might* act, and how
the natives *might* respond, Peckham went on to reveal what he must
have considered the more likely course of events:

But if after these good and fayre meanes used, the Savages nevertheles
will not be heerewithall satisfied, but barbarously wyll goe about to prac-
tise violence either in repelling the Christians from theyr Portes and safe
Landinges or in withstanding them afterwardes to enjoye the rights for
which both painfully and lawfully they have adventured themselves
thether; Then in such a case I holde it no breache of equitye for the
Christians to defende themselves, to pursue revenge with force, and to
doo whatsoever is necessary for attayning of theyr safety: For it is allowable
by all Lawes in such distresses, to resist violence with violence.

With earlier statements of the gentle and receptive qualities of the
Indians almost beyond recall, Peckham reminded his countrymen of
their responsibility to employ all necessary means to bring the natives
from "falsehood to truth, from darknes to lyght, from the hieway of
death, to the path of life, from superstitious idolatry, to sincere christianity, from the devill to Christ, from hell to Heaven." Even more
revealing of his essentially negative image of the Indian, he wrote
that the English, in planting their civilization, would aid the Indians
by causing them to change "from unseemly customes, to honest
maners, from disordred riotous rowtes and companies, to a wel governed common wealth."

Thus, two conflicting images of the Indian were wrestling for as-
cendance in the English mind as the first attempts to colonize in the
New World began. At times the English tended to see the native as a
backward but receptive man with whom amicable and profitable relations might be established. This image originated not only in the uto-

pian anticipation of the New World but in the desire to trade with the Indians. The early voyages were not primarily intended for the purpose of large-scale settlement and agricultural production. A careful reading of the promotional literature of this period will show that the English were primarily interested in a mercantile relationship. Trade with the Indians, the search for gold and silver, and discovery of the Northwest Passage were the keys to overseas development. Trade was expected to be a major source of profit. Not only would the natives provide a new outlet for English woolens, but all of the rich and varied commodities of the New World would flow back to England in ample measure. Since trade was the key to success in these bold new adventures, a special incentive existed for seeing the Indian as something more than an intractable savage. For the Spanish and Portuguese colonizers in the New World (and for the English in Ireland) land had been the key. But land conquest did not figure importantly in Elizabethan planning. In fact, it would undermine attempts to establish a mercantile relationship. Instead well-fortified trading posts would be established at the heads of rivers where the natives would come to trade. In this mercantile approach to overseas adventuring the English promoters were strongly influenced by English participation in the Levantine and Muscovy trade where English merchants had operated profitably for half a century, not invading the land of foreign peoples and driving them from it, but "trafficking" among them without challenging their possession of the land. In Hakluyt's *Notes on Colonization,* written five years prior to the Roanoke voyages, the recommendations for approaching the natives are almost identical to those given for adventurers seeking the Northeast Passage in 1580.

Thus, one side of the image of the native had its source not only in the idyllic visions of the New World, but in the intentions of the Elizabethan adventurers. It was only a friendly Indian who *could* be a trading Indian. If trade was the key to overseas development, then it is not surprising that English promoters suggested that the Indian might be receptive and generous—a man who could be wooed and won to the advantages of trade.

But the creation of a tractable Indian, amenable to trade, could never blot from the English mind the image of the hostile savage who awaited Christian adventurers. Most of the Elizabethan adventurers had been involved in the English invasions of Ireland and the Netherlands where they had learned that indigenous peoples do not ordinarily accept graciously those who come to dominate them. They had special reasons for anticipating the darker side of the Indian's nature because they were familiar with the literature on the "savages" of the New World and were well acquainted with the Spanish and Portuguese overseas experience. With hostility on their minds, it was impossible to picture the Indian as a purely benign creature. Regardless of the natural temperament of the New World man, his contact with Europeans thus far had rarely been pacific. To imagine the Indian as a savage beast was a way of predicting the future and preparing for it and of justifying what one would do, even before one caused it to happen.

The experience at Roanoke Island between 1584 and 1587 illustrates how preconceptions affected the initial Anglo-Indian contacts. For Englishmen it was their first settlement in the New World. Initially, several hundred men attempted to maintain themselves on the island while making exploratory trips into the mainland wilderness. For three years the settlement struggled for existence, kept alive by fresh infusions of men and supplies from England. But left to its own resources, when the Spanish Armada prevented provisioning ships from leaving England in 1588, the tiny colony perished.

Three accounts of the Roanoke experience survive. Because they were written at least partially as promotional pamphlets, intended to inspire further attempts at settlement, they must be used cautiously as a source of information. Though differing in detail, all of the accounts agree that the Indians of the Carolina region were receptive to the English. Arthur Barlowe, a member of the first expedition, wrote that "we were entertained with all love, and kindnes, and with as much bountie, after their manner, as they could possibly devise. Wee found the people most gentle, loving, and faithfull, void of all guile, and treason," and noted that the Indians were "much grieved" when their hospitality was shunned by the suspicious English. Other accounts, though less roseate, also suggest that the natives were eager to learn about the artifacts of the Europeans, and, though wary, extended their hospitality. Since the English came in small numbers, the Indians probably did not regard them as much of a threat. They were no doubt as curious about the English as the English were about them. So far as one can tell from the surviving evidence, no conflict occurred until the English, upon discovering a silver cup missing, dispatched a punitive expedition to a nearby Indian village. When the Indians denied taking the cup, the English, determined to make a show of force, burned the village to the ground and destroyed the Indians' supply of corn. After that, relations deteriorated. Aware of their numerical disadvantage and the precariousness of their position, the English used force in large doses to convince the natives of their invulnerability. As one member of the voyage admitted, "Some of our companie towardes the ende of the yeare, shewed themselves too fierce, in slaying some of the people, in some towns, upon causes that on our part, might easily enough have bene borne withall."

In spite of these difficulties, the principal members of the Roanoke colony who returned to England entertained considerable respect for Indian culture. Thomas Hariot wrote that "although they have no such tooles, nor any such craftes, sciences and artes as wee; yet in those things they doe, they shewe excellencie of wit." John White, a painter of some skill, who had accompanied the Roanoke expedition, brought back more explicit testimony of the Indians' culture—in the form of scores of sketches and watercolors which show the Indians at various aspects of work and play. White's drawings reveal a genuine appreciation of the Indians' ability to control their environment through their methods of hunting and agriculture, their family and communal life, and other aspects of their culture.

For two decades after the failure at Roanoke, Englishmen launched no new colonial adventures. Although a few English ship captains, who represented merchants dabbling in the West Indies trade, looked in on the coast of North America in hopes of bartering with the natives, and reported that their relations with them were generally friendly, the next attempt at colonization did not come until the Virginia Company of London completed its plans in December 1606. The arrival of the first Virginia expedition in April 1607, with more than one hundred men in three ships, marked the beginning of permanent English presence in North America. Henceforward, Indians and Englishmen would be in continuous contact.

The crucial difference between the Roanoke colony of the 1580s and the settlement at Jamestown in 1607 was that the latter, after the first few years, was planned as a permanent community. From this point onward, Englishmen came to America not merely to trade with the natives or to extract the riches of the land but to build an enduring society—an extension of England overseas. It was this shift in intention that reshaped the nature of the contacts between English and Indians and consequently altered the English image of the native as well as the Indian perception of the Englishman. Permanent settlement required acquisition by whites of land—land which was in the possession of the Indian. That single fact was the beginning of a chain of events which governed the entire sociology of red-white relations.

For Englishmen, the Indians' occupation of the land presented a problem both of law and morality. Even in the 1580s, George Peckham, an early promoter of colonization, had admitted that many Englishmen doubted their right to take possession of the land of others. In 1609 the thought was amplified by Robert Gray, who asked rhetorically, "By what right or warrant we can enter into the land of these Savages, take away their rightfull inheritance from them, and plant ourselves in their places, being unwronged or unprovoked by them." It was a logical question to ask, for Englishmen, like other Europeans, had organized their society around the concept of private ownership of land and regarded this as an important characteristic of their superior culture. They were not blind to the fact that they were entering the land of another people, who by prior possession could lay sole claim to all the territory of mainland America. To some extent the problem was resolved by arguing that the English did not intend to take the Indians' land but wanted only to share with them the resources of the New World where there was land enough for all. In return, they would extend to the Indians the advantages of a richer culture, a more advanced civilization, and, most importantly, the Christian religion. Thus, in 1610 the governing council in Virginia advertised to those at home that the English "by way of marchandizing and trade, doe buy of them [the Indians] the pearles of earth, and sell to them the pearles of heaven." A few decades later, Samuel Purchas, who took up the Hakluyts' work of promoting colonization in the seventeenth century, gave classic expression to this explanation: "God in wisedome having enriched the Savage Countries, that those riches might be attractive for Christian suters, which there may sowe spirituals and reape temporals." Spirituals to be sown, of course, meant Christian doctrines; temporals to be reaped meant land.

A second and far more portentous way of resolving the problem of land possession was to deny the humanity of the Indians. Thus, Robert Gray, who had asked if Englishmen were entitled to "plant ourselves in their places," answered by arguing that the Indians' inhumanity disqualified them from the right to possess land. "Although the Lord hath given the earth to children of men, . . . the greater part of it [is] possessed and wrongfully usurped by wild beasts, and unreasonable creatures, or by brutish savages, which by reason of their godles ignorance, and blasphemous Idolatrie, are worse then those beasts which are of most wilde and savage nature." This was an argument fraught with danger for the Indian, for whereas other Englishmen, such as William Strachey, secretary of the resident council in Virginia at this time, were arguing that "every foote of Land which we shall take unto our use, we will bargayne and buy of them," Gray was suggesting that present and future acts of godlessness or savagery, as defined by the English, would entitle the colonists unilaterally to seize or occupy land. This notion that by their nature the "savages" had forfeited their right to the land was only occasionally mentioned in the early years. But in the 1620s, after a major war had been fought, the idea would gain greater acceptance.

Little evidence exists on which to base unequivocal assertions about English attitudes toward the Indians in 1607, at the moment of initial contact. But it seems likely that given their belief that the Roanoke colony had been reduced to a pile of bones by the Indians a generation earlier, the English were not very optimistic about the receptiveness of the indigenous people. This pessimistic view must have been greatly intensified when the Jamestown expedition was attacked near Cape Henry, following their first debarkation in the New World. Hereafter, the English would proceed with extreme caution, as well they might, given the size of their expedition. Violence was anticipated, and when Indians approached the English in outwardly friendly ways, the worst was suspected. Thus, when Christopher Newport led the first exploratory trip up the newly named James River, just weeks after a tiny settlement had been planted at Jamestown, he was confused by what he encountered. The Indians, a member of his group wrote, "are naturally given to trechery, howbeit we could not finde it in our travell up the river, but rather a most kind and loving people." This account reveals that the English were wined and dined by the Indians who explained that they were "at oddes" with other tribes, including the Chesapeake tribe that had attacked the English at Cape Henry, and were willing to ally with the English against their enemies. It is clear from ethnological research that the Indians of the Chesapeake region, composing some thirty different tribes, were not monolithic in cultural characteristics and were undergoing internal reorganization. The most powerful tribe, the Pamunkey, of which Powhatan was chief, had been attempting for some time before the arrival of the English to consolidate its hold on lesser tribes in the area, while at the same time warding off the threats of westerly tribes of the Piedmont. From the available ethnographic evidence, it appears that Powhatan saw an alliance with the English as a means of extending his power in the tidewater area while neutralizing the power of his western enemies.

But the English, who were quick to comprehend the intertribal tensions as well as the linguistic differences among the Indians of the region, could apparently not convince themselves that some tribal leaders regarded the English as threatening while others found their arrival potentially to their advantage. Perhaps because they viewed their position as so precarious (the Jamestown settlement was in a state of internal crisis almost from the moment of landfall), they could only afford to regard all Indians as threatening. Thus, hostile and friendly Indians seemed different only in their outward behavior. Inwardly they were identical. The hostile Indian revealed his true nature while the friendly Indian feigned friendship while waiting for an opportunity to attack, thus proving even more than his openly warlike brother the treacherous nature he possessed.

Over the first few years of contact, during which time the Jamestown settlement was reprovisioned from England with men and supplies, the confusion in the English mind was revealed again and again. In the summer of 1607, when food supplies were running perilously low and all but a handful of the Jamestown settlers had fallen too ill to work, the colony was saved by the Indians who brought sufficient food to keep the struggling settlement alive until the sick recovered. This, too, was seen by many as an example of Powhatan's covert hostility rather than an attempt to serve his own interests through an alliance with the English. "It pleased God (in our extremity)," wrote Smith, "to move the Indians to bring us Corne, ere it was halfe ripe, to refresh us, when we rather expected . . . they would destroy us." As a man of military experience among "barbarian" people in all parts of the world, Smith was not willing to believe that the Indians, in aiding the colony, might have found the survival of the English in their own interest. Hostility was on his mind, sporadic hostility had already been experienced, and thus all acts, friendly or foul, were perceived as further evidence of the natives' irreversible hostility and innate savagery. The records left by the English would be couched hereafter in these terms. Outright conflict was taken as the norm because it represented the logical result of contact with a people who were hostile and treacherous by nature. Friendly overtures by Powhatan and other tribal leaders, who hoped to use the English to consolidate their own position, were seen as further examples of the dissembling nature of the Indians. One reads of "these cunning tricks of their Emperour of *Powhatan*," or of "their slippery designes," or of "perfidious Savages," or that "I know their faining love is towards me not without a deadly hatred." Increasingly, of course, this was true, as Powhatan, finding his efforts to build a mutually profitable relationship fading, withheld trading privileges and assumed an uncooperative stance.

It was John Smith who, more than any other figure, wrought the most significant change in English attitudes and policy toward Powhatan. As the Jamestown settlement struggled for existence in 1607 and 1608, plagued by hunger, disease, dissension, and a remarkable refusal of most of its participants to work for their own survival, Smith emerged as the "strong man." Experienced in military exploits, skilled in cartography, seemingly indestructible, Smith initiated an aggressive Indian policy, based on the burning of Indian canoes, fields, and villages, in order to extort food supplies and to cow Powhatan and other tribal leaders. "The patient Councel, that nothing would move to warre with the Salvages," was replaced by a policy of terrorization, which "brought them [the Indians] in such feare and obedience, as his very name would sufficiently affright them." It is not easy to fathom Smith's perception of the situation, especially since so much of the information available for this period must be gleaned from his own accounts. But certainly important in Smith's assessment of the Indians' intentions was the petty theft of English implements by Indians who circulated in the English settlements in the first year, the confession of two Indians in May 1608 (under duress if not torture) that Powhatan was the recipient of the stolen objects and was secretly plotting to wipe out the colony, and Smith's worldwide military experience, which convinced him that with "heathen" people the best defense was a good offense. On the last point Smith wrote that "the Warres in *Europe, Asia,* and *Affrica,* taught me how to subdue the wilde Salvages in *Virginia* and *New-England,* in *America.*"

In the short run most of the colonists thought that Smith's policy of intimidation paid off. As it was later written, "Where before, wee had sometime peace and warre twice in a day, and very seldome a weeke but we had some trecherous villany or other," now the Indians, both the openly hostile and the professedly friendly, were tamed. But Smith's ruthless and indiscriminate approach disturbed some Virginia leaders who thought that on several occasions he mercilessly killed and attacked Indians who had done the English no harm and thus destroyed chances of profitable trade with the Indians while sowing the seeds for future discord. But Smith convinced most in the colony, as well as the managers of the London-based Virginia Company, of the efficacy of his strategy. The new attitude toward the Indians is apparent in the orders for Sir Thomas Gates, who sailed from England in 1609 to take command of the colony. In 1606 the Company had instructed: "In all your passages you must have great care not to offend the naturals, if you can eschew it." Now Gates was ordered to effect a military occupation of the Chesapeake region, to make all tribes tributary to him rather than Powhatan, to extract corn, furs, dye, and labor from each tribe in proportion to its number, and, if possible, to mold the natives into an agricultural labor force as the Spanish had attempted in their colonies. As the English settlement gained in strength following the arrival of six hundred additional colonists in 1610, Gates continued Smith's policy of intimidation, as did his successor, Sir Thomas Dale. In 1610, and 1611, following sporadic violence by both sides, three attacks by the English took the lives of a significant part of the population of three tribes and destroyed the tribal centers of Appomattucks and Kecoughtan. In 1613, the English kidnapped Powhatan's favorite daughter, Pocahontas, who had acted as intervening savior in 1608 when Powhatan conducted a mock execution of the captured John Smith. Pocahontas immediately won the love of John Rolfe, a leader in the colony, and Powhatan was reluctantly persuaded of the political advantages of allowing the first, and perhaps the only, Anglo-Indian marriage in Virginia's early history. A period of peace followed, and this, one suspects, further confirmed many in their view that the English policy, as it had evolved, was the best that could be devised.

In spite of this tendency to read hostility and savagery into the Indians' character, the early leaders of the Virginia colony manifested a strong curiosity about native culture and in their writings did not suppress their respect for it. John Smith, as has been indicated, was the foremost proponent in the early years of cowing the Indians through repeated demonstrations of the English martial spirit and superiority in weapons. But in his descriptions of Indian culture Smith revealed a genuine respect for the native way of life. He marveled at the Indians' strength and agility, their talent for hunting and fishing, their music and entertainment. He noted that civil government was practiced by them, that they adhered to religious traditions, and that many of their customs and institutions were not unlike those of the Europeans. Smith's statement that "although the countrie people be very barbarous; yet have they amongst them such government, as that their Magistrats for good commanding, and their people for du subjection, and obeying, excell in many places that would be counted very civill" illustrates the tendency to define the native as a hostile savage but still to retain an avid interest in his way of life. William Strachey, who served as secretary to the colony from 1610 to 1611, and Henry Spelman, who lived among the Indians for four years, also wrote appreciatively about Indian life. Borrowing liberally from Smith and other authors, Strachey wondered how the Indians could have effected "so generall and grosse a defection from the true knowledg of God." But with this off his chest, he went on to portray the natives as "ingenious enough in their owne workes" and in possession of much of the apparatus of "civilized" society. Alexander

Whitaker, an Anglican minister who proselytized among the Indians, wrote that some men "are farre mistaken in the nature of these men, for besides the promise of God, which is without respect of persons, made as well to unwise men after the flesh, as to the wise, etc. let us not thinke that these men are so simple as some have supposed them: for they are of body lustie, strong, and very nimble: they are a very understanding generation, quicke of apprehension, suddaine in their dispatches, subtile in their dealings, exquisite in their inventions, and industrious in their labour." Whitaker's comments indicate the division of opinion that may have been growing in Virginia, with some men beginning to blot from their minds some of the positive characteristics of Indian society they had earlier observed.

Notwithstanding misconceptions on both sides, the English and the Indians lived in close contact during the first years. Neither mutual distrust nor intermittent conflict nor casualties on both sides kept the English from trading with the Indians when they could, from sporadically conducting experiments in proselytizing and educating the Indians, and even from fleeing to Indian villages where some of the settlers found life more agreeable than at Jamestown where a military regimen prevailed after 1608. After the colony's ability to survive and overmatch the Indians was established, Indians were frequently admitted to the white settlements as day laborers. Though perhaps accepting hostility as the norm after the first few years, both sides were tacitly agreeing to exploit the dangerous presence of the other as best they could.

Although the documentary record becomes much thinner after 1612, it appears that it was in the decade following this date that a major change in Indian relations occurred in Virginia. The Virginia Company of London gave up its plans for reaping vast profits through Indian trade or the discovery of minerals and instead instituted a liberal land policy designed to build the population of the colony rapidly and ultimately to make it an agricultural province of such productivity that land sales would enrich its investors. When the cultivation of tobacco was perfected, giving Virginia a money crop of great potential, and further promotional efforts were rewarded with a new influx of settlers after 1619, the availability of land became a critical question for the first time in the colony's existence. As more and more men began pushing up the James River and its tributaries in the second decade of settlement to carve tobacco plantations out of the wilderness, the Indians of the region perceived that what had heretofore been an abrasive and often violent relationship might now become a disastrous one. It was the tension of a rapidly growing—and

spreading—population that provided the highly combustible atmosphere that in 1622 was ignited by the murder of a greatly re-
spected Indian of the Powhatan confederacy. The result was a well-
coordinated, all-out attack on the white settlements in that year.

In studying the colonial image of the Indian, the details of the
"massacre" of 1622 are less important than the effect it had on English perceptions of the natives. It was, of course, a genuine disaster
for the Virginia Company of London, which was shortly to go bank-
rupt, and for the weary Virginia settlement, which lost about one-
third of its inhabitants. But more important, it confirmed beyond
doubt what most Englishmen had suspected from the beginning: that
all Indians were inherently treacherous, cunning, and infinitely hostile. No longer would it be necessary to acknowledge an obligation to
civilize and Christianize the native. Even though several leaders in
the colony confided that the real cause of the Indian attack was "our
owne perfidiouse dealing with them," it was generally agreed that
henceforward the English would be free to hunt down the native
wherever he could be found. A no-holds-barred approach to "the Indian problem" was now adopted. Whereas before the colonists claimed
(at least officially) that they followed the principle of retributive justice, only engaging in attacks against the natives when they had been
assaulted, now they were entitled to put aside all restraint and take
the offensive. As one leader wrote revealingly after the Indian attack:

Our hands which before were tied with gentlenesse and faire usage, are
now set at liberty by the treacherous violence of the Sausages. . . . So
that we, who hitherto have had possession of no more ground then their
waste and our purchase at a valuable consideration to theire owne con-
tentment, gained; may now by right of Warre, and law of Nations, in-
vade the Country, and destroy them who sought to destroy us: whereby
wee shall enjoy their cultivated places, turning the laborious Mattocke
into the victorious Sword (wherein there is more both ease, benefit, and
glory) and possessing the fruits of others labours. Now their cleared
grounds in all their villages (which are situate in the fruitfullest places
of the land) shall be inhabited by us, whereas heretofore the grubbing of
woods was the greatest labour.

A note of grim satisfaction that the Indians had succeeded in wiping
out one-third of the English settlement can be detected. Now the colonizers were entitled to devastate Indian villages and to take rather
than buy the best land of the area. John Smith, writing two years
after the attack, noted that some men held that the massacre "will be
good for the Plantation, because now we have just cause to destroy
them by all meanes possible."

Another writer gave clear expression to his genocidal intent when he reasoned that the Indians had done the colonists a favor by sweeping away the previous English reluctance to annihilate the Indians. Now the colony would prosper. The author relished in enumerating the ways that the "savages" could be exterminated. "Victorie," he wrote, "may bee gained many waies: by force, by surprize, by famine in burning their Corne, by destroying and burning their Boats, Canoes, and Houses, by breaking their fishing Weares, by assailing them in their huntings, whereby they get the greatest part of their sustenance in Winter, by pursuing and chasing them with our horses, and blood-Hounds to draw after them, and Mastives to teare them."

Once the thirst for revenge was slaked, the only debatable question was whether the extermination of the Indians would work to the benefit or disadvantage of the colony. John Martin, a prominent planter, offered several "Reasons why it is not fittinge utterlye to make an exterpation of the Savages yett," and then assured his readers that it was not genocide he was against but the destruction of a people who, if properly subjected, could enrich all of the Virginians through their labor. Martin's advice was ignored and during each summer in the decade following the attack of 1622, the provincial government dispatched raiding parties to destroy Indians and their crops wherever they could be found. In 1629 a peace treaty was negotiated but then rejected because it was decided by the Virginia Council that a policy of "perpetual enmity" would serve the colony better. Rather than interpret the massacre of 1622 as the culmination of conflicting interests and acts of violence on both sides, the Virginians sought its origins in the nature of the native man. Because of the attack he had launched, the Indian had defined himself in a way that justified any course of action that the English might devise.

In the aftermath of the massacre of 1622 an unambiguously negative image of the Indian appeared. It would be strengthened and confirmed by later Indian attacks in 1644 and 1675. Words such as "perfidious," "cunning," "barbarous," and "improvident" had been used heretofore in describing the native, but his culture still commanded considerable respect in English eyes. After 1622, the Indians' culture was seldom deemed worthy of consideration. More and more abusive words crept into English descriptions of the Indian. Negative qualities were projected onto him with increasing frequency. Words like "beastly," "brutish," and "deformed" can be found in descriptions of the Indians after 1622. Whereas John Smith and others had described them as "ingenious," "industrious," and "quick of apprehension," Edward Waterhouse, writing after the massacre, informed his readers that the Indians "are by nature sloathfull and idle, vitious, melancholy, slovenly, of bad conditions, lyers, of small memory, of no constancy or trust . . . by nature of all people the most lying and most inconstant in the world, sottish and sodaine: never looking what dangers may happen afterwards, lesse capable then children of sixe or seaven yeares old, and lesse apt and ingenious." This vocabulary of abuse reflects not only the rage of the decimated colony but an inner need to provide a justification for colonial policy for generations to come. Hereafter, the elimination of the Indians could be rationalized far more easily, for they were seen as vicious, cultureless, unreconstructible savages rather than merely as hostile and primitive men, though men with an integral culture and a way of life worthy of notice.

The psychological calculus by which intentions governed white attitudes can be seen more clearly by studying the views of Englishmen who genuinely desired amicable relations with the Indians. The Quakers of Pennsylvania and West New Jersey, who were the most important early practitioners of pacifism in the New World, threatened no violence to the Indians when they arrived in the Delaware River Valley in the last quarter of the seventeenth century. It was pacifism, not violence, that was on the minds of the Quakers. Eager to avoid the conflict which had beset other colonies and committed ideologically to banishing violence and war, the Quakers viewed the Indian in a different light. Though regarding him as backward and "under a dark Night in things relating to Religion," they also saw him as physically attractive, generous, mild tempered, and possessed of many admirable traits. William Penn, the proprietor of the colony, gave new expression to old speculations that the Indians were the "Jews of America," the descendants of the Lost Tribes of Israel. He found their language "lofty" and full of words "of more sweetness or greatness" than most European tongues. Though Quaker relations with the Indians were not so benign as some historians have suggested, it is significant that not a single incident of organized violence between Indians and Quakers occurred during the colonial period. The deterioration of Indian relations in Pennsylvania can be traced primarily to the rapid influx after 1713 of German and Scotch-Irish settlers whose land hunger and indifference toward the Indians combined with the Anglo-French wars of the mid-eighteenth century set the frontier in flames for a quarter century.

In the southern colonies the image of the Indian also began to change once the resistance of the natives to the territorial encroachment of white settlers faded. In almost all the colonies, concerted attacks by the Indians lasted only into the third generation. Thereafter the Indians who had survived contact with European culture either moved beyond the reach of the colonizers, at least temporarily, or lived within white communities in a subservient status. Thus, in Virginia the last significant Indian attack came in 1675. In South Carolina, settled six decades later, the last major Indian offensives were mounted in the Tuscarora and Yamasee Wars of the early eighteenth century. Later in the eighteenth century Indian tribes fought English settlers on numerous occasions, but always as adjuncts of their French or Spanish allies who armed, directed, and controlled them, rather than as independent nations.

When the precariousness of the English position was eliminated as a significant factor in Anglo-Indian relations and when large-scale attacks on white communities had subsided, the image of the Indian began to change, at least among the literate or reflective element of society. Because the social context of Indian-white relations was changing, the white community was far better disposed emotionally to see the Indian as another cultural group rather than simply as the enemy. In the first half of the eighteenth century a number of colonial observers began to develop a new image of the Indian. Unlike later writers, who from seaboard cities or European centers of culture sentimentalized the native into a "noble savage," these men knew of Indian life from first-hand experience as missionaries, provincial officials, and fur traders. Close to Indian culture, but not pitted against the native in a fight for land or survival, they developed clearer perspectives on aboriginal life. Not yet seized by the certainty that they were fulfilling a divine mission in North America, they were able to take a more anthropological approach to Indian society rather than assaying it only in terms of its proximity to English culture.

All of the components in the revised image of the Indian emerging in the eighteenth century were linked together by the basic assumption that the Indians' culture was worth examining on its own terms. This in itself was a significant change, since during the period of Indian attacks most colonists had regarded the Indians as cultureless. Samuel Purchas's charge of 1625 that the Indians were "bad people, having little of humanities but shape, ignorant of Civilitie, or Arts, or Religion: more brutish then the beasts they hunt, more wild and unmanly then that unmanned wild Countrey, which they range rather then inhabite" was a classic statement of the earlier view of the worthlessness or absence of Indian culture. But now Englishmen began to discover all of the missing elements in the Indians' cultural makeup—government, social structure, religion, family organization, codes of justice and mortality, crafts and arts.

So far as can be ascertained from the surviving sources, an unpublished anonymous account of 1689, perhaps by the Anglican minister John Clayton, was the first attempt since John Smith's description of 1612 to take Indian culture seriously. "The Indians in Virginia . . ." assumed a reportorial tone and described Indian customs, though not the Indians' character, in a neutral way. Far more significant was Robert Beverley's *The History and Present State of Virginia . . . ,* published in 1705, almost a century after the planting of the Jamestown settlement and at a time when the Indian population of the settled regions of the colony had declined from an estimated eighteen thousand in 1607 to about two thousand. Even in the chapter headings he used—"Religion and Worship," "Laws and Authority," "Learning and Language," "Marriage and Children," and "Crafts"— Beverley revealed a new attitude toward the native. Much of what he saw in Indian culture reminded him of classical Spartan life. Beverley used words like "strange" or "remarkable" to describe Indian customs, but completely absent from his account were those earlier adjectival indicators such as "beastly," "savage," "primitive," "monstrous," and "idolatrous." In Beverley's description can be seen the beginning of a new genre of literature on the Indian—a genre which included a foretaste of the "noble savage" tradition, but which was more fundamentally rooted in a desire to describe the Indians' culture than to use it as a foil for demonstrating the decadence of western civilization.

Four years later, John Lawson, a proprietary officeholder who traveled extensively among the tribes of South Carolina and Georgia, published a lengthier description of Indian culture. In *A New Voyage to Carolina,* Lawson attempted to describe the material culture of the southern tribes and to examine their social, political, and religious institutions. Lawson's account was not free of judgmental statements about the "imbecilities" of certain native customs or their "lazy, idle" habits. But like Beverley he seems to have made a conscious attempt to step back from his own cultural standards when observing the music, dancing, games, marriage and family customs, medicine, religion, and government of the southeastern tribes among which he traveled for eight years.

Some eighteenth-century writers were, however, still employing words like "savage," "monstrous," and "idolatrous" to describe the Indians. William Stith's *The History of the First Discovery and Settle-*

ment of Virginia . . . , published in 1747, pictured the Indian as inherently treacherous and barbarous. Relying heavily on the early accounts of Virginia by John Smith and Thomas Hariot, Stith insisted that the English had always treated the Indians "with the utmost Humanity and Kindness, out of the Hope and Desire, of thereby alluring and bringing them over, to the Knowledge of God and his true Religion." At Jamestown, the Indians had been "fed at their Tables, and even lodged in their Bedchambers; so that they seemed, entirely to have coalesced, and to live together, as one People." The Indians had repaid this generous treatment, Stith claimed, with perfidious attacks on the English settlement. The Anglican minister, Hugh Jones, writing in 1724, was equally prepared to assign blame for Anglo-Indian hostility to the natives and to describe them as savage and idolatrous. But Jones also found the Indians serious in debate and possessed of "tolerable good notions of natural justice, equity, honor, and honesty." Although he could not persuade himself that the Indians would ever rise to the level of Christianity, Jones was far more appreciative of native culture than his seventeenth-century predecessors.

The most complete statement of the integrity of Indian culture came from James Adair in his *History of the American Indians* . . . , published in 1775 and based on forty years of experience as an Indian trader on the frontiers of South Carolina and Georgia. In an argument extending to more than two hundred pages, Adair labored to prove the descent of the American Indians from the ancient Jews. In matters as widely separated as adherence to theocratic governments, genius for language and rhetoric, and manner of embalming the dead, Adair found links between Semitic and Indian culture. Like a number of others who were describing the Indians, Adair was impressed with the "plain and honest law of nature" which governed native society and by the strong sense of religion that gave meaning and coherence to native life.

Just as a new view of native culture was appearing in the eighteenth century, ideas about the Indians' character traits—or what would come to be called personality—were undergoing a marked change. Widespread agreement cannot be found among colonial writers, of course, for each was influenced by his own background and by his special purposes in writing about the Indians. Moreover, the personality of the Indian was in the process of change as he struggled to adapt to the presence of more and more Europeans and African slaves in his ancestral lands. But despite significant differences, eighteenth-century colonial observers of Indian character were far more favorable than those of an earlier period, when the ultimate outcome of Anglo-Indian confrontation had still been in doubt.

On one point agreement was nearly unanimous: the Indians were extraordinarily brave. Both men and women were fired with the most unswerving loyalty to their tribe and endowed with incredible stoicism under torture and duress. At the same time, most observers thought the Indians were revengeful, never forgetting an ill deed or an injustice. Agreement was general that this was a weakness in the Indian, though to identify this as a defect was ironic inasmuch as colonial Indian policy was unambiguous on the need to administer swift and severe retribution for every Indian offense.

Predictably, observers took a variety of positions on the honesty of the natives. The old image of the cunning, deceitful, treacherous Indian retained its currency. But other observers insisted that the Indians were more straightforward and honorable in matters of trade and land exchange than the English. For example, Edmond Atkin, who was appointed southern superintendent of the Indians in 1756, was convinced that "in their publick Treaties no People on earth are more open, explicit and Direct. Nor are they excelled by any in the observance of them."

In the more favorable image of the Indian that was emerging, an element of considerable importance, because it related to the origins of Anglo-Indian hostility, concerned the attitude of Indians toward strangers. After the first concerted Indian attacks of the seventeenth century, writers had characterized the native as brutish, vicious, and hostile by nature. But in the eighteenth century, men who traveled among or negotiated with the Indians discovered that hospitality and generosity were important in the Indians' structure of values. Robert Beverley made the point explicitly by noting that the Indians had been "at first very fair and friendly" and provided the provisions that kept the struggling Jamestown colony alive during the first hard winter. Edmond Atkin charged that the English had received "a very hospitable Reception" at Roanoke Island but were rewarded for their pains by the leader of the colony, Richard Grenville, who punished the Indians for the action of a native "who did not know the difference of Value between [the silver cup] and a horn Spoon." Missionaries of the Society for the Propagation of the Gospel, the evangelical arm of the Anglican church, also reported on the equable temperament and generosity of the natives. In 1706, for example, Francis Le Jau's first impressions of the Yamasee Indians in South Carolina were of a "very quiet, sweet humor'd and patient [people], content with little."

Physical attractiveness also commanded the attention of eighteenth-century commentators. In the previous century the Indian had not been regarded as physically repulsive, as was the African in some cases, but neither had the Indian women been generally regarded as suitable for marriage. Now, early in the eighteenth century, it was proposed that the Indians had an uncommonly handsome physique which commended them for racial intermixture. William Byrd, one of Virginia's largest plantation owners and a man who kept the pleasures of the flesh and the mind in exquisite balance, described the Indians as strong, handsome, and at least as attractive as the first English settlers. Byrd was sufficiently impressed by the Indians' features to suggest that intermarriage should offend the tastes of nobody. If practiced earlier, he argued, a century of bloodshed might have been avoided. Their fine bodies, wrote Byrd in a revealing comment, "may make full Amends for the Darkness of their Complexions." If the English had not been "so Squeamish" and imbued with a "false Delicacy," they might have made a "prudent alliance" with the Indians of the Chesapeake region to everyone's benefit. Byrd believed the Indians had been offended by this rejection and could never "perswade themselves that the English were heartily their Friends, so long as they disdained to intermarry with them." He advised that a lost opportunity might still be reclaimed by intermarriage—the "Modern Policy" in French Canada and Louisiana. Robert Beverley took a similar view. He described Indian males as "straight and well proportion'd, having the cleanest and most exact limbs in the World." As for the native woman, she was "generally Beautiful, possessing uncommon delicacy of Shape and Features, and wanting no Charm, but that of a fair Complexion." Like Byrd, Beverley regretted that intermarriage had not occurred. Lawson was another who remarked on the admirable stature of the Indian men, commenting on their "full and manly" eyes, their "sedate and majestick" gait, and their strength and agility. Indian women were no less appealing. They were described as "fine shap'd Creatures . . . as any in the Universe" and their smiles "afford the finest Composure a Face can possess."

Closely tied to physical attractiveness in the mind of white writers was the notion of cleanliness—both of body and mind. Earlier colonists, perhaps projecting their own feelings of embarrassment and guilt, had frequently remarked on the nakedness and open sexual relations of the Indians, concluding that the natives were dirty and lewd. Beverley, however, wrote that Indian marriage was "most sacred and inviolable" and that the women were relaxed, good humored, and full of dignity. Though white men charged unmarried Indian women with promiscuity, he was convinced that this was only a projection of "the guilt of their own consciences," and added that white men, who kept their women in tight rein, were "not very nice in distinguishing betwixt guilt, and harmless freedom" when they saw the familiarity and openness of young Indian girls. Adair was in agreement. He found the native women "of a mild amiable soft disposition: exceedingly soft in their behaviour," and compared Indian marriage and divorce traditions with those of the ancient Hebrews. The tribes of southeastern America had high moral standards, inhabited "clean, neat dwelling houses," and were critical, with much cause, of the laxity of white morals. The Anglican missionary Le Jau, after observing both white and red settlements in South Carolina for a year, concluded that the Indians "make us ashamed by their life, Conversation and Sense of Religion." Whereas English settlers talked about religion and morality, the Indians lived it. Lawson, however, was offended by the Indian practice of fornication before marriage and the readiness of Indian women to prostitute themselves to fur traders. But in personal habits he found the natives clean and "sweet."

The ability to take a more dispassionate view of the Indian allowed discussion of the effects of white society on the Indians' way of life. Earlier, when the Indian had been seen simply as a savage, it was logical to assume that the confrontation of cultures could only benefit the indigenous man. If Europeans were civilized and Indians were heathen, cultural interaction would necessarily improve the inferior group. But eighteenth-century observers, more wont to take Indian culture on its own terms, frequently concluded that colonizing Europeans had perverted rather than converted the Indian. The English had introduced drunkenness and covetousness, Beverley complained, and robbed the natives of much of their "Felicity, as well as their innocence." Almost every pre-Revolutionary eighteenth-century writer agreed that the Indians had been debauched by rum, and educated in thievery, avariciousness, and immorality. The lowest elements of white society, in most frequent contact with the natives, gave the Indians cause to suspect the superiority of white Christian culture to which they were incessantly urged to aspire. Fur traders were no better, constituting a "Wretched sort of Men," as one Anglican missionary put it. Agreement was general among the Society for the Propagation of the Gospel that it was impossible to convert the native until the "white barbarians" of the frontier areas, as Benjamin Franklin called them, had been brought within the pale of civilization.

Ironically, the new image of the Indian was emerging at a time when the native qualities most likely to gain the admiration or respect of white society were disappearing. Ravaged by alcohol and European diseases, decimated by wars in which they fought at a technological disadvantage, the tribes of the coastal area were losing many of the age-old skills and cultural attributes which commended them to eighteenth-century observers. Even while the new view of him formed, the indigenous American was in some areas slipping into a state of dependency which eroded white respect enormously. As the gun and knife replaced the bow and arrow, as the kettle and fishhook replaced handfashioned implements, and as rum became the great pain killer for those whose culture was undergoing rapid change, the grudging respect of white culture turned to contempt. While the colonial intelligentsia was discovering the integrity of native culture in the eighteenth century, the ordinary farmer and frontiersman found less and less to admire in Indian life. For the Indian the limited respect of European colonizers had come too late to halt the process of cultural change which would leave his image impaired and his power to resist further cultural and territorial aggrandizement fatally weakened. For the colonist, the image of the native, so useful in the past, would continue to reflect the needs and intentions of a restless, ambitious people.

WINTHROP D. JORDAN
Unthinking Decision
Enslavement of Negroes in America to 1700

At the start of English settlement in America, no one had in mind to establish the institution of Negro slavery. Yet in less than a century the foundations of a peculiar institution had been laid. The first Negroes landed in Virginia in 1619, though very, very little is known about their precise status during the next twenty years. Between 1640 and 1660 there is evidence of enslavement, and after 1660 slavery crystallized on the statute books of Maryland, Virginia, and other colonies. By 1700 when African Negroes began flooding into English America they were treated as somehow deserving a life and status radically different from English and other European settlers. The Negro had been debased to a condition of chattel slavery; at some point, Englishmen in America had created a legal status which ran counter to English law.

Unfortunately the details of this process can never be completely reconstructed; there is simply not enough evidence (and very little chance of more to come) to show precisely when and how and why Negroes came to be treated so differently from white men, though there is just enough to make historians differ as to its meaning. Concerning the first years of contact especially we have very little infor-

"Unthinking Decision: Enslavement of Negroes in America to 1700," reprinted by permission from Winthrop D. Jordan, *White Over Black: American Attitudes Toward the Negro 1550-1812* (Chapel Hill: University of North Carolina Press for the Institute of Early American History and Culture, Williamsburg, Virginia, 1968), pp. 44–45, 71–82, 91–97.

mation as to what impression Negroes made upon English settlers: accordingly, we are left knowing less about the formative years than about later periods of American slavery. That those early years were crucial ones is obvious, for it was then that the cycle of Negro debasement began; once the Negro became fully the slave it is not hard to see why white men looked down upon him. Yet precisely because understanding the dynamics of these early years is so important to understanding the centuries which followed, it is necessary to bear with the less than satisfactory data and to attempt to reconstruct the course of debasement undergone by Negroes in seventeenth-century America. . . .

ENSLAVEMENT: VIRGINIA AND MARYLAND

In Virginia and Maryland the development of Negro slavery followed a very different course [from that found in New England], for several reasons. Most obviously, geographic conditions and the intentions of the settlers quickly combined to produce a successful agricultural staple. The deep tidal rivers, the long growing season, the fertile soil, and the absence of strong communal spirit among the settlers opened the way. Ten years after settlers first landed at Jamestown they were on the way to proving, in the face of assertions to the contrary, that it was possible "to found an empire upon smoke." More than the miscellaneous productions of New England, tobacco required labor which was cheap but not temporary, mobile but not independent, and tireless rather than skilled. In the Chesapeake area more than anywhere to the northward, the shortage of labor and the abundance of land—the "frontier"—placed a premium on involuntary labor.

This need for labor played more directly upon these settlers' ideas about freedom and bondage than it did either in the West Indies or in New England. Perhaps it would be more accurate to say that settlers in Virginia (and in Maryland after settlement in 1634) made their decisions concerning Negroes while relatively virginal, relatively free from external influences and from firm preconceptions. Of all the important early English settlements, Virginia had the least contact with the Spanish, Portuguese, Dutch, and other English colonies. At the same time, the settlers of Virginia did not possess either the legal or Scriptural learning of the New England Puritans whose conception of the just war had opened the way to the enslavement of Indians. Slavery in the tobacco colonies did not begin as an adjunct of captivity; in marked contrast to the Puritan response to the Pequot War the settlers of Virginia did *not* generally react to the Indian massacre of 1622 with propositions for taking captives and selling them as "slaves." It was perhaps a correct measure of the conceptual atmosphere in Virginia that there was only one such proposition after the 1622 disaster and that that one was defective in precision as to how exactly one treated captive Indians.

In the absence, then, of these influences which obtained in other English colonies, slavery as it developed in Virginia and Maryland assumes a special interest and importance over and above the fact that Negro slavery was to become a vitally important institution there and, later, to the southwards. In the tobacco colonies it is possible to watch Negro slavery *develop,* not pop up full-grown overnight, and it is therefore possible to trace, very imperfectly, the development of the shadowy, unexamined rationale which supported it. The concept of Negro slavery there was neither borrowed from foreigners, nor extracted from books, nor invented out of whole cloth, nor extrapolated from servitude, nor generated by English reaction to Negroes as such, nor necessitated by the exigencies of the New World. Not any one of these made the Negro a slave, but all.

In rough outline, slavery's development in the tobacco colonies seems to have undergone three stages. Negroes first arrived in 1619, only a few days late for the meeting of the first representative assembly in America. John Rolfe described the event with the utmost unconcern: "About the last of August came in a dutch man of warre that sold us twenty Negars." Negroes continued to trickle in slowly for the next half century; one report in 1649 estimated that there were three hundred among Virginia's population of fifteen thousand—about 2 per cent. Long before there were more appreciable numbers, the development of slavery had, so far as we can tell, shifted gears. Prior to about 1640, there is very little evidence to show how Negroes were treated—though we will need to return to those first twenty years in a moment. After 1640 there is mounting evidence that some Negroes were in fact being treated as slaves, at least that they were being held in hereditary lifetime service. This is to say that the twin essences of slavery—the two kinds of perpetuity—first become evident during the twenty years prior to the beginning of legal formulation. After 1660 slavery was written into statute law. Negroes began to flood into the two colonies at the end of the seventeenth century. In 1705 Virginia produced a codification of laws applying to slaves.

Concerning the first of these stages, there is only one major historical certainty, and unfortunately it is the sort which historians find hardest to bear. There simply is not enough evidence to indicate with any certainty whether Negroes were treated like white servants or not. At least we can be confident, therefore, that the two most common assertions about the first Negroes—that they were slaves and that they were servants—are *unfounded,* though not necessarily incorrect. And what of the positive evidence?

Some of the first group bore Spanish names and presumably had been baptized, which would mean they were at least nominally Christian, though of the Papist sort. They had been "sold" to the English; so had other Englishmen but not by the Dutch. Certainly these Negroes were not fully free, but many Englishmen were not. It can be said, though, that from the first in Virginia Negroes were set apart from white men by the word *Negroes.* The earliest Virginia census reports plainly distinguished Negroes from white men, often giving Negroes no personal name; in 1629 every commander of the several plantations was ordered to "take a generall muster of all the inhabitants men woemen and Children as well *Englishe* as Negroes." A distinct name is not attached to a group unless it is regarded as distinct. It seems logical to suppose that this perception of the Negro as being distinct from the Englishman must have operated to debase his status rather than to raise it, for in the absence of countervailing social factors, the need for labor in the colonies usually told in the direction of non-freedom. There were few countervailing factors present, surely, in such instances as in 1629 when a group of Negroes were brought to Virginia freshly captured from a Portuguese vessel which had snatched them from Angola a few weeks earlier. Given the context of English thought and experience, . . . it seems probable that the Negro's status was not ever the same as that accorded the white servant. But we do not know for sure.

When the first fragmentary evidence appears about 1640 it becomes clear that *some* Negroes in both Virginia and Maryland were serving for life and some Negro children inheriting the same obligation. Not all Negroes, certainly, for Nathaniel Littleton had released a Negro named Anthony Longoe from all service whatsoever in 1635, and after the mid-1640's the court records show that other Negroes were incontestably free and were accumulating property of their own. At least one Negro freeman, Anthony Johnson, himself owned a Negro. Some Negroes served only terms of usual length, but others were held for terms far longer than custom and statute permitted with white servants. The first fairly clear indication that slavery was practiced in the tobacco colonies appears in 1639, when a Maryland statute declared that "all the Inhabitants of this Province being Christians (Slaves excepted) Shall have and enjoy all such rights liberties immunities privileges and free customs within this Province as any naturall born subject of England." Another Maryland law passed the same year provided that "all persons being Christians (Slaves excepted)" over eighteen who were imported without indentures would serve for four years. These laws make very little sense unless the term *slaves* meant Negroes and perhaps Indians.

The next year, 1640, the first definite indication of outright enslavement appears in Virginia. The General Court pronounced sentence on three servants who had been retaken after absconding to Maryland. Two of them, a Dutchman and a Scot, were ordered to serve their masters for one additional year and then the colony for three more, but "the third being a negro named John Punch shall serve his said master or his assigns for the time of his natural life here or else where." No white servant in any English colony, so far as is known, ever received a like sentence. Later the same month a Negro (possibly the same enterprising fellow) was again singled out from a group of recaptured runaways; six of the seven culprits were assigned additional time while the Negro was given none, presumably because he was already serving for life.

After 1640, when surviving Virginia county court records began to mention Negroes, sales for life, often including any future progeny, were recorded in unmistakable language. In 1646 Francis Pott sold a Negro woman and boy to Stephen Charlton "to the use of him . . . forever." Similarly, six years later William Whittington sold to John Pott "one Negro girle named Jowan; aged about Ten yeares and with her Issue and produce duringe her (or either of them) for their Life tyme. And their Successors forever"; and a Maryland man in 1649 deeded two Negro men and a woman "and all their issue both male and Female." The executors of a York County estate in 1647 disposed of eight Negroes—four men, two women, and two children—to Captain John Chisman "to have hold occupy posesse and injoy and every one of the afforementioned Negroes forever." The will of Rowland Burnham of "Rapahanocke," made in 1657, dispensed his considerable number of Negroes and white servants in language which clearly differentiated between the two by specifying that the whites were to serve for their "full terme of tyme" and the Negroes "for ever." Nothing in the will indicated that this distinction was exceptional or novel.

Further evidence that some Negroes were serving for life in this period lies in the prices paid for them. In many instances the valuations placed on Negroes (in estate inventories and bills of sale) were far higher than for white servants, even those servants with full terms yet to serve. Higher prices must have meant that Negroes were more highly valued because of their greater length of service. Negro women may have been especially prized, moreover, because their progeny could also be held perpetually. In 1643, for example, William Burdett's inventory listed eight servants, with the time each had still to serve, at valuations ranging from 400 to 1,100 pounds of tobacco, while a "very anntient" Negro was valued at 3,000 and an eight-year-old Negro girl at 2,000 pounds, with no time remaining indicated for either. In the late 1650's an inventory of Thomas Ludlow's estate evaluated a white servant with six years to serve at less than an elderly Negro man and only one half of a Negro woman. Similarly, the labor owned by James Stone in 1648 was evaluated as follows:

	lb tobo
Thomas Groves, 4 yeares to serve	1300
Francis Bomley for 6 yeares	1500
John Thackstone for 3 yeares	1300
Susan Davis for 3 yeares	1000
Emaniell a Negro man	2000
Roger Stone 3 yeares	1300
Mingo a Negro man	2000

The 1655 inventory of Argoll Yeardley's estate provides clear evidence of a distinction between perpetual and limited service for Negroes. Under the heading "Servants" were listed "Towe Negro men, towe Negro women (their wifes) one Negro girle aged 15 yeares, Item One Negro girle aged about teen yeares and one Negro child aged about sixe moneths," valued at 12,000 pounds, and under the heading "Corne" were "Servants, towe men their tyme three months," valued at 300 pounds, and "one Negro boye ['about three yeares old'] (which by witness of his godfather) is to bee free att twenty foure yeares of age and then to have towe cowes given him," valued at 600 pounds. Besides setting a higher value on Negroes, these inventories failed to indicate the number of years they had still to serve, presumably because their service was for an unlimited time.

Where Negro women were involved, higher valuations probably reflected the facts that their issue were valuable and that they could be used for field work while white women generally were not. This latter discrimination between Negro and white women did not necessarily involve perpetual service, but it meant that Negroes were set apart in a way clearly not to their advantage. This was not the only instance in which Negroes were subjected to degrading distinctions not immediately and necessarily attached to the concept of slavery. Negroes were singled out for special treatment in several ways which suggest a generalized debasement of Negroes as a group. Significantly, the first indications of this debasement appeared at about the same time as the first indications of actual enslavement.

The distinction concerning field work is a case in point. It first appears on the written record in 1643, when Virginia almost pointedly endorsed it in a tax law. Previously, in 1629, tithable persons had been defined as "all those that worke in the ground of what qualitie or condition soever." The new law provided that *all* adult men were tithable and, in addition, *Negro* women. The same distinction was made twice again before 1660. Maryland adopted a similar policy beginning in 1654. This official discrimination between Negro and other women was made by men who were accustomed to thinking of field work as being ordinarily the work of men rather than women. As John Hammond wrote in a 1656 tract defending the tobacco colonies, servant women were not put to work in the fields but in domestic employments, "yet som wenches that are nasty, and beastly and not fit to be so employed are put into the ground." The essentially racial character of this discrimination stood out clearly in a law passed in 1668 at the time slavery was taking shape in the statute books:

Whereas some doubts, have arisen whether negro women set free were still to be accompted tithable according to a former act, *It is declared by this grand assembly* that negro women, though permitted to enjoy their Freedome yet ought not in all respects to be admitted to a full fruition of the exemptions and impunities of the English, and are still lyable to payment of taxes.

Virginia law set Negroes apart from all other groups in a second way by denying them the important right and obligation to bear arms. Few restraints could indicate more clearly the denial to Negroes of membership in the white community. This first foreshadowing of the slave codes came in 1640, at just the time when other indications first appeared that Negroes were subject to special treatment.

Finally, an even more compelling sense of the separateness of Negroes was revealed in early reactions to sexual union between the races. Prior to 1660 the evidence concerning these reactions is equivocal, and it is not possible to tell whether repugnance for intermixture preceded legislative enactment of slavery. In 1630 an angry Virginia court sentenced "Hugh Davis to be soundly whipped, before an assembly of Negroes and others for abusing himself to the dishonor of God and shame of Christians, by defiling his body in lying with a negro," but it is possible that the "negro" may not have been female. With other instances of punishment for interracial union in the ensuing years, fornication rather than miscegenation may well have been the primary offense, though in 1651 a Maryland man sued someone who he claimed had said "that he had a black bastard in Virginia." (The court recognized the legitimacy of his complaint, but thought his claim for £20,000 sterling somewhat overvalued his reputation and awarded him 1500 pounds "of Tobacco and Cask.") There may have been no racial feeling involved when in 1640 Robert Sweet, a gentleman, was compelled "to do penance in church according to laws of England, for getting a negroe woman with child and the woman whipt." About 1650 a white man and a Negro woman were required to stand clad in white sheets before a congregation in lower Norfolk County for having had relations, but this punishment was sometimes used in cases of fornication between two whites. A quarter century later in 1676, however, the emergence of distaste for racial intermixture was unmistakable. A contemporary account of Bacon's Rebellion caustically described one of the ringleaders, Richard Lawrence, as a person who had eclipsed his learning and abilities "in the darke imbraces of a Blackamoore, his slave: And that in so fond a Maner, . . . to the noe meane Scandle and affrunt of all the Vottrisses in or about towne."

Such condemnation was not confined to polemics. In the early 1660's when slavery was gaining statutory recognition, the assemblies acted with full-throated indignation against miscegenation. These acts aimed at more than merely avoiding confusion of status. In 1662 Virginia declared that "if any christian shall committ Fornication with a negro man or woman, hee or shee soe offending" should pay double the usual fine. . . . Two years later Maryland banned interracial marriages: "forasmuch as divers freeborne English women forgettfull of their free Condicion and to the disgrace of our Nation doe intermarry with Negro Slaves by which alsoe divers suites may arise touching the Issue of such woemen and a great damage doth befall the Masters of such Negros for prevention whereof for deterring such freeborne women from such shamefull Matches," strong language indeed if "divers suites" had been the only problem. A Maryland act of 1681 described marriages of white women with Negroes as, among other things, "always to the Satisfaccion of theire Lascivious and Lustfull desires, and to the disgrace not only of the

English butt allso of many other Christian Nations." When Virginia finally prohibited all interracial liaisons in 1691, the Assembly vigorously denounced miscegenation and its fruits as "that abominable mixture and spurious issue."

From the surviving evidence, it appears that outright enslavement and these other forms of debasement appeared at about the same time in Maryland and Virginia. Indications of perpetual service, the very nub of slavery, coincided with indications that English settlers discriminated against Negro women, withheld arms from Negroes, and—though the timing is far less certain—reacted unfavorably to interracial sexual union. The coincidence suggests a mutual relationship between slavery and unfavorable assessment of Negroes. Rather than slavery causing "prejudice," or vice versa, they seem rather to have generated each other. Both were, after all, twin aspects of a general debasement of the Negro. Slavery and "prejudice" may have been equally cause and effect, continuously reacting upon each other, dynamically joining hands to hustle the Negro down the road to complete degradation. Much more than with the other English colonies, where the enslavement of Negroes was to some extent a borrowed practice, the available evidence for Maryland and Virginia points to less borrowing and to this kind of process: a mutually interactive growth of slavery and unfavorable assessment, with no cause for either which did not cause the other as well. If slavery caused prejudice, then invidious distinctions concerning working in the fields, bearing arms, and sexual union should have appeared *after* slavery's firm establishment. If prejudice caused slavery, then one would expect to find these lesser discriminations preceding the greater discrimination of outright enslavement. Taken as a whole, the evidence reveals a process of debasement of which hereditary lifetime service was an important but not the only part.

White servants did not suffer this debasement. Rather, their position improved, partly for the reason that they were not Negroes. By the early 1660's white men were loudly protesting against being made "slaves" in terms which strongly suggest that they considered slavery not as wrong but as inapplicable to themselves. The father of a Maryland apprentice petitioned in 1663 that "he Craves that his daughter may not be made a Slave a tearme soe Scandalous that if admitted to be the Condicon or tytle of the Apprentices in this Province will be soe distructive as noe free borne Christians will ever be induced to come over servants." An Irish youth complained to a Maryland court in 1661 that he had been kidnapped and forced to sign for fifteen years, that he had already served six and a half years and was now twenty-one, and that eight and a half more years of service was "contrary to the lawes of God and man that a Christian Subject should be made a Slave." (The jury blandly compromised the dispute by deciding that he should serve only until age twenty-one, but that he was now only nineteen.) Free Negro servants were generally increasingly less able to defend themselves against this insidious kind of encroachment. Increasingly, white men were more clearly free because Negroes had become so clearly slave.

Certainly it was the case in Maryland and Virginia that the legal enactment of Negro slavery followed social practice, rather than vice versa, and also that the assemblies were slower than in other English colonies to declare how Negroes could or should be treated. These two patterns in themselves suggest that slavery was less a matter of previous conception or external example in Maryland and Virginia than elsewhere.

The Virginia Assembly first showed itself incontrovertibly aware that Negroes were not serving in the same manner as English servants in 1660 when it declared "that for the future no servant comeing into the country without indentures, of what christian nation soever, shall serve longer then those of our own country, of the like age." In 1661 the Assembly indirectly provided statutory recognition that some Negroes served for life: "That in case any English servant shall run away in company with any negroes who are incapable of making satisfaction by addition of time," he must serve for the Negroes' lost time as well as his own. Maryland enacted a closely similar law in 1663 (possibly modeled on Virginia's) and in the following year, on the initiative of the lower house, came out with the categorical declaration that Negroes were to serve "Durante Vita." During the next twenty-odd years a succession of acts in both colonies defined with increasing precision what sorts of persons might be treated as slaves. Other acts dealt with the growing problem of slave control, and especially after 1690 slavery began to assume its now familiar character as a complete deprivation of all rights. As early as 1669 the Virginia Assembly unabashedly enacted a brutal law which showed where the logic of perpetual servitude was inevitably tending. Unruly servants could be chastened by sentences to additional terms, but "WHEREAS the only law in force for the punishment of refractory servants resisting their master, mistris or overseer cannot be inflicted upon negroes, nor the obstinacy of many of them by other then violent meanes supprest," if a slave "by the extremity of the correction should chance to die" his master was not to be adjudged guilty of felony "since it cannot be presumed that prepensed malice (which alone makes murther Felony) should induce any man to destroy his owne estate." Virginia planters felt they acted out of mounting necessity: there were disturbances among slaves in several areas in the early 1670's.

By about 1700 the slave ships began spilling forth their black cargoes in greater and greater numbers. By that time, racial slavery and the necessary police powers had been written into law. By that time, too, slavery had lost all resemblance to a perpetual and hereditary version of English servitude, though service for life still seemed to contemporaries its most essential feature. In the last quarter of the seventeenth century the trend was to treat Negroes more like property and less like men, to send them to the fields at younger ages, to deny them automatic existence as inherent members of the community, to tighten the bonds on their personal and civil freedom, and correspondingly to loosen the traditional restraints on the master's freedom to deal with his human property as he saw fit. In 1705 Virginia gathered up the random statutes of a whole generation and baled them into a "slave code" which would not have been out of place in the nineteenth century. . . .

RACIAL SLAVERY: FROM REASONS TO RATIONALE

In scanning the problem of *why* Negroes were enslaved in America, certain constant elements in a complex situation can be readily, if roughly, identified. It may be taken as given that there would have been no enslavement without economic need, that is, without persistent demand for labor in underpopulated colonies. Of crucial importance, too, was the fact that for cultural reasons Negroes were relatively helpless in the face of European aggressiveness and technology. In themselves, however, these two elements will not explain the enslavement of Indians and Negroes. The pressing exigency in America was labor, and Irish and English servants were available. Most of them would have been helpless to ward off outright enslavement if their masters had thought themselves privileged and able to enslave them. As a group, though, masters did not think themselves so empowered. Only with Indians and Negroes did Englishmen attempt so radical a deprivation of liberty—which brings the matter abruptly to the most difficult and imponderable question of all: what was it about Indians and Negroes which set them apart, which rendered them *different* from Englishmen, which made them special candidates for degradation?

To ask such questions is to inquire into the *content* of English attitudes, and unfortunately there is little evidence with which to build an answer. It may be said, however, that the heathen condition of the Negroes seemed of considerable importance to English settlers in America—more so than to English voyagers upon the coasts of Africa—and that heathenism was associated in some settlers' minds with the condition of slavery. This is not to say that the colonists enslaved Negroes because they were heathens. . . .

The importance and persistence of the tradition which attached slavery to heathenism did not become evident in any positive assertions that heathens might be enslaved. It was not until the period of legal establishment of slavery after 1660 that the tradition became manifest at all, and even then there was no effort to place heathenism and slavery on a one-for-one relationship. Virginia's second statutory definition of a slave (1682), for example, awkwardly attempted to rest enslavement on religious difference while excluding from possible enslavement all heathens who were not Indian or Negro. Despite such logical difficulties, the old European equation of slavery and religious difference did not rapidly vanish in America, for it cropped up repeatedly after 1660 in assertions that slaves by becoming Christian did not automatically become free. By about the end of the seventeenth century, Maryland, New York, Virginia, North and South Carolina, and New Jersey had all passed laws reassuring masters that conversion of their slaves did not necessitate manumission. These acts were passed in response to occasional pleas that Christianity created a claim to freedom and to much more frequent assertions by men interested in converting Negroes that nothing could be accomplished if masters thought their slaves were about to be snatched from them by meddling missionaries. This decision that the slave's religious condition had no relevance to his status as a slave (the only one possible if an already valuable economic institution was to be retained) strongly suggests that heathenism was an important component in the colonists' initial reaction to Negroes early in the century. . . .

In the early years, the English settlers most frequently contrasted themselves with Negroes by the term *Christian,* though they also sometimes described themselves as *English;* here the explicit religious distinction would seem to have lain at the core of English reaction. Yet the concept embodied by the term *Christian* embraced so much more meaning than was contained in specific doctrinal affirmations that it is scarcely possible to assume on the basis of this linguistic contrast that the colonists set Negroes apart because they were heathen. The historical experience of the English people in the six-teenth century had made for fusion of religion and nationality; the qualities of being English and Christian had become so inseparably blended that it seemed perfectly consistent to the Virginia Assembly in 1670 to declare that "noe negroe or Indian though baptised and enjoyned their owne Freedome shall be capable of any such purchase of christians, but yet not debarred from buying any of their owne na-tion." Similarly, an order of the Virginia Assembly in 1662 revealed a well-knit sense of self-identity of which Englishness and Christi-anity were interrelated parts: "METAPPIN a Powhatan Indian being sold for life time to one Elizabeth Short by the king of Wai-noake Indians who had no power to sell him being of another nation, *it is ordered* that the said Indian be free, he speaking perfectly the English tongue and desiring baptism."

From the first, then, vis-à-vis the Negro the concept embedded in the term *Christian* seems to have conveyed much of the idea and feeling of *we* as against *they*: to be Christian was to be civilized rather than barbarous, English rather than African, white rather than black. The term *Christian* itself proved to have remarkable elas-ticity, for by the end of the seventeenth century it was being used to define a species of slavery which had altogether lost any connec-tion with explicit religious difference. In the Virginia code of 1705, for example, the term sounded much more like a definition of race than of religion: "And for a further christian care and usage of all christian servants, *Be it also enacted, by the authority aforesaid, and it is hereby enacted,* That no negroes, mulattos, or Indians, although christians, or Jews, Moors, Mahometans, or other infidels, shall, at any time, purchase any christian servant, nor any other, except of their own complexion, or such as are declared slaves by this act." By this time "Christianity" had somehow become intimately and ex-plicitly linked with "complexion." The 1705 statute declared "That all servants imported and brought into this country, by sea or land, who were not christians in their native country, (except Turks and Moors in amity with her majesty, and others that can make due proof of their being free in England, or any other christian country, before they were shipped, in order to transportation hither) shall be ac-counted and be slaves, and as such be here bought and sold notwith-standing a conversion to christianity afterwards." As late as 1753 the

Virginia slave code anachronistically defined slavery in terms of religion when everyone knew that slavery had for generations been based on the racial and not the religious difference.

It is worth making still closer scrutiny of the terminology which Englishmen employed when referring both to themselves and to the two peoples they enslaved, for this terminology affords the best single means of probing the content of their sense of difference. The terms *Indian* and *Negro* were both borrowed from the Hispanic languages, the one originally deriving from (mistaken) geographical locality and the other from human complexion. When referring to the Indians the English colonists either used that proper name or called them *savages,* a term which reflected primarily their view of Indians as uncivilized, or occasionally (in Maryland especially) *pagans,* which gave more explicit expression to the missionary urge. When they had reference to Indians the colonists occasionally spoke of themselves as *Christians* but after the early years almost always as *English.*

In significant contrast, the colonists referred to *Negroes* and by the eighteenth century to *blacks* and to *Africans,* but almost never to Negro *heathens* or *pagans* or *savages.* Most suggestive of all, there seems to have been something of a shift during the seventeenth century in the terminology which Englishmen in the colonies applied to themselves. From the initially most common term *Christian,* at mid-century there was a marked drift toward *English* and *free.* After about 1680, taking the colonies as a whole, a new term appeared—*white.*

So far as the weight of analysis may be imposed upon such terms, diminishing reliance upon *Christian* suggests a gradual muting of the specifically religious element in the Christian-Negro disjunction in favor of secular nationality: Negroes were, in 1667, "not in all respects to be admitted to a full fruition of the exemptions and impunities of the English." As time went on, as some Negroes became assimilated to the English colonial culture, as more "raw Africans" arrived, and as increasing numbers of non-English Europeans were attracted to the colonies, the colonists turned increasingly to the striking physiognomic difference. By 1676 it was possible in Virginia to assail a man for "eclipsing" himself in the "darke imbraces of a Blackamoore" as if "Buty consisted all together in the Antiphety of Complections." In Maryland a revised law prohibiting miscegenation (1692) retained *white* and *English* but dropped the term *Christian*—a symptomatic modification. . . .

What had occurred was not a change in the justification of slavery from religion to race. No such justifications were made. There seems to have been, within the unarticulated concept of the Negro as a different sort of person, a sutble but highly significant shift in emphasis. Consciousness of the Negro's heathenism remained through the eighteenth and into the nineteenth and even the twentieth century, and an awareness, at very least, of his different appearance was present from the beginning. The shift was an alteration in emphasis within a single concept of difference rather than a development of a novel conceptualization. The amorphousness and subtlety of such a change is evident, for instance, in the famous tract, *The Negro's and Indians Advocate,* published in 1680 by the Reverend Morgan Godwyn. Baffled and frustrated by the disinterest of planters in converting their slaves, Godwyn declared at one point that "their *Complexion,* which being most obvious to the sight, by which the *Notion* of things doth seem to be most certainly conveyed to the Understanding, is apt to make no *slight* impressions upon rude Minds, already prepared to admit of any thing for *Truth* which shall make for Interest." Altering his emphasis a few pages later, Godwyn complained that "these two words, *Negro* and *Slave*" are "by custom grown Homogeneous and Convertible; even as *Negro* and *Christian, Englishman* and *Heathen,* are by the like corrupt Custom and Partiality made Opposites." Most arresting of all, throughout the colonies the terms *Christian, free, English,* and *white* were for many years employed indiscriminately as metonyms. A Maryland law of 1681 used all four terms in one short paragraph!

Whatever the limitations of terminology as an index to thought and feeling, it seems likely that the colonists' initial sense of difference from the Negro was founded not on a single characteristic but on a congeries of qualities which, taken as a whole, seemed to set the Negro apart. Virtually every quality in the Negro invited pejorative feelings. What may have been his two most striking characteristics, his heathenism and his appearance, were probably prerequisite to his complete debasement. His heathenism alone could never have led to permanent enslavement since conversion easily wiped out that failing. If his appearance, his racial characteristics, meant nothing to the English settlers, it is difficult to see how slavery based on race ever emerged, how the concept of complexion as the mark of slavery ever entered the colonists' minds. Even if the colonists were most unfavorably struck by the Negro's color, though, blackness itself did not urge the complete debasement of slavery. Other qualities—the utter strangeness of his language, gestures, eating habits, and so on—

certainly must have contributed to the colonists' sense that he was very different, perhaps disturbingly so. In Africa these qualities had for Englishmen added up to *savagery;* they were major components in that sense of *difference* which provided the mental margin absolutely requisite for placing the European on the deck of the slave ship and the Negro in the hold. . . .

T. H. BREEN
A Changing Labor Force and Race Relations in Virginia, 1660-1710

Seventeenth-century Virginians were an unruly lot. While New Englanders lived in relative peace with one another, Virginians rioted and rebelled; even in periods of apparent calm, they were haunted by the specter of social unrest. These men witnessed a series of disorders between 1660 and 1683, most of which were local in character, some were only threats of violence, but a few involved several counties and one escalated into a colony-wide civil war.

Wealthy planters and political officeholders at the time offered a simple explanation for these events. In each case opportunists had played upon the hopes and fears of the "giddy multitude," an amalgam of indentured servants and slaves, of poor whites and blacks, of landless freemen and debtors. Nathaniel Bacon was the most successful and therefore the most notorious of these agitators, but there were others. A gang of desperate *"Oliverian* Soldiers" supposedly organized the servant uprising of 1663, and high governing officials believed Robert Beverley, Sr., clerk of the House of Burgesses, had sparked the tobacco cutting riots of 1683. No one will ever know whether the mass of discontented workers fully supported, or even understood, the demands of a Bacon or Beverley. The "giddy multitude" may have taken advantage of divisions within the ruling class to express its anger over economic and social conditions beyond its control.

T. H. Breen, "A Changing Labor Force and Race Relations in Virginia," *Journal of Social History,* Fall (1973), pp. 3–25. Copyright © 1973 by Peter N. Stearns; reprinted by permission of the publisher.

Whatever its goals, control of this group preoccupied the Virginia gentry for nearly a quarter century.

During the 1680s Virginia's time of troubles drew to a close, and by the beginning of the eighteenth century the colony had achieved remarkable social stability. The Glorious Revolution in America which disrupted New York and Massachusetts in 1689 passed almost unnoticed in Virginia. To be sure, the tobacco planters were apprehensive about a band of black Maroons that harrassed the settlers of the northern counties, but there was little talk of a general uprising of poor whites, indentured servants and Negro slaves. The "giddy multitude" which a few years earlier had caused Governor William Berkeley to despair of ever controlling "a People wher six parts of seaven at least are Poore Endebted Discontented and Armed" had ceased to threaten the colony's internal peace.

Many elements contributed to the transformation of Virginia society during the last half of the seventeenth century, but none seems more curious than the disappearance of the "giddy multitude." This group of malcontents requires closer investigation, but unfortunately, the judicial records and tax lists from this period are incomplete, making it difficult to determine the precise identity of these people. The sources are rich enough, however, to provide substantial information about the general character of the "giddy multitude." By examining this material one begins to understand why the great planters regarded the lower classes as such a serious threat to Virginia's internal security. This analysis should also suggest how the changing composition of the colony's labor force between 1660 and 1710 affected Virginia's progress from chronic disorder to stability and more, how it fundamentally altered the relationship between blacks and whites.

A pamphleteer writing about Virginia at mid-century observed the colony's earliest years had been marked by failure and disappointment. But those unhappy days, he argued, were gone forever, and Virginians could anticipate a new era of prosperity. Evidence seemed to support his claims. The colonists had recently reduced the once powerful Powhatan Confederacy to impotence, pushing local Indians to the frontiers of white settlement. Planters rushed to develop the fertile tobacco-producing lands along the rivers north of the James, first the York and then the Rappahannock and Potomac. What Virginia needed—what it had always needed—was a large inexpensive labor force, workers who could perform the tedious tasks necessary to bring tobacco to market.

In the middle of the seventeenth century, the solution to this problem was the importation of white indentured servants. Some historians have claimed that Virginia planters preferred white laborers to Negro slaves, but the argument is not persuasive. Before the mid-1680s, the mainland colonies did not possess a reliable, inexpensive source of blacks. White Englishmen were available, however, in large numbers. Beginning in the 1650s, indentured servants flooded into Virginia at a faster rate than ever before, several thousand arriving annually. Many came voluntarily. They were people who, in Governor Berkeley's words, arrived in America with a "hope of bettering their conditions in a Growing Country." Most signed their indentures while still in the mother country, promising to work for a stated number of years in exchange for the costs of transportation, food, clothes and shelter in Virginia. Almost nothing is known about the class of people who found this offer attractive, but many were probably middling sorts.

Other servants found themselves in Virginia even though they had little or no desire to be there. Unscrupulous merchants called "spirits" took advantage of the labor boom, dumping over the years many English laborers onto the colonial market. The "spirits" operated out of England's major port cities, preying upon the poor, young and unsuspecting. Some victims were enticed to the New World with stories of quick riches; others were coerced. One man testified before Parliament in 1660 that he had been sent "against his will to Virginia" by his sister's "cruell contrivance." Once a vessel left England, the "spirited" servants reportedly received just enough food to stay alive. It was even rumored in the mother country that if a storm threatened the ship, the sailors were likely to throw an old person overboard as a suspected witch. That seventeenth-century Englishmen found such stories credible indicates that the servants' voyage to America could often be a terrible ordeal. Since the "spirits" seldom kept records of their dealings, their share of the servant commerce is difficult to estimate. Historians minimize the extent of this illicit trade, but a contemporary describing the colony in 1649 claimed that the "spirits" were the planters' chief source of indentured servants.

Great Virginia planters expressed disappointment with the quality of their servants regardless of the means by which they had been recruited. The owners of large tobacco plantations wanted hardworking, honest and obedient laborers, but the merchants seemed to be delivering "the very scum and off-scouring" of England. The planters, no doubt, were guilty of hyperbole, combining poor and ignorant persons with a few known criminals into a single category of undesirables. Throughout Berkeley's administration, leaders complained about the "importacon of Newgateers" and "Jaylebirds" whom they regarded as a serious threat to the colony's security. The gentry came to see the servants as a dangerous and untrustworthy group requiring constant surveillance. How much these attitudes affected relations between individual masters and servants is impossible to determine, but the planters' representation of the indentured workers as a bunch of "desperate villans" may have been a self-fulfilling description.

Many servants were as disappointed with their masters as their masters were with them. As early as 1649, rumors circulated in England that "all those servants who are sent to *Virginia* are sold as slaves." Tales of harsh treatment were probably the source of such stories. One man who returned to the mother country reported that he had "served as a slave" in Virginia for nine years and had "endured greate hardshipp." But the servants' unhappiness had deeper roots than hard labor and poor food. Many were not psychologically prepared for life in Virginia, and the frustrations they experienced led in time to bitterness and depression. For a majority of servants the colony had represented a new start, an opportunity to achieve wealth and status denied them in England. Propagandists fed these hopes, depicting Virginia as a land of milk and honey. Indeed, one writer observed that servants about to emigrate spoke of the colony as "a place where food shall drop into their mouthes." Many expected free land at the end of their service. The reality never matched the dreams. Virginia at mid-century burst inflated expectations and shocked all but the well-informed. William Bullock, a pamphleteer writing in 1649, understood this problem and warned planters about purchasing servants who "not finding what was promised, their courage abates, & their minds being dejected, their work is according."

The servants' life did not necessarily improve when they reached the end of their contracts. What the new freeman desired most was land, but no one in Virginia seemed willing to furnish it. Successful planters were not eager to establish commercial rivals. Indeed, contemporaries condemned the covetousness of those members of the Virginian gentry who engrossed "great Tracts of land" and deprived others of the means to achieve economic independence. In his account of Bacon's Rebellion, William Sherwood denounced the colony's "Land lopers" who claimed thousands of acres yet "never cultivated any part of itt . . . thereby preventing others seateing, soe that too many rather then to be Tennants, seate upon remote barren Land." Since before 1680 remote lands meant constant danger from the Indians, many ex-servants chose to work for wages or rent land

in secure areas rather than to settle on the frontier. It has been estimated that no more than six percent of this group ever became independent planters. Landless laborers more often became overseers on
the plantations, supervising servants and slaves whose condition dif-
fered little from their own.

Freemen found themselves tied to an economic system over which
they had little control. Fluctuations in the price of tobacco could reduce wage earners and small planters to abject poverty. It was not a
question of work habits. According to an account in 1667, a man, on
the average, could produce 1,200 pounds of tobacco each year, which
after taxes left him with approximately 50 shillings. It left so little,
in fact, that the colony's secretary marvelled, "I can attribute it to
nothing but the great mercy of God . . . that keeps them [the small
planters] from mutiny and confusion." In 1672 Governor Berkeley
explained to the English Privy Council that single freemen could
hardly maintain themselves by their own labor. They fell into debt,
unable to purchase necessary imported goods—especially clothing.
Whatever hopes they once entertained of becoming prosperous planters gave way to anger. Their numbers swelled, and their disappointment must have discouraged those persons who were still indentured.
Certainly, no one seemed surprised when the king's commissioners,
investigating in 1677 the causes of Bacon's Rebellion, discovered a
major part of the rebel army had been "Free men that had but lately
crept out of the condition of Servants."

Another component of the "giddy multitude" was Virginia's Negroes. Historians know relatively little about this group. Governor
Berkeley thought there were some 2,000 blacks in the colony in 1671,
but recent scholarship regards that estimate as high. By the early
1680s, the Negro population had probably risen to three or four thousand. A majority of the blacks in this period appear to have come to
Virginia from the West Indies. Around the turn of the century, for
example, it was reported on the authority of one planter that before
1680 "what negroes were brought to Virginia were imported generally from Barbados." There is no way of ascertaining how long the
blacks had lived on Barbados before transferring to the mainland, but
it is doubtful Virginia planters would have invested what little capital they possessed in expensive "unseasoned" laborers who could
easily die after a single summer in the tobacco fields. If the blacks
had stayed a year or two on Barbados, they probably learned to speak
some English. Morgan Godwyn, a minister who had visited the island colony in the 1670s, noted that many Negroes there not only
spoke English, but did so "no worse than the natural born subjects of

that Kingdom." Their facility with the English language could have played an important part in Virginia's unrest, for it would have enabled blacks to communicate with indentured servants and poor whites.

The status of black men in mid-seventeenth-century Virginia remains obscure; a few were free, some were indentured servants and most were probably slaves. After 1660 the Virginia legislature began to deprive black people of basic civil rights. Although the process of total debasement was not completed until the 1700s, it has generally been assumed that Negroes were a separate and subordinate group within Virginia as early as Governor Berkeley's second administration (1662–1677). The problem with this interpretation is that it relies too heavily upon statute law as opposed to social practice, and dismisses the fact that some whites and blacks cooperated—even conspired together—until the late 1670s.

No one could deny that many whites saw Negroes as property to be exploited, and these men may have been responsible for shaping Virginia legislation. On the lowest levels of colonial society, however, race prejudice may have developed more slowly than it did among the successful planters. Black and white field hands could hardly have overlooked the things they had in common. For the Negroes the original trip from Africa to the West Indies had been a terrible ordeal. Few whites had experienced a psychological shock of this magnitude, but some of them had been forcibly abducted and confined in foul quarters until a ship was prepared to sail, and were then transported to the New World under conditions vaguely similar to those endured by Africans. Although little is known about the relative treatment of whites and blacks in Virginia before Bacon's Rebellion, it is doubtful that English servants fared better than Negroes. Evidence from Barbados at this time reveals that planters there regarded white servants as a short-term investment to be exploited ruthlessly and thus, "for the time the servants have the worser lives [than the Negroes], for they are put to very hard labour, ill lodging, and their dyet very sleight." If such conditions prevailed on the mainland, it would help explain why some poor and indentured whites voluntarily joined with black men to challenge the planters' authority. One should understand, of course, that a willingness to cooperate under certain circumstances does not mean white laborers regarded Negroes as their equals. Indeed, such actions only indicate that economic grievances could sometimes outweigh race prejudice.

Between 1660 and 1685, members of the colony's labor force expressed their discontent in a variety of ways, some by isolated, spontaneous acts of violence, others by larger conspiratorial ventures. If an individual became desperate enough, he or she might strike a master. Disaffected servants and slaves also ran away. The problem of fleeing bondsmen became quite serious in Berkeley's Virginia, and numerous colonial statutes tried to curb the practice. People often ran away in groups, fearing perhaps the Indians or the wilderness itself. Servants and slaves, eager for freedom and lured by rumors of a better life somewhere else, slipped away into the forests. Blacks and whites sometimes fled together, conscious that without cooperation their bid for freedom and escape might fail and bring instead immediate physical punishment and probably additional years of drudgery. Whatever the terrors of flight, there were always persons desperate enough to take the chance. Some even plotted escape on shipboard before seeing America. Planters assumed that the desire for freedom was contagious and that unless runaways were quickly suppressed, other men—black and white—would soon imitate them. When a group of fugitive slaves frustrated all attempts to retake them in 1672, the planters' greatest concern was that "other negroes, Indians or servants . . . [might] fly forth and joyne with them."

Insurrection offered another means by which discontented workers expressed unhappiness with conditions in Virginia. While such organized disturbances were relatively infrequent, an occasional uprising reinforced the planters' fears and remained a source of uneasiness years after the violence had been quelled. During the early 1660s, servants upset the peace in several counties. The first disorder occurred in York and appears to have been sparked by complaints among indentured workers of "hard usage" and inadequate diet. Several conspirators, weary of "corne & water," demanded meat at least two or three times a week. The leader, an indentured servant named Isaac Friend, suggested that his followers petition the king for redress. This idea was dropped when someone pointed out that even if Charles II would listen, the group could never get a letter out of Virginia. Friend then decided that 40 servants should band together and "get Armes & he would be the first & have them cry as they went along, 'who would be for Liberty, and free from bondage,' & that there would be enough come to them & they would goe through the Countrey and kill those that made any opposition, & that they would either be free or die for it." Someone apparently revealed the plans before Friend and the others began their freedom march through Virginia. When the commissioners of York questioned the leader about his actions, he admitted making seditious speeches, but protested that he never intended to put the scheme into operation. Despite Friend's assurance, York officials refused to regard the episode as a servants' prank. They ordered Friend's master to keep close watch over him and warned the heads of all families in the county to take note of "like dangerous discourses."

Two years later officials in Gloucester County, a fast growing region north of York, discovered another conspiracy. The causes of this disturbance are difficult to reconstruct since most of the Gloucester records have been lost and the surviving testimony is inconsistent. In his history of Virginia published in 1705, Robert Beverley, Jr., claimed that veterans of Cromwell's army who had been transported to the colony as indentured servants stirred up "the poor People . . . [and] form'd a villanous Plot to destroy their Masters, and afterwards to set up for themselves." Presumably Beverley drew his information from old planters and local tradition, but the available contemporary documents do not mention "*Oliverian* Soldiers." A Gloucester court in 1663 accused nine "Laborers" of conspiring to arm 30 persons to overthrow the government of Virginia. While extant depositions reveal nothing about the political ideas of this group, they do suggest that some participants regarded bondage as their primary grievance. For example, one member reported that the conspirators had secretly pledged to seize weapons, march on the colonial capital and "demand our freedome." If the royal governor denied this request, the rebels planned to leave Virginia.

The reaction to the attempted servant uprising of 1663 appears excessive unless one considers it in the context of the strained relationship between the major tobacco planters and colonial laborers. After the organizers of the plot had been captured and several executed, the servant who had warned the planters received his freedom and £200. The day on which the conspirators were arrested became an annual holiday. Virginia officials notified Charles II of the details of the insurrection in such exaggerated terms that the king immediately ordered the colonists to construct a fortress to protect the governor and his loyal officials. As late as 1670, the memory of the servant plot could still unnerve the gentry of Gloucester, Middlesex and York. Indeed, when it appeared that the mother country had allowed too many criminals and undesirables to emigrate to Virginia, the leading planters of these counties protested and reminded royal officials of "the horror yet remaining amongst us of the barbarous designe of those villaines in September 1663 who attempted at once the subversion of our Religion, Lawes, libertyes, rights and priviledges."

During the 12 years preceding Bacon's Rebellion, fear of the labor force increasingly affected the character of Virginian society. Although no organized violence against the planters or the government occurred in this period, the laborers—black and white—constituted a subversive element. They were essential to the colony's economic well-being, but at the same time, no one trusted them. It was a foolish plantation owner who did not recognize the danger, for in a community in which so many men were unhappy, even seemingly contented workers might be potential conspirators. The tobacco gentry tried to regulate the lives of their bondsmen, and according to colonial statute, any servant who attended an unlawful meeting or traveled about the countryside without a pass risked arrest. But these measures were insufficient to insure domestic tranquillity. Even if the behavior of the slaves and servants could have been closely controlled (a doubtful proposition at best), the poor freemen remained a threat.

The extent of Virginia's social instability was revealed by events in 1676. Indian raids exacerbated long-standing grievances, and when a young planter named Nathaniel Bacon came forward as spokesman for the discontented, he sparked a civil war. Because Bacon's Rebellion was the most momentous event in seventeenth-century Virginia, it has been the object of intense investigation. Historians concerned chiefly with the behavior of the colony's elite have offered several interpretations of what motivated the leaders of this insurrection. Such analysis is of little value in understanding the "giddy multitude," however, since whatever the aims of Bacon and his lieutenants, there is little evidence their goals were the same as those of their followers. Contemporaries, in fact, believed Bacon had aroused popular fears and frustrations to achieve his own private ends. The House of Burgesses concluded in 1677 that this rebellion, like others before it, resulted from "false Rumors, Infused by ill affected persons provoking an itching desire" in the common people. Indeed, the loyal planters around Berkeley despised Bacon not so much because he was ambitious or even because he had led an unauthorized march against local Indians, but because he had carried his case to the populace. After Bacon had been captured in June 1676, the governor pardoned him; and even though the rebel leader had defied Berkeley's orders several times and slaughtered a village of friendly Occaneechee Indians, Berkeley believed Bacon's submission to be sincere. But Bacon had already stirred forces beyond his control. His followers demanded action. Within two days of receiving his pardon, Bacon "heard what an incredible Number of the meanest of the People were every where Armed to assist him and his cause." He did not disappoint them. Had Bacon somehow confined the dispute to the upper class, he might have been forgiven for his erratic behavior, but once the servants, slaves and poor freemen became involved, he had to be crushed.

Participants on both sides of the conflict believed it had pitted the rich against the poor, the privileged against the oppressed or, as Berkeley described it, the "Rabble" against "the better sort people." There is no reason to doubt the validity of this assessment. To many persons, the Rebellion must have seemed the type of class confrontation which Berkeley and his friends had long feared. "The poverty of the Country is such," Bacon declared, "that all the power and sway is got into the hands of the rich, who by extorious advantages, having the common people in their debt, have always curbed and oppressed them in all manner of wayes." Although historians may discover the Virginian gentry was not as selfish as Bacon claimed, the leader's class rhetoric appealed to a large number of colonists.

It would be interesting to identify these people, to know more about their social status, but the rebels have preserved their anonymity. Surviving records have yielded only a few names out of the hundreds who took up arms against the government. Contemporaries, however, insisted Bacon's troops had been recruited from the lowest ranks of Virginia society. They were the rabble, the disaffected, the vulgar, the indigent. In June 1676, loyalist William Sherwood reported "Now tag, rag, and bobtayle carry a high hand." Philip Ludwell, another prominent colonial official, told an English correspondent that Bacon had raised 500 soldiers "whose fortunes & Inclinations being equally desperate, were fit for the purpose there being not 20 in the whole Route, but what were Idle & will not worke, or such whose Debaucherie or Ill Husbandry has brought in Debt beyond hopes or thought of payment." Another account described the rebel army as a body composed of three parts: "freemen, searvants, and slaves."

The lower-class origins of Bacon's troops receives additional verification from a narrative written by an English sea captain, Thomas Grantham. This rough adventurer arrived in Virginia just as the Rebellion was ending. Bacon had already died, and groups of dispirited rebels throughout the colony were debating whether to surrender or carry on the fight. Grantham volunteered to serve as an intermediary between Berkeley and his enemies. The governor accepted the offer, and the captain set off in his thirty-gun ship, the *Concord*, in search of the rebel bands. At a fortified position called West Point, he persuaded Joseph Ingram and "about 250" soldiers to submit to the governor's authority in exchange for a full pardon. Grantham then traveled three miles more to the plantation of Colonel John West, the rebels' "Chiefe Garrison and Magazine." At West's home he encountered approximately 400 "English and Negroes in Armes." In fact, he confronted the very sort of men that Berkeley's followers had often claimed supported Bacon.

The soldiers complained about Ingram's capitulation, and some urged shooting Grantham on the spot. But the captain knew how to talk himself out of difficult situations and brazenly informed "the negroes and Servants, that they were all pardoned and freed from their Slavery." With other such "faire promises" and a liberal supply of brandy, Grantham won most of the discouraged rebels over to the government, but "eighty Negroes and Twenty English . . . would not deliver their Armes." Perhaps these holdouts realized the captain had no power to grant bondsmen freedom; perhaps they believed fighting in a desperate cause better than returning to their masters. Whatever their reasoning, Grantham was one step ahead of the rebels. He tricked them onto a small boat by promising safe passage across the York River, and when the Negroes and servants were aboard, he threatened to blow them out of the water with the guns of the *Concord* unless they immediately surrendered. His account closes with the return of the captured "Negroes & Servants . . . to their Masters."

The presence of so many black rebels at West's plantation provides evidence that many Virginians in Berkeley's time regarded economic status, not race, as the essential social distinction. Even the gentry seems to have viewed the blacks primarily as a component of the "giddy multitude." If the large tobacco planters could have played the white laborers off against the Negroes, they surely would have. The governor's supporters charged Bacon with many failings: atheism, hypocrisy, pride, avarice; but no one attacked the rebel leader for partiality toward black men. One loyalist account of the Rebellion noted that Richard Lawrence, one of Bacon's advisers, had indulged in "the darke imbraces of a Blackamoore, his slave," but in the narrative literature of this period, such racial comments were rare.

If the colonial gentry had been as worried about the danger of black insurrection in 1676 as they were in the eighteenth century, one would have expected some writer to have condemned Bacon's arming the slaves. The silence on this point is especially strange since it had long been illegal in Virginia for Negroes to bear arms. Englishmen such as Captain Grantham appear to have been more conscious of the mixed racial character of Bacon's army than were the local planters. Possibly the colonists had come to view the entire labor force, not just a part of it, as the threat to their safety. The absence of racial slurs does not indicate that Virginia leaders in 1676 felt no prejudice against Negroes. Rather, the planters may have taken for granted the cooperation of slaves, servants and poor freemen.

Bacon's Rebellion has often been described as a turning point in Virginia's history. The settlement of the insurrection did bring about important political changes, especially in the colony's relationship to England; but it did almost nothing to allay the gentry's fear of the "giddy multitude." The social and economic conditions that had originally caused the labor force to participate in the disorder persisted after calm supposedly had been restored. In 1677, a small and relatively insignificant disturbance near Albemarle Sound in Carolina revealed the degree of the planters' uneasiness about maintaining order within their own colony. The disruption, known as Culpeper's Rebellion, grew out of several local grievances, the chief being the collection of a Parliamentary tax. What bothered the Virginians was not the rebels' specific demands, but the character of the rebels themselves. Observers in Carolina reported that Culpeper's force included the worst elements in colonial society. One person warned that if this band of impoverished whites and blacks succeeded in Carolina, it might soon "make Inroads and dayly Incursions" on Virginia.

An even graver danger was the temptation which the Albemarle community presented to the poor laborers and bondsmen in other colonies. As one Carolinian explained, Virginia leaders hoped for a quick suppression of the rebels, "Being exceeding sensible of the dangerous consequences of this Rebellion, as that if they be not suddenly subdued hundreds of idle debtors, theeves, Negros, Indians and English servants will fly unto them." There is no evidence that Virginia workers actually ran to the Albemarle settlements. The fear of a lower-class exodus, however, is more significant than the fact. The colony's elite assumed a coalition of "servants, Slaves & Debtors" would defy established authority if the opportunity arose, and since Virginia's economy had not improved following Bacon's Rebellion, no one knew when a confrontation might occur.

In 1681, five years after Bacon's death, Virginia's leaders were still worried about the possibility of a general servant uprising. At one point they urged the king to allow the foot companies originally sent to Virginia in 1677 to remain so that the Redcoats could "prevent or suppress any Insurrection that may otherwise happen during the necessitous unsettled condition of the Colonie." And Thomas Lord Culpeper, the colony's royal governor (no relation to the leader of the Carolina disorder), regarded the labor force as the chief threat to internal peace. In 1679 the king had instructed Culpeper to "take care that all Planters and Christian Servants be well and fitly provided with Arms." But after living in Virginia only a short time, the governor realized the crown's order was impractical, if not counterproductive. In 1681 Culpeper scribbled in the margin next to this instruction: "Masters have arms. Servants not trusted with them."

The lower classes once again turned to violence in the spring of 1682. The primary cause of this disturbance was chronic economic depression, although the political ambitions of Robert Beverley, Sr., clerk of the House of Burgesses, probably served as a catalyst for unrest. For several years, over-production of tobacco had brought hard times to everyone. In an effort to raise prices, some Virginians advocated the voluntary cessation of planting. Royal officials, however, discouraged these plans in the belief they would reduce customs revenue (a tax based on the volume of trade). When the colony's governor prorogued the Burgesses, preventing any legislation on the issue, people in Gloucester took matters into their own hands. Mobs marched from plantation to plantation, cutting tobacco plants as they went. Each victim immediately became a fervid "cutter," since once his crop had been destroyed, he wanted to insure that his neighbors did not profit by his loss. The panic spread to other counties, and although Deputy Governor Henry Chicheley quickly dispatched cavalry units to apprehend the leading "mutineers" and to frustrate further "Insurrection and outrages," the rioting and "night mischiefs" continued for well over a month.

After 1682 the character of social violence changed in Virginia. Never again would the "giddy multitude"—indentured servants, black slaves and poor freemen—make common cause against the colony's ruling planters. In fact, the plant-cutting riots were the last major disturbance in which white laborers of any sort took part. Over the next two decades, white men came to regard blacks—and blacks alone—as the chief threat to Virginia's tranquillity.

The transformation came slowly; for several years colonial leaders were hardly aware of it. Late in the summer of 1682, Secretary Spencer predicted new disorders simply because it was the season when "All plantations [are] flowing with Syder." He even thought he detected a spirit of unrest that "Bacon's Rebellion left itching behind it." But no rebellion occurred. In 1683, Governor Culpeper reported that all was calm in Virginia. "All hands are at worke," he wrote, "none excepted. And yet there is an evil spiritt at Worke, who governed in our Time of Anarchy." Again, no disorder followed. Two years later, Governor Francis Effingham asked William Blathwayt, secretary of the Lords of Trade, for a special force of 20 men "in Case any disorder should accidenteally happen," but the Governor undermined the urgency of his request by admitting "all things here are in a peaceable and Quiett Condition." The lower-class whites, the common people, seemed interested in planting tobacco, settling frontier lands and raising families, and none showed much inclination toward organized violence. Not even the Glorious Revolution or rumors that hordes of Maryland Catholics planned to descend upon the colony could stir the "giddy multitude." In 1697, the governor's council in Virginia reported: "The country is in peace and happiness." By 1700, the general uprisings of whites, sometimes supported by a few Negroes, were no more than an unpleasant memory. The eighteenth-century Virginia gentry feared the blacks and the policies of certain aggressive royal governors, but no one expressed apprehension about the poor whites, the tenants, the indentured servants or the debtors. The problem is to explain how this change came about.

Many elements contributed to the transformation of Virginia, but none was more important than the rise of tobacco prices after 1684. In Berkeley's time, the tobacco market had generally been poor. Some years were better than others, but prices never regained the level achieved in 1660. During the last two decades of the seventeenth century, economic conditions improved. The demand for Virginia crops expanded, and poor yields and natural disasters occurred often enough to prevent market saturation. These were not boom years as the 1620s had been, but tobacco prices were high enough to raise the lower classes out of the poverty that had been so widespread before the 1680s. Contemporaries appreciated the relationship between economic improvement and social tranquillity. Governor Culpeper informed crown officials in 1683 that "peace and quietness" would continue in Virginia "so long as tobacco bears a price." The next year Spencer observed that the people had calmed down since they had begun working for a full harvest.

While rising prices reduced social tensions, they did not in themselves bring about the disappearance of the "giddy multitude." The character of the labor force also changed during this period. Before Bacon's Rebellion, planters imported thousands of indentured servants; and because the demand for workers exceeded the supply, planters accepted whomever merchants delivered. After 1680, however, commercial developments outside Virginia altered the servant trade. English companies achieved the capacity to ship Negroes directly from Africa to the mainland colonies and, during the last years of the seventeenth century, tobacco planters purchased slaves in increasingly larger numbers. This new source of labor was not only more economic than the indentured servants had been, but it also allowed planters greater selectivity in the choice of servants. William Fitzhugh, for example, one of the colony's major slave holders, refused to take "ordinary servants," warning a trader, "I would have a good one or none."

A second element affecting the quality of indentured servants was England's crackdown on the "spirits." In 1682 Charles II issued a proclamation regulating the recruitment of servants. No indenture would be valid unless signed before a magistrate in the mother country, and no person under 14 years old could be shipped to America without parental consent. The king's humanitarian act may in part have been an attempt to protect legitimate merchants from fraudulent suits by individuals claiming to have been abducted. In the early 1680s a group calling itself "the Principall Merchants of England traders to the Plantacions" protested that unnecessary prosecutions had so discouraged traders from carrying servants to the New World that some colonies would soon find themselves with "few white men to Governe & direct the Negroes."

Whatever the causes, the number of indentured servants arriving in Virginia dwindled. Those who did immigrate, however, were of a higher social rank than those who flooded the colony at mid-century. Large planters wanted servants with special skills. In 1687 Fitzhugh advised an Englishman how to establish a plantation in Virginia: "the best methods to be pursued therein is, to get a Carpenter & Bricklayer Servants, & send them in here to serve 4 or five years, in which time of their Service they might reasonably build a substantial good house . . . & earn money enough besides in their said time, at spare times from your work . . . as will purchase plank, nails & other materials." Of the seven indentured servants mentioned in Fitzhugh's will, one was a carpenter, one a glazier and another the planter's own cousin. Unlike the planters of Berkeley's time, Fitzhugh's contemporaries seldom complained that their servants were "desperate villans" recruited from the "very scum" of England. Conditions had changed. The indentured workers who emigrated after the mid-1680s escaped the crushing poverty and frustrations that so embittered the previous generation of servants. For these later arrivals Virginia may well have appeared a land of opportunity.

The poor freemen also became less disruptive in this period. Landless and indebted persons, many of them former servants, had once flocked to Bacon's standard. Yet, by the mid-1680s, no one seems to have regarded them as a serious threat to Virginia's internal security. These people benefited greatly from improved economic conditions. Few at the lowest levels of white society experienced the grinding poverty that a decade earlier had driven desperate men to violence. Food was abundant and clothes easier to obtain. Indeed, by the beginning of the eighteenth century, Virginians boasted of eradicating poverty. The planter-historian, Robert Beverley, Jr., noted in 1705 that the colonists "live in so happy a Climate, and have so fertile a Soil, that no body is poor enough to beg, or want Food, though they have abundance of People that are lazy enough to deserve it." Beverley concluded that compared to European nations, Virginia was "the best poor man's Country in the World." Foreign visitors corroborated Beverley's observation. When a French Protestant, Francis Louis Michel, traveled through Virginia in 1702, he reported finding no poor people and wrote: "It is indeed said truthfully that there is no other country, where it is possible with so few means and so easily to make an honest living and be in easy circumstances." As tobacco prices improved, the less prosperous freemen found wealthier neighbors willing to advance credit. And if a person possessed a special skill or trade, he could command a good wage. "I have seen a common journeyman paid annually 30 lbs. sterling, including his board," one man wrote. "But I have heard of master workmen who receive above a guinea daily."

As always, freemen wanted land. In Berkeley's time, hostile Indians along the frontier and "Land lopers" among the gentry frustrated this desire. After the mid-1680s, however, changes in Virginia reduced these obstructions—the colonists simply removed the Indians. A foreign traveller at the turn of the century discovered that Indians "have not come into the colony to inflict damage, because for one thing they are afraid of the English power, but especially because they are unable to flee from the cavalry." As early as 1687, Virginians counselled prospective colonists that Indians "are not greatly to be feared."

Often the colony's most influential planters, such as William Byrd, William Fitzhugh and Ralph Wormeley, claimed the vacated Indian lands. One means to obtain large tracts in the west was to lead the militia in a successful march against the Indians. "The colonels of these troops," a Frenchman explained, "claimed the plantations of the savages & had them surveyed, so that at the present time [1687] there are large tracts of very good land for sale in Virginia." Some of these men held onto the land, building the vast estates that became an integral part of the Virginia aristocracy in the eighteenth century, but much of the acreage was sold. Several Virginians, in fact, became speculators and showed no desire to discourage small farmers from settling the newly secured territory. Fitzhugh, one of the colony's largest landowners, urged an English associate to promote the planter's Virginia lands, for any transfer "will be doubly advantageous to me first by meeting with an opportunity to serve you through your friends, & secondly, by profitably either selling or tenementing my Land, which till so done, is rather a charge than profit." Easy and flexible terms were offered to interested buyers. Ralph Wormeley, for example, was willing to sell "ten thousand acres of ground he owned . . . for one écu an acre."

If landless freemen could not afford acreage in Virginia, they could move to Carolina or Pennsylvania, areas largely inaccessible before 1680. This practice was fairly common. In 1695, Governor Francis Nicholson complained "many families, but especially young men" were leaving Virginia and Maryland for Pennsylvania where land could be purchased at a lower rate. A visitor to Virginia in 1702 "heard many good reports about Pennsylvania and that some people from Virginia moved there." Whichever option the ex-servant chose—buying land in Virginia or moving—he could anticipate becoming an independent planter. Although relatively few advanced to the highest ranks of society, the freeman's horizons were broader in 1700 than they had been in 1670.

After the 1680s the experience of the blacks in Virginia was increasingly different from that of other colonists. Improved tobacco prices raised white laborers out of poverty, making their servitude endurable and their freemanship secure. But the same economic conditions brought large numbers of Negroes into the colony as slaves. No one knows exactly how rapidly the black population grew after 1680. There seem to have been about 4,000 slaves at the time of the tobacco-cutting riots. Estimates of the size of the Negro population in 1700 range as high as 20,000. Even if this figure is excessive, the number of Africans arriving in Virginia expanded substantially in the last two decades of the seventeenth century.

The leading tobacco planters required no encouragement to make the transition from white to black labor. The wealthiest among them had accumulated enough capital to purchase and maintain large gangs of Negroes. For the first time in the century, English trading companies were able to supply blacks on a reasonably regular basis. The colonists bought all the Negroes the slavers could transport and then demanded more. In 1696, a group of Chesapeake planters and merchants petitioned Parliament to lift restrictions on the African trade, since the company holding the monopoly (the Royal African Company) could not meet the escalating demand for blacks in Maryland and Virginia.

The changes in the slave community were more complex than revealed by population statistics alone. In fact, the sheer growth in numbers only partially explains why whites no longer joined with blacks to threaten planter society. An equally important element in understanding race relations in this period was the Negroes' experience before arriving in Virginia. With each passing year an increasing proportion of slaves came directly from Africa. These immigrants had no stopover in Barbados to learn English or to adjust either physically or mentally to an alien culture. They were simply dumped on the wharves of the river plantations in a state of shock, barely alive after the ocean crossing. Conditions on the slave ships were terrible. One vessel from Guinea unloaded 230 blacks, but reported that a hundred more had died at sea. No white servant in this period, no matter how poor, how bitter or badly treated, could identify with these frightened Africans. The terrors they had so recently faced were beyond comprehension. The sale of the blacks emphasized the difference between races. "The negroes are brought annually in large numbers," a visitor to Virginia recounted at the turn of the century. "They can be selected according to pleasure, young and old, men and women. They are entirely naked when they arrive, having only corals of different colors around their necks and arms." These strange, helpless blacks repulsed the writer who noted that even the Indians seemed preferable to these "animal-like people." His reactions, no doubt, were shared by many white Virginians. In 1699, members of the House of Burgesses described the blacks in a manner unknown in Berkeley's time, claiming it unnecessary to expose slaves to Christianity, since "the gross barbarity and rudeness of their manners, the variety and strangeness of their languages and the weakness and shallowness of their minds rendered it in a manner impossible to attain to any progress in their conversion."

Language became a major barrier between white laborers and the thousands of new black immigrants. Before the 1690s, no one recorded any problem in communicating with Negroes. Indeed, it is difficult to comprehend how servants and slaves could have conspired to run away or rebel had they been unable to understand one another. The flood of Africans directly into Virginia not only made it difficult for whites to deal with blacks, but also hindered communications between blacks. The colonists apparently regarded the great variety of African tongues as a protection against black insurrection. Early in the eighteenth century, Governor Alexander Spotswood, convinced of the need for stricter controls over the labor force, warned Virginians that the slaves' "Babel of Languages" offered no real security, since "freedom Wears a Cap which can without a Tongue, Call Together all Those who long to Shake off the fetters of Slavery."

The blacks hated their status. They ran away whenever possible, and on at least one occasion, formed a small band that terrorized the colonists of Rappahannock County. Rumors of Negro plots made the planters uneasy, with good reason. A group of slaves could easily have seized a plantation and murdered the master and his family before troops could have been summoned. But there was little chance that the blacks at this time could have overrun the colony; without the support of poorer whites and indentured servants, they were badly outnumbered. The white cavalry that hunted down the Indians could have done the same to the slaves. The changes in Virginia society after the mid-1680s had set whites against blacks, the armed, organized forces of the planters against the small, isolated groups of slaves. In Berkeley's time the militia had been regarded as a means of protecting the elite from the entire labor force, but early in the eighteenth century, historian Hugh Jones reported that "in each county is a great number of disciplined and armed militia, ready in case of any sudden irruption of Indians or insurrection of Negroes." The labor force was still the major threat to internal security in Virginia, but now the laborers were predominantly black.

Like the Barbadians, the seventeenth-century Virginians exchanged white servants for Negro slaves, and in so doing, exchanged a fear of the "giddy multitude" for a fear of slave rebellion. By 1700, whites had achieved a sense of race solidarity at the expense of blacks. Negroes were set apart as objects of contempt and ridicule. The whites, even the meanest among them, always knew there was a class of men permanently below them. But the story of Virginia's labor force between 1660 and 1710 was more than a dreary narrative of suffering and oppression. For a few decades, it had been possible to overlook racial differences, a time when a common experience of desperate poverty and broken dreams brought some whites and blacks together. Such conditions were present in the American South during the 1890s, and it is not unlikely that they will appear again.

PETER H. WOOD

Black Labor—White Rice
Colonial Manpower and
African Agricultural Skill in Early Carolina

I

No development had greater impact upon the course of South Carolina history than the successful introduction of rice. The plant itself, shallow-rooted and delicate, is now rare on the landscape it once dominated, but its historical place in the expansion of the colony and state is deep-seated and secure, hedged round by a tangle of tradition and lore almost as impenetrable as the wilderness swamps near which it was first grown for profit. Despite its eventual prominence, the mastery of this grain took more than a generation, for rice was a crop about which Englishmen, even those who had lived in the Caribbean, knew nothing at all. White immigrants from elsewhere in northern Europe were equally ignorant at first, and local Indians, who gathered small quantities of wild rice, had little to teach them. But gradually, after discouraging initial efforts, rice emerged as the mainstay of the lowland economy during the first fifty years of settlement, and the cultivation of this grain for export came to dominate Carolina life during the major part of the eighteenth century. "The only Commodity of Consequence produced in South Carolina is

"Black Labor—White Rice: Colonial Manpower and African Agricultural Skill in Early Carolina," from *Black Majority: Negroes in Colonial South Carolina from 1670 through the Stono Rebellion* by Peter H. Wood. Copyright © 1974 by Peter H. Wood; reprinted by permission of Alfred A. Knopf, Inc.

Rice," commented James Glen in 1761, "and they reckon it as much their staple Commodity, as Sugar is to Barbadoes and Jamaica, or Tobacco to Virginia and Maryland."

Throughout the eighteenth century white Carolinians marveled at their own industry and good fortune in having conjured this impressive trade from a single bushel of rice, and they debated which Englishman should wear the laurels for introducing the first successful bag of seed. In 1726 a Swiss correspondent stated that "it was by a woman that Rice was transplanted into Carolina," and occasional mention was made of the idea that the first seeds came aboard a slaving ship from Africa. "Opinions differ about the manner in which rice hath been naturalized in Carolina," wrote the Abbé Raynal at the end of the eighteenth century. "But whether the province may have acquired it by a shipwreck, or whether it may have been carried there with slaves, or whether it be sent from England, it is certain that the soil is favourable for it."

Since rice cultivation had a halting beginning which stretched over several decades, numerous bags of imported seed could have contributed to its growth. Documentary evidence is scanty, and it therefore seems likely that minor issues of individual precedence may never be fully resolved. One fact which can be clearly documented, however, and which may have considerably greater significance, is that during precisely those two decades after 1695 when rice production took permanent hold in South Carolina, the African portion of the population drew equal to, and then surpassed, the European portion. Black inhabitants probably did not actually outnumber whites until roughly 1708 [when the total population was still slightly below 10,000 persons]. But whatever the exact year in which a black majority was established, the development was unprecedented within England's North American colonies and was fully acknowledged long before the English crown took control of the proprietary settlement in 1720.

The fact that the mastery of rice paralleled closely in time the emergence of a black majority in the colony's population has not been lost upon scholars of the early South. But while few have failed to note it, none can be said to have explained it adequately. What could either be a mere coincidence on the one hand, or a crucial interrelation on the other, has been bypassed with short passages carefully phrased. Verner W. Crane observed that in 1700 "The transition from mixed farming and cattle raising to rice culture was just beginning, and with it the development of negro slavery." W. Frank Craven stated that "South Carolina's especially heavy commitment to the use of Negro labor coincided closely with the development of rice as a new and profitable staple." Similarly, Aubrey C. Land concluded that despite an earlier preference for Negro labor, white "South Carolinians did not import Negroes in large numbers until after the introduction of rice in the 1690's." In short, there appears to be an ongoing consensus among the leading southernists that somehow "rice culture turned planters increasingly to slave labor," but the causal relationships suggested, or perhaps skirted, by such observations have received little analysis.

Were Negro slaves simply the cheapest and most numerous individuals available to a young colony in need of labor? Or were there other variables involved in determining the composition of the Carolina work force? In exploring such questions it is first necessary to examine the different sorts of potential labor—red, white, and black—which existed in the early years. It will then be possible, by focusing on the process of rice cultivation at the end of this essay, . . . to suggest a separate factor which may have contributed far more than has been acknowledged in fostering the employment of African slaves.

II

Although persons from Africa had been enmeshed in New World colonization for more than a century and a half before the founding of Carolina [in 1670], alternative sources of labor were very real possibilities during the early years of the lowland settlement. The option closest at hand was that presented by the numerous Indian tribes which had inhabited the area for centuries. Their interaction with white and black foreigners during the colonial era constitutes a separate story, but it is clear that they provided some much-needed support in the early years. English trade goods could be used to purchase their services cheaply, and no expensive importation costs were incurred. Difficulties in verbal communication were offset by the Indians' impressive knowledge of the land; they could provide ready food, suitable medicine, and safe passage in a semitropical wilderness environment which was unfamiliar to Europeans. Several neighboring tribes, with a pragmatic eye upon English firearms and woolens, were quick in coming forward to assist the new colonists, offering "to fish, and hunt their Game for a Trifle; to fell Tim[ber, to plant] Corn, and to gather in their Crop: as also to Pilot, and convey them from on[e place] to another." Louis Thibou's letter of September 20, 1683, described the European settler's situation:

If he wishes to hunt or to have an Indian hunt for him there is no lack of venison or game. An Indian will provide a family of 30 with enough game and venison, as much as they can eat, all the year round for 4 crowns. . . . We have 15 or 16 nations of Indians round us who are very friendly and the English get on well with them; the largest number is not more than 500 strong. They bring them a great quantity of deer skins and furs.

Settlers were greedy for involuntary as well as voluntary Indian labor, despite obvious disadvantages. Acts of enslavement were risky, since any provocations in the earliest years contained the danger of retaliation. In later decades, as the colony became slightly more secure, local slaving ventures presented a threat to the growing Indian trade. Moreover, women and children were more likely than men to be taken alive during intertribal wars and sold to the colonists. Even when white traders promoted intertribal conflicts to obtain cheap slaves, the likelihood of later escape by the captives reduced their value in the vicinity.

But when Indians were sold to an unfamiliar region where they were less likely to run away, their value as slaves went up. Therefore a small commerce developed in exchanging Indian captives abroad for more tractable white or black labor, or for additional livestock which would encroach further upon Indian land. During the late seventeenth century, in fact, Carolina was more active than any other English colony in the export of Indian slaves. In 1679, for example, the Carolina bark *Mary* carried "goods and slaves" to Virginia to exchange for several mares and a hold full of neat cattle. At the Proprietors' insistence, a system of permits was established to regulate these deportations. It provided that no slave was to be exported "without his owne consent," but among the victims fear of their Indian captors and ignorance of their white purchasers seems to have made this consent readily obtainable.

Although the Proprietors in London had few scruples about slavery as an institution, they protested strenuously against the "evill men" who "made a trade of enslaving & sending away the pore Indians." In part they were fearful of prompting hostilities with local tribes or the nearby Spanish (fears realized when a combined force of Spaniards, Indians, and Negroes attacked the settlement in 1686), and in part they were anxious to protect their peaceful trade in deer-skins, which provided the colony's first source of direct revenue to England. With the opening up of this lucrative Indian trade to more people in the 1690s, the European settlers themselves became increasingly willing to curtail their limited reliance upon Native American labor. Although enslavement of Indians continued on into the settlement's second generation, any thought of utilizing such laborers as the core of the colonial work force had dissipated well before the end of the seventeenth century.

The alternative of a white labor force presented a different set of variables. Simple reasons of custom, language, and religion naturally made Europeans prefer to have other Europeans working with and under them. But it was one thing to promote independent migration from Europe and another to contract serviceable labor from there. Some of the difficulties became apparent with the first fleet that paused at Kinsale in Ireland to obtain several dozen servants. The attempt failed totally, and Robert Southwell wrote to Lord Ashley that the Irish there had been so "terrified with the ill practice" of being shipped to the Caribbean islands "where they were sold as slaves that as yet they will hardly give credence to any other usage." Not even offers of brief service and generous land grants could offset this negative publicity entirely.

For the overall availability of white labor in the colony, the number of Europeans recruited was less important than the terms of indenture under which they came. Individual contracts varied widely. Some whites may have signed on as servants for the outward passage in order to help someone else obtain land through the headright system, only to be released upon arrival to take up lands of their own. (Hugh Carteret received a warrant for 325 acres on March 20, 1683, which included "70 acres for his wife arriveing a sert: upon his acco^{tt}: in August 1671 [and] 70 acres allowed his wife at the expiracon of her servitude.") Others worked until the cost of their passage was paid. It was not unheard-of for elderly people to indent themselves for life, but generally a specific term of service was set. Among colonies competing for European labor such terms of service had to be roughly comparable, and they tended to decrease through time. The usual term in Barbados dropped from five to seven years before the Restoration to three to five years after, with bargains for as little as one year's labor being struck in certain instances. Carolina contracts diminished similarly: in an indenture surviving from 1682 a London sawyer promised to serve for two years in the Charlestown settlement.

Such brief contracts resulted in a rapid turnover in the dependent white work force, and Gov. Archdale, addressing the commons in 1695, was not the first to complain of the "Servants that Dayley became free." More important, even a steady flow of indentured servants failed to increase the available pool of unfree manpower beyond a certain fixed point; it merely replenished the small supply of persons serving work-terms, while the overall population continued to grow. To maintain even this supply it was necessary for the colony to avoid the risk of adverse rumors about extended servitude. In 1687, therefore, a statute was passed which set maximum limits upon terms of service for new white arrivals according to their age. The same act imposed a further expense upon the employer by requiring him to provide each servant at the end of his term with "one suite of Apparell, one barrel of Indian Corne, one Axe and one Hoe."

Even before their terms expired, English servants who sensed their value in a labor-scarce economy could often better their lot. One man appealed successfully to the grand council for a change of household, since his current master "could not at present maintaine him with convenient & necessary provisions, and clothes." And many who could not bargain for their well-being must have stolen instead, for "Servants purloyning their masters goods" became an early topic of concern. Occasional disappearances and acts of flagrant disobedience were other matters of common anxiety. Severe penalties deterred most, though by no means all, white servants from attempting to flee the colony altogether, but many shared the disposition of Philip Orrill, who was sentenced to twenty-one lashes for threatening his mistress, tossing his rations to the dogs, "and divers other Gross abuses and destructive practices." Masters felt the odds for such ill behavior to be stronger among certain groups than among others. Joseph West, for example, having complained openly about the first servants drawn from England, held those from Barbados in even lower repute. He wrote the Proprietors in 1671:

I hope yo[r] Honn[rs] are thinking of sending a supply of Serv[ts] from England, for some of these wilbe out of their time the next yeare, and wee find that one of our Serv[ts] we brought out of England is worth 2 of ye Barbadians, for they are soe much addicted to Rum y[t] they will doe little but whilst the bottle is at their nose.

General lethargy seems to have constituted a particular vice among whites (and was by no means confined to servants). It now seems likely that the Europeans were not simply diverted from their Protestant ethic of work by the mild climate, but instead actually sacrificed some measure of their physical health (see Wood, *Black Majority*, chapter III). The observation concerning laziness was commonplace. "Inhabitants toil not in summer to accommodate themselves with Winter's Provision," wrote Gascoyne, and Archdale observed bluntly that the "natural Fertility and easy Manurement, is apt to make the

People incline to Sloth." Thus in quality, as well as in quantity, white indentured labor clearly left something to be desired.

III

The alternative of African labor was a plausible one from the outset. It appeared natural to colonizers from the West Indies and intriguing to those from Western Europe, and it afforded certain advantages to both. Since Africans came from a distance, their exploitation did not present the serious diplomatic and strategic questions posed by Indian labor, yet their Caribbean sources were closer and their transportation costs lower than those of white workers. Unlike white servants Negroes could be held for unlimited terms, and there was no means by which word of harsh or arbitrary treatment could reach their homelands or affect the further flow of slaves. Moreover, Africans had long had the reputation of being able to fend for themselves more readily than Europeans in the subtropical southern Atlantic climate—a valuable asset when provisions were scarce. For example, a century earlier (June 4, 1580) the Council of the Indies in Madrid, in urging that thirty slaves be sent out from Havana to work on the fortifications at St. Augustine, remarked that, "With regard to their food, they will display diligence as they seek it in the country, without any cost to the royal treasury."

The barriers posed by language were scarcely more formidable for Africans than for other non-English-speakers and had often been reduced through time spent in the West Indies. The useful effects of this Caribbean "seasoning" are noted in a letter of 1688. Edmund White wrote from London to Joseph Morton, two-time governor of the Carolina colony, offering the chance for investment in a slave ship which was sailing directly to the Guinea Coast, but acknowledging that Morton might rather venture his capital on Negroes already in the West Indies. If that were the case, White went on to recommend that Morton contact one Col. Johnson in Barbados, asking whether, "when any bargaine of negroes is to be had, he would buy them for you and keep them upon his plantation till he can send them." This, White assured Morton, "he can doe with much care & the negroes will be the better after they have been ashore for sometime and their work will be worth their keeping." It is notable that White added, "Let y^r negroes be taught to be smiths shoemakers & carpenters & bricklayers: they are capable of learning anything & I find when they are kindly used & have their belly full of victualls and [possess suitable] clothes, they are the truest servants." Of course few Europeans in the seventeenth century were likely to concede—or even suspect—that such Negro skills with metal, leather, wood, and masonry could well be the result of prior familiarity. Still, it was soon granted among whites that, by one means or another, blacks seemed to "understand most handycrafts."

The actual methods of obtaining black labor were quite varied at first, and many of the colony's earliest Negro slaves, like certain European and Indian workers, were secured by dubious means. Piracy was at its height in the Caribbean during the period of Carolina's early white settlement, and there is little doubt that colonists occasionally offered shelter and provision to buccaneers in exchange for portions of their spoils. In 1684 the governor of Jamaica, protesting the increase of piracy to the Lords of Trade and Plantations, "represented to them the great damage that does arise in His Majesty's service by harbouring and encouraging of Pirates in Carolina." A year later the Proprietors wrote their colony concerning some accused pirates, transported from Charlestown to London for trial, who reportedly "had negroes gould and other things which were seized in Carolina," all of which would fall to the Proprietors if the men were found guilty. A large pirate fleet had plundered Vera Cruz in 1683, and according to the depositions made by several runaway English servants at St. Augustine in January 1686, South Carolina obtained roughly two hundred Negroes from this and other raids. (The appearance of Spanish names among early slaves supports such testimony.) Raiding parties carried off Negroes from New Providence, the nearest English slave island in the Bahamas, twice during 1684, and again in 1703.

A few Negroes no doubt came to Carolina through the practice of "salvaging" for resale slaves who had been abandoned to their own devices in the Caribbean as a result of natural disasters or shipboard rebellions. Other blacks were imported to Carolina from as far away as England upon occasion. As for imports directly from Africa, it is possible that interlopers in the slave trade who were turned away from Barbados by the Royal African Company might have traveled as far as Carolina, but this seems unlikely, for the colony's economy would not reach a scale capable of absorbing and paying for a large shipload of slaves on short notice until well after the turn of the century. One or two small vessels from Charlestown may have risked an Atlantic crossing to seek a cargo of African workers before 1700, but any such efforts were exceptional during the colony's first generation.

Throughout the first twenty-five years after 1670 the documentary evidence suggests that most Negroes arriving in Carolina were brought in small numbers, by specific owners, from points in the western hemisphere. For example, in 1683 the ship *Betty*, "rideing att Anchor in the Roade of Barbadoes & bound for Ashley River in Carolina," took aboard six Negroes, along with two half-barrels of flour and two barrels of rum," for delivery "unto Bernard Schenckingh or to his Assignes." Upon their arrival, Schenckingh was to pay what must have been the standard shipping charge of fifty shillings per head for the group of slaves, which included four men (June, Meningo, Walle, Bache), one young woman (Cumboe), and a boy (Popler). Because of the direction of Carolina's mercantile ties and the broader patterns of the English slave trade, Barbados served as the main source for this small-scale commerce in Negro labor. Due to the increased exertions of the Royal African Company and the growing number of separate traders, that island entrepot received more than seventy thousand slaves between 1670 and 1695. (In the last quarter of the seventeenth century Barbados accounted for almost 40 per cent of the British slave trade, a trade which itself still represented less than 30 per cent of the entire Atlantic commerce in Africans during the period.) Barbadian disdain for Irish labor ("commonly very idle") was expressed to the Lords of Trade and Plantations in 1676 by Sir Jonathan Atkins, who claimed that sugar planters had found by experience that black slaves worked better at one third the cost. In 1680 he observed that "since people have found out the convenience and cheapness of slave labour they no longer keep white men, who formerly did all the work on the Plantations."

The preferences of the Caribbean landlords, although geared to a very different economy, must have been widely known to their Carolina cousins. Carolina's reliance upon Barbados for what slaves its white colonists could afford served to strengthen further the existing ties to the sugar island, and these bonds—in a circular fashion—helped predispose would-be planters in the mainland colony to black labor. Since little social hierarchy was possible at first in the southern wilderness, slave ownership quickly became a means for Englishmen to establish status distinctions in the mainland settlement. Their food, clothing, and shelter became more similar with migration; the destitute lived somewhat better, and the well-to-do somewhat worse, than they had before. At Bridgetown in Barbados, where more than 90 per cent of white householders owned Negroes—almost twice the percentage that possessed white labor—the pattern counted for little, but in Charlestown, where white servants represented a smaller, safer, and more common investment than black, the possession of Negroes assumed additional social connotations.

Since an African retinue, however forlorn, served to distinguish and to reinforce authority patterns among whites, it is not surprising that at first local officials were among the largest individual importers of slaves. Among the early governors, Sayle brought several slaves despite his brief tenure; Yeamans and Morton owned dozens between them. James Colleton employed black laborers on his extensive barony and probably left most of them there when he returned to Barbados; while Seth Sothell possessed at least ten slaves even before he replaced Colleton. Sir Nathaniel Johnson, who would become governor in 1702, had imported over several decades more than one hundred "Servants & Negroes at Sundry times on his account in this parte of the province," and when the Rev. Samuel Thomas visited Johnson's Cooper River estate of "Silk Hope," he noted that "his family is very large many servants and slaves."

Such status-seeking had certain implications for the slaves purchased to fill symbolic roles. Several hundred Negroes must have belonged to the handful of whites who each owned more than a dozen black workers before 1695. These slaves apparently lived upon large tracts in remote areas, where contacts with other Africans were limited but where the nucleus of a social unit larger than a family could already exist. Supervision was partial and activities varied, for new crops were being tried and new land cleared annually. (It is misleading to glorify—or damnify—any of these isolated seventeenth-century holdings as "plantations.") For slaves who had served on sugar plantations the uncertainties of the frontier must have posed a welcome contrast to the harsh routine of the islands, and for those who were dressed handsomely and employed superficially in ways calculated to enhance their master's stature, there were the small gratifications which the patronizing and the patronized always share.

But labor was too scarce for any but the most highly placed to restrict Negroes to symbolic or genteel functions as yet. If certain masters purchased blacks to announce their social arrival, most employed them to better their economic well-being. Some prosperous craftsmen owned whole black families, more than one member of which may well have been employed in the business. Stephen Fox, a tanner from Barbados, brought four men, four women, and four children with him aboard the *Mary* in May 1679; the extensive estate left by James Beamer, a "joyner," in 1694 included three men, three women, and six children; a carpenter named Thomas Gunstone owned two men, two women, and four children who were sold together in 1698.

In general, therefore, slaves simply shared the calling of the white household to which they were annexed, participating fully in the colony's growing number of specialized trades.

IV

There were, however, numerous impediments to the use of African labor in Carolina, and widespread enslavement of Negroes was by no means a foregone conclusion from the start. An inexperienced Huguenot settler claimed that "any man who has a couple of negroes, a ready-made plantation, [and] a maid-servant . . . can live very happily . . . in this country at small outlay." But in fact the outlay required for black labor was by no means small. Indeed, it was their price, more than anything else, that limited the viability of slave laborers at first. If African labor was recognized in the Caribbean as potentially more profitable than European labor over the long run, it still entailed a larger initial investment, and many early settlers in Carolina who could not afford to bring slaves brought indentured servants instead. A Negro purchased outright for an unlimited period could be worked harder, maintained more cheaply, and retained longer than a white servant under a limited indenture, but only after several years of steady labor would these comparative advantages begin to carry weight. The additional cost and responsibility of such a purchase had limited appeal in a frontier colony where money was scarce, risks were high, and the future nature of the economy was still uncertain.

Whenever slave labor could be purchased cheaply, it usually represented an excessive gamble. The Canteys, an Irish family of small means who reached Carolina by way of Barbados in the 1670s, acquired along the way a slave named Marea and her infant son, Jacke. This "Sicke Dropsecall diseased Negro woman" was later appraised at two pounds and could hardly have been a valuable asset. Moreover, even white Carolinians with sufficient capital to import healthy Negro labor could not always find sound investments at hand. Barbadian planters, who reckoned the mortality of their bondsmen at one in twenty annually, had prior call upon their island's expanding supply of imported slaves. As a result, other settlements, as close to Barbados as Nevis, complained about the price and quality of Negroes available through re-export. In the more distant and less wealthy mainland colony these problems were still greater.

Foreign competition compounded these difficulties. Not only were the English colonies in the Caribbean, to which Jamaica had been added in 1655, exploiting Africans in growing numbers, but the mainland colonies of Spain were obtaining an increasing percentage of their slaves through British merchants. Although the Navigation Acts of 1661 excluded foreign ships from trading with English colonies, several thousand of the Royal African Company's slaves were annually diverted into "assientist" vessels, and in 1685 the Lords of Trade officially exempted from seizure "Spanish ships that are come to buy negroes" at English ports in the Caribbean. Since the Spaniards could generally pay high prices in hard coin without requesting credit, they received priority over English planters and pushed the cost of Company Negroes upward. When the planters resorted to interlopers to supply their own demand, the expense of procuring slaves in Africa was also increased. Overall slave prices among the English appear to have risen more than 20 per cent during the 1680s. Therefore, advantages related to employing Negroes in Carolina were largely offset by increasing demands for their services elsewhere.

And indeed, in Carolina itself the attraction of foreign demand was felt. Although the re-export of slaves from Charlestown for profit would not prove generally feasible for another three quarters of a century, the first generation of white settlers were never free from the thought of exchanging valuable Negro labor for Spanish bullion. Lord Shaftesbury, himself associated with the Royal African Company, had commerce with the Florida Catholic settlement in mind when he considered establishing his barony in Carolina. "You are to endeavour," he instructed Andrew Percivall in 1674, "to begin a Trade with the Spaniards for Negroes, Clothes or other Commodyties they want." In the 1680s when eleven blacks (members of a larger contingent of "diverse negroe slaves" which had run away from South Carolina) appeared at St. Augustine, embraced Catholicism, and sought permanent asylum there, Maj. William Dunlop negotiated to sell them to the Spanish for sixteen hundred pieces of eight. After the Spanish raid of 1686, in which thirteen of Landgrave Morton's slaves were carried off, his brother-in-law killed, and "great desolation . . . made in the South part of this Settlem^t," Gov. Colleton reopened trading relations so quickly that eyebrows were raised. "The truth is," confirmed a later report, "there was a design on foot to carry on a Trade with the Spaniard." Strategic considerations finally outweighed commercial interests, however, and no regular profits came to the English from selling slaves to their nearby Spanish rivals.

Next to the high initial cost, it was the frequency of disappearances which presented the greatest drawback to employing black labor, and these two factors were of course related. The unlimited term which raised the price of the slave also increased his motivation to escape; unlike the indentured servant's his situation contained no prospect of predictable improvement. Since settlement conditions were harsh and means of social control superficial, disappearances were frequent for all varieties of unfree labor in the new province, but the departure of a servant with several years left to serve was less costly to his white master than the absence of a lifetime slave. Some newcomers were undoubtedly deterred from running away by ignorance of local geography, but many were knowledgeable and realistic about the prospects for escape, if only because of the regulations which forbade it. The likely refuge of St. Augustine was a constant subject of public discussion in early years, and the appearance of Carolina slaves and servants there gives evidence that its whereabouts was not overlooked. By 1689 the red, white, and black populations of the Spanish settlement totaled almost fifteen thousand, and outside St. Augustine there already existed the makings of a distinct Negro community which would grow with time. Although more distant and less inviting, Virginia was also known, particularly to those laborers who had been brought from that direction. As early as 1671, when Yeamans sent Dr. Henry Woodward on a secret overland journey to the north, Gov. West had expressed to Lord Ashley that "if he arrives safe in Virginia, there is a way laid for o^r Serv^{ts} to range in, wee have lost two allready."

Similar concerns are borne out in the colony's first legislation devoted entirely to slavery, an "Act for the Better Ordering of Slaves" passed by the Assembly in 1690 and quickly disallowed by the Proprietors for political reasons. This statute represented little more than a reworking by the local West Indian faction of a strict law drawn up by whites in Barbados after a suspected Negro plot in 1688. Significantly, the law initiated a system of tickets for slaves sent on errands, despite the absence of any effectual means of enforcement, and it sanctioned such brutal corporal punishments as branding, nose-slitting, and emasculation at a time when very few slaveowners in the wilderness colony were yet in a secure enough position to resort to punishments more severe than whipping. Section V of the law required masters to search regularly for weapons in "all the slaves houses" at a time when it is likely that few Carolina Negroes yet lived in such separate and solid dwellings. Other portions of the act, however, pertained more closely to the local situation: masters were ordered to issue every slave a convenient set of clothes annually and to refrain from giving slaves Saturday afternoons free as had been the custom in Carolina until that time.

Since piracy was so rampant during this first generation it is worth noting here that pirates occasionally conspired with Negroes to mutual advantage. There is even an instance on record of a Negro and an Indian helping a captured pirate to escape. Having benefited in some instances from the slaves' arrival, the buccaneers were not above profiting from their escape, and more than one black was transported away to be sold again elsewhere or retained as a crewman. Nor was the line between pirate and non-pirate particularly clear in this turbulent era. The French pirate ship *La Trompeuse,* which included Negroes and Indians as well as Europeans among its crew, served briefly as an official man-of-war in 1684. On the other hand, H.M.S. *Drake,* although assigned to protect the Carolina coast, engaged in this illegal traffic on the side. A letter of 1690 denounces her commander as a "Piraticall villain" who "seases carys abroad and receaves of Negros Runing from their Masters 2000 lib [pounds] worth to the ruining [of] many famalies."

The attitudes of neighboring Indians, more than the activities of pirate groups, were crucial to the retention of black labor during this first generation. Local tribes could assist runaway Negroes or else capture and return them, depending upon a variety of factors. It quickly became apparent to white colonists that the nature of this response would in large measure determine the frequency and success of slave departures, and efforts were undertaken to have the surrounding native population assume, in effect, the confining function performed by the sea in the West Indies. The fact "that the Indians will be of great Use to ye Inhabitants of our province for the fetching in againe of such Negro Slaves as shall Runn away from their masters" was regarded by the Proprietors as grounds for improving relations with the Indians and curtailing their enslavement. The Proprietors, through selfish concern for the growing fur trade, offered constant reminders that without good Indian relations "you can never get in yor Negroes that run away." By the 1690s, as Negro numbers expanded and the trade in furs opened up, the white colonists took concrete steps to set black and red at cross purposes. Gov. Thomas Smith reported to the commons at the start of its fall session 1693 that he had "by the Advice of the Councill Sumond all ye neighbouring Indians to Receive Some Comands from ye Councill relateing to

Runaway slaves." Yet despite such dealings, Indian relations with the white slavemasters remained ambiguous, and the disappearance of black servants from the isolated colony continued. An inventory com piled the following spring for an extensive Charlestown estate in- cludes, at a value of twenty-nine pounds, "one negro man named will now rund away."

Despite these various drawbacks, hundreds of Negroes were brought to Carolina to supplement labor from other sources. Fre- quently during the first generation black and white workers were im- ported on the same boat by the same planter, as was the case with "Tom: Samboe: Betty & Peter," who arrived at Charlestown in Sep- tember 1682 alongside their master and his six European servants. Already it was generally understood that indentured servants were white and their terms were short, while nonwhite laborers served for life; but anomalies remained common. A European could be bound to a life term; an Indian could obtain an indenture. And regardless of formal status, the actual conditions of life and labor did not yet vary greatly between servant and slave, free and unfree. The fact that few new residents were so well stationed as to be exempt from hardship, or so insignificant as to be expendable, is underscored by the letter of a young Huguenot girl who arrived in 1685. Judith Giton wrote to her brother in Europe:

After our arrival in Carolina we suffered all sorts of evils. Our eldest brother died of a fever, eighteen months after coming here, being unac- customed to the hard work we were subjected to. We ourselves have been exposed, since leaving France, to all kinds of afflictions, in the forms of sickness, pestilence, famine, poverty, and the roughest labor. I have been for six months at a time in this country without tasting bread, laboring meanwhile like a slave in tilling the ground. Indeed, I have spent three or four years without knowing what it was to eat bread whenever I wanted it.

Where white migrants "worked like slaves," black arrivals labored in many respects like hired hands, and there were numerous house- holds in which captured Indians, indentured Europeans, and en- slaved Africans worked side by side during these first years. For example, the estate of John Smyth, who died in 1682, included nine Negroes, four Indians, and three whites. Even though such de- pendents were not all engaged in the same tasks or accorded equal status, they must have fulfilled complementary functions at close quarters. In the final balance, therefore, no one form of labor seemed sufficiently cheap or superior or plentiful to preclude the others.

V

Just as no single type of manpower predominated within the colony at first, no single economic activity preoccupied the varied work force of the early years. Given this context, the large-scale transitions to a slave labor force and to a rice-growing economy during the second generation take on particular interest. Both changes depended upon a great number of separate variables, and it is certainly conceivable that these parallel developments, so thoroughly intertwined in later years, had little causal relation at the outset. Every colony was in search of a staple, and South Carolina's commitment to rice developed only gradually; as late as 1720 there was probably more labor engaged in the production of meat exports and naval stores than in the growing of rice. Likewise every colony was in search of labor, and if each obtained from the nearest source workers who were accustomed to the prevailing climate, it was natural that the northern colonies would draw servants from Europe while the southern colonies were taking slaves from the West Indies and Africa. In South Carolina, there were logical reasons for the appearance of black laborers irrespective of the tasks intended for them. More than any mainland colony, its roots of settlement and early commercial ties stretched toward Barbados and the other islands of the English Caribbean. African labor was already in steady supply there, and English colonists from the West Indies who were economically unable to bring Negroes with them at least brought along the social aspiration of slave ownership. Laborers from the British Isles were in shorter supply during the period of South Carolina's early settlement than they had been during the initial years of the Virginia or Maryland colonies, and after the end of the government monopoly on the slave trade in 1699, the mainland colony closest to the Caribbean stood to benefit most from the participation of private English traders in the traffic in unfree labor.

Even reduced to briefest form, these points are logical enough, and in themselves they suggest little more than a temporal association between the development of rice and slavery. But one possible link has never been fully explored. Scholars have traditionally implied that African laborers were generally "unskilled" and that this characteristic was particularly appropriate to the tedious work of rice cultivation. It may well be that something closer to the reverse was true early in South Carolina's development. Needless to say, most of the work for all colonists was what one Scotsman characterized as simple "labor and toyl of the body," but if highly specialized workers were not required, at the same time there was hardly a premium on being unskilled. It seems safe to venture that if Africans had shown much less competence in, or aptitude for, such basic frontier skills as managing boats, clearing land, herding cattle, working wood, and cultivating fields, their importation would not have continued to grow. [See Wood, *Black Majority*, chap. 4.] But it is worthwhile to suggest here that with respect to rice cultivation, particular know-how, rather than lack of it, was one factor which made black labor attractive to the English colonists.

Though England consumed comparatively little rice before the eighteenth century, the cheap white grain had become a dietary staple in parts of southern Europe by 1670, and Carolina's Proprietors were anticipating a profit from this crop even before the settlement began. The colonists sent out from London in 1669 did not possess rice among their experimental samples, although an enticing pamphlet for the Cape Fear settlement several years earlier had suggested that "The meadows are very proper for Rice." Nevertheless, a single bushel or barrel of rice was shipped by the Proprietors along with other supplies aboard the *William & Ralph* early in 1672. This quantity may have been planted rather than eaten, for one of several servants who defected to St. Augustine two years later told the Spanish governor that the new colony produced "some rice" along with barrel staves and tobacco. But by 1677 the colonists still had little to show for their experimental efforts, and their sponsors wrote impatiently from London: "wee are Layinge out in Severall places of ye world for plants & Seeds proper for yor Country and for persons that are Skill'd in plantinge & producinge . . . Rice oyles & Wines." There is no direct evidence, however, that the Proprietors followed through on this promise, or that they responded helpfully to later requests for guidance.

During the 1680s, perhaps after the arrival of a better strain of rice seed from Madagascar, the colonists renewed their rice-growing efforts. The mysteries of cultivation were not unraveled quickly, however, as is shown by several letters from John Stewart in 1690. Stewart had been managing Gov. James Colleton's "Wadboo Barony" and was taking an active part in rice experimentation. He claimed to have cultivated the crop in twenty-two different places in one season to ascertain the best location and spacing of the plant. Stewart boasted, perhaps truthfully, that already "Our Ryce is esteem'd of in Jamaica," but even this arch promoter did not yet speak of the grain as a logical export staple. Instead he proposed that rice could be used for the distilling of beer and ale ("from what I observ'd in Russia"), and he went on to suggest that planters "throw by Indian corne to feed slaves with rice as cheaper."

The processing as well as the planting of rice involved obstacles for the Europeans, which may explain why they had discarded the crop initially. "The people being unacquainted with the manner of cultivating rice," recalled an Englishman during the eighteenth century, "many difficulties attended the first planting and preparing it, as a vendable commodity, so that little progress was made for the first nine or ten years, when the quantity produced was not sufficient for home consumption." Similarly, Gov. Glen would later claim that even after experimenters had begun to achieve plausible yields from their renewed efforts around 1690, they still remained "ignorant for some Years how to clean it." In 1691 a Frenchman named Peter Jacob Guerard received a two-year patent on "a Pendulum Engine, which doth much better, and in lesse time and labour, huske rice; than any other [that] heretofore hath been used within this Province," but there is no indication that the device itself succeeded, or that it helped to spur further invention as hoped.

By 1695 Carolina was not yet one of the sources from which England drew her moderate supply of rice, and the colonial legislature was still urging diversity of output as it cast about for a suitable economic base. In 1698 the Assembly was seeking information on such possible activities as whale fishing and the raising of Smyrna currants. Although a request was also made that the Proprietors "Procure and Send . . . by ye first oppertunity a moddell of a Rice mill," it is doubtful that any such thing was ever found or sent. More than a decade later, Thomas Nairne mentioned the practice of cleaning rice in mills turned by oxen or horses, but no such labor-saving machines came into common use. It is notable that Nairne, like many others in South Carolina at the start of the eighteenth century, continued to view rice in large part as an adjunct to the livestock economy. " 'Tis very much sow'd here," he wrote in 1710, "not only because it is a vendible Commodity, but thriving best in low moist Lands, it inclines People to improve that Sort of Ground, which being planted a few Years with Rice, and then laid by, turns to the best Pasturage."

In contrast to Europeans, Negroes from the West Coast of Africa were widely familiar with rice planting. Ancient speakers of a proto-Bantu language in the sub-Sahara region are known to have cultivated the crop. An indigenous variety (*Oryza glaberrima*) was a staple in the western rain-forest regions long before Portuguese and French navigators introduced Asian and American varieties of *O. sa-*

tiva in the 1500s. By the seventeenth and eighteenth centuries, West Africans were selling rice to slave traders to provision their ships. The northernmost English factory on the coast, James Fort in the Gambia River, was in a region where rice was grown in paddies along the river-banks. In the Congo-Angola region, which was the southernmost area of call for English slavers, a white explorer once noted rice to be so plentiful that it brought almost no price.

The most significant rice region, however, was the "Windward Coast," the area upwind or westward from the major Gold Coast trading station of Elmina in present-day Ghana. Through most of the slaving era a central part of this broad stretch was designated as the Grain Coast, and a portion of this in turn was sometimes labeled more explicitly as the Rice Coast. An Englishman who spent time on the Windward Coast (Sierra Leone) at the end of the eighteenth century claimed that rice "forms the chief part of the African's sustenance." He went on to observe, "The rice-fields or *lugars* are prepared during the dry season, and the seed sown in the tornado season, requiring about four or five months growth to bring it to perfection." Throughout the era of slave importation into South Carolina references can be found concerning African familiarity with rice. Ads in the local papers occasionally made note of slaves from rice-growing areas, and a notice from the *Evening Gazette,* July 11, 1785, announced the arrival aboard a Danish ship of "a choice cargo of windward and gold coast negroes, who have been accustomed to the planting of rice."

The most dramatic evidence of experience with rice among enslaved Africans comes from the famous rebels aboard the *Amistad* in the nineteenth century. Thirty-six slaves from the Sierra Leone region were shipped illegally from Lomboko to Cuba, and in the wake of their successful shipboard uprising they eventually found themselves imprisoned in New Haven, Connecticut. There they were interrogated separately, and excerpts from the interviews drive home this familiarity with rice in personal terms:

He was a blacksmith in his native village, and made hoes, axes and knives; he also planted rice.

There are high mountains in his country, rice is cultivated, people have guns; has seen elephants.

He was caught in the bush by four men as he was going to plant rice; his left hand was tied to his neck; was ten days going to Lomboko.

He was seized by four men when in a rice field, and was two weeks in traveling to Lomboko.

He is a planter of rice.

His parents are dead, and he lived with his brother, a planter of rice.

He was seized by two men as he was going to plant rice.

5 ft. 1 in. high, body tattoed, teeth filed, was born at Fe-baw, in Sando, between Mendi and Konno. His mother's brother sold him for a coat. He was taken in the night, and sold to Garlobá, who had four wives. He staid with this man two years, and was employed in cultivating rice. His master's wives and children were employed in the same manner, and no distinction made in regard to labor.

Needless to say, by no means every slave entering South Carolina had been drawn from an African rice field, and many, perhaps even a great majority, had never seen a rice plant. But it is important to consider the fact that literally hundreds of black immigrants were more familiar with the planting, hoeing, processing, and cooking of rice than were the European settlers who purchased them. Those slaves who were accustomed to growing rice on one side of the Atlantic, and who eventually found themselves raising the same crop on the other side, did not markedly alter their annual routine. When New World slaves planted rice in the spring by pressing a hole with the heel and covering the seeds with the foot, the motion used was demonstrably similar to that employed in West Africa. In summer, when Carolina blacks moved through the rice fields in a row, hoeing in unison to work songs, the pattern of cultivation was not one imposed by European owners but rather one retained from West African forebears. And in October when threshed grain was "fanned" in the wind, the wide, flat winnowing baskets were made by black hands after an African design.

Those familiar with growing and harvesting rice must also have known how to process it, so it is interesting to speculate about the origins of the mortar-and-pestle technique which became the accepted method for removing rice grains from their husks. Efforts by Europeans to develop alternative "engines" proved of no avail, and this process remained the most efficient way to "clean" the rice crop throughout the colonial period. Since some form of the mortar and pestle is familiar to agricultural peoples throughout the world, a variety of possible (and impossible) sources has been suggested for this device. But the most logical origin for this technique is the coast of Africa, for there was a strikingly close resemblance between the traditional West African means of pounding rice and the process used by slaves in South Carolina. Several Negroes, usually women, cleaned the grain in a small amount at a time by putting it in a wooden mortar which was hollowed from the upright trunk of a pine or cypress. It was beaten with long wooden pestles which had a sharp edge at one end for removing the husks and a flat tip at the other for whitening the grains. Even the songs sung by the slaves who threshed and pounded the rice may have retained African elements.

In the establishment of rice cultivation, as in numerous other areas, historians have ignored the possibility that Afro-Americans could have contributed anything more than menial labor to South Carolina's early development. Yet Negro slaves, faced with limited food supplies before 1700 and encouraged to raise their own subsistence, could readily have succeeded in nurturing rice where their masters had failed. It would not have taken many such incidents to demonstrate to the anxious English that rice was a potential staple and that Africans were its most logical cultivators and processors. Some such chain of events appears entirely possible. If so, it could well have provided the background for Edward Randolph's comment of 1700, in his report to the Lords of Trade, that Englishmen in Carolina had "now found out the true way of raising and husking Rice."

GERALD W. MULLIN
The Plantation World of William Byrd II

Great planters like William Byrd II would "live in a kind of Independence on Every one but Providence" even though they were des-
tined to be colonial staple producers and slaveowners in a mercantilist
empire. This was the central paradox of their careers. As colonists,
Byrd and his countrymen understood that authority for the most important political and economic decisions for Virginia originated outside its boundaries, in England. As staple producers, they were
subject to the mother-country's mercantile community and its manufactured goods, credit, and prices. As slaveowners, they exploited
Africa as a cheap and consistent source of labor, only to gradually
realize how thoroughly dependent they were on slaves.

To achieve a measure of control over their circumstances, wealthy
slaveowners sought to make themselves patriarchs of plantations
which were far more self-contained than their nineteenth-century
counterparts. These economically diversified plantations, which the
gentry worked so hard to create and maintain, were absolutely dependent on acculturated, skilled slaves. They were also the vehicle by
which the great planters would realize their dream of self-sufficiency—
and ultimately of mastery—over a society in which this was largely
impossible. Not only were they colonial agriculturalists but most important, their leading objective, the autarkic plantation community

"The Plantation World of William Byrd II," from *Flight and Rebellion: Slave
Resistance in Eighteenth-Century Virginia* by Gerald Mullin, pp. 3–33. Copyright © 1972 Oxford University Press, Inc.; reprinted by permission.

and its corollary, acculturated artisans, created a cruel dilemma: cultural change made Negroes less suitable for plantation slavery.

"THIS SILENT COUNTRY"

Africans in slavers entered Virginia on majestic tidal rivers that carried them from the Chesapeake Bay to the great planters' wharves in a land which, even a century after its settlement, remained a densely forested, sparsely populated wilderness. Waterways and forests, the tidewater region's most distinctive features, provoked the images whites used to convey their awed impressions of primeval splendor and vast distances. "The land, an immense forest extend[s] on a flat plain, almost without bounds," wrote an Englishman in 1787, "Nature here being on such a scale that what are called great rivers in Europe, are here considered only as inconsiderable creeks or rivulets. . . . The Rivers," he continued, "large expanses of water of enormous extent spread . . . under the eye as far as it can comprise." Another late eighteenth-century traveler, the Marquis de Chastellux, saw, "the great part of Virginia [as] very low and flat and so divided by creeks and great rivers, that it appears in fact redeemed from the sea and entirely of very recent creation."

Carved in the last glacial age, the Chesapeake Bay and its great tributaries, the Potomac, Rappahannock, York, and James rivers, comprise over 1,100 miles of waterways. The Bay (the ancient bed of the Susquehanna River) is 200 miles long and at one point 40 miles wide. The four rivers rise as fresh-water streams high in the gently rolling hills of the piedmont, the transitional zone between the Blue Ridge mountains and the tidewater. At the head of navigation their character changes. They widen, deepen, and become brackish; shrimp, oysters, and clams appear off the docks of such fall-line towns as Alexandria, Fredericksburg, Richmond, and Petersburg. Fall-line towns on the Potomac and Rappahannock could accommodate the largest ships built in the colonial period. At their mouths the rivers lose their identity altogether, and roll into the Great Bay in estuaries, which divide the coastal area into necks of land, or peninsulas, where the large slaveowners built their homes.

Accessibility to distribution points largely determines the character of staple-producing regions. In New England the well-worn coastal ranges in some areas march nearly to the beaches; the terrain is rocky and difficult to farm extensively, and marked by few rivers navigable by ocean-going vessels. Here Englishmen settled in communities and turned to the sea for their livelihood. In contrast the rich alluvial soil and web of waterways in Virginia drew the people into the interior, where they built plantations, not towns. Jamestown too, unlike Massachusetts-Bay Colony, was founded as a commercial venture by a London corporation intent on making a swift, neat profit on its investment. Although the Company's settlers initially tried to establish such staples as precious metals, wine, silk, and glass, by the 1620's tobacco became the cash crop. Tobacco planters also grew Indian corn, grain, and fruit and raised horses, cattle, and swine. By the late seventeenth century the supply of African slaves increased rapidly and the more profitable large plantations—often at the expense of the yeoman's farm—came to dominate the arable land in the tidewater and to move inexorably west up the river basins. But as late as 1750 the fresh-water sources for the great rivers sprang from an interior that was still largely unknown. In a report to the Board of Trade, a wealthy planter described his country's western boundary by reference to the mysterious "South Sea": "Virginia is Bounded by the Great Atlantic Ocean to the East, by North Carolina to the South, by Maryland and Pennsylvania to the North, and by the South Sea to the West, including California."

Political divisions, trade, and the plantations themselves were oriented to the river courses. Large slaveowners like Byrd, who once described Westover as "two miles above where the great ships ride," preferred to build on "roads," sections where the rivers broadened to two or three miles. A location on deep water had obvious economic advantages: the planter could control slave sales, and serve as a distributor for his inland neighbors' commodities. But a mansion situated on a tidal river had its own magical appeal. While explaining his countrymen's aversion to town life, one contemporary historian noted that Virginians preferred their "dispers'd way of living," because they would not be "coop'd up." Indeed, wrote Hugh Jones, another early eighteenth-century historian, "they love to build near water."

Most of the great home plantations of the one hundred wealthiest eighteenth-century Virginians were clustered off the coastline, a few miles downstream from the head of navigation on the great rivers. Professor Jackson Turner Main's analysis of the wealthiest taxpayers in the 1780's indicates that the median value of their property was about £25,000 (based on a computation of their amounts of taxable property in land, slaves, cattle, horses, and carriage wheels. One pound sterling equaled roughly $50 in food, clothing, and shelter in 1965). Slaves made up slightly more than one-fifth of the total sum of the gentry's property. These men owned an average of 70 slaves at home and 60 elsewhere. Only about one in ten owned 300 or more slaves; the largest with 785 was a Carter. George Mason of Gunston Hall was a representative member of the "One Hundred." He paid taxes on 7,649 acres, 118 slaves, 63 horses, 116 cattle, and a four-wheeled carriage.

Slaves and land were widely dispersed along the river basins. Only 58 slaveowners kept more than 100 slaves in a single county; and the average wealthy planter owned about 3,000 acres, both in the county where he lived and in counties upriver from his estate. Nearly all manors were broken up into small, isolated tracts referred to as "quarters." Half of the men on Main's list, for example, held land in 4 or more counties; and only 4 (less than 1 in 20) owned all of their property in one county. These non-resident quarters were usually west of the home plantation. The river courses also largely determined where land was held: Potomac River planters speculated in Northern Neck properties, while aristocrats on the James River developed quarters along that waterway.

Rivers, the main arteries of trade and travel for more than two hundred years, had tidal estuaries that opened up the interior, drew people into the land, and dispersed population.

Population density remained low even in the most populous counties throughout the colonial period. These were located in the oldest areas of settlement in the tidewater south of the Rappahannock River. These counties, which included the colony's few leading towns, were Gloucester (with 10,292 inhabitants), Elizabeth City (2,439), York (4,857), and James City (4,041). There were approximately 40 people per square mile in the first three; and James City County had about 30 people per square mile.

In 1699 when large importations of Africans were under way, there were about 70,000 inhabitants in the colony; and nearly 138,000 a quarter-century later. In the first year of the American Revolution the population was about half a million, of whom 40 per cent were slaves. Town life did not influence many colonists. In 1790 after a perceptible growth of port and fall-line towns following the war, only 19,000 of nearly half a million whites lived in nine of the new state's largest towns. The ninth was a hamlet of 669 souls.

The important connection between the colony's severe shortage of towns and free artisans, on the one hand, and staple production with slaves, self-sufficient plantations, and the lack of capital accumulation, on the other, was understood as early as 1698. *The Present State of Virginia and the College,* written by colonists for the Board of Trade, began, "[tobacco] swallows up all other Things"—towns, port facilities, educational institutions, and tradesmen. Artisans were especially "dear," because "for want of Towns, Markets, and Money," they had to be part-time farmers. Where else would they buy their meat, milk, corn, "and all other things"? Skilled laborers were perforce itinerants, "going and coming to and from their Work" in the "dispers'd Country." Instead of wages they were paid "straggling parcels of Tobacco," or worse, sides of beef, which had to be immediately salted and preserved. Planters refused to pay cash or even smaller quantities of payment in kind. The white artisan's loss, however, was the skilled slave's gain. Assimilated slaves, those who were sufficiently conversant in English to be taught work skills, were used in mines, salt- and rope-works; and they trained as shipwrights, blacksmiths, and as various kinds of woodworkers, including carpenters, coopers, wheelwrights, and sawyers.

But the lack of town life and urban services was not an insurmountable problem for the large slaveowners, for the articles which they did not produce on their own plantations were shipped to their wharves directly from Europe. Hugh Blair Grigsby, a late eighteenth-century Virginia historian and an acute observer, used a comparison of habits of dress to call attention to the great planters' pre-eminence based on their slave-artisans, self-sufficiency, and strategic location. "You can tell the men who come from the bay counties and from the banks of the large rivers, and who, from the facility with which they could exchange their products for British goods are clothed in foreign fabrics," he wrote. "You can also tell those who live off the great arteries of trade, far in the interior, in the shadow of the Blue Ridge, in the Valley. . . . These are mostly clad in homespun, or in the most substantial buckskin."

"A KIND OF INDEPENDENCE ON EVERY ONE BUT PROVIDENCE"

Conspicuous in a European finery symbolic of their dependence on metropolitan areas overseas, the great planters were also well known for their vaunted individualism which they displayed in all major aspects of their lives. "The public or political character of the Virginians," the Reverend Andrew Burnaby understood, "corresponds with their private one: they are haughty and jealous of their liberties, impatient of restraint and can scarcely bear the thought of being controuled by any superior power." Dependence on British culture, ministers, and merchants sharpened the Virginians' fears about becoming anyone else's "slaves"—a concept they often used in the Revolutionary era.

In order to master forces that were actually for the most part beyond their influence, the large planters became exemplary entrepreneurs in what C. Vann Woodward has aptly labeled "The Age of the Puritan Ethic." "I cannot allow myself," Robert "King" Carter wrote his London factor, "to come behind any of these gentlemen in the planter's trade." His son Landon understood that the quixotic quest for autonomy in a slave society began at home: Sabine Hall, he remarked, was "an excellent little Fortress . . . built on a Rock . . . of *Independency*." Indeed, the planters' economically diversified plantations, as well as their subsidiary business roles as slave dealers, home manufacturers, and retailers of European goods to their less fortunate neighbors, were ultimately the source of their power, their life style, and the means by which they would resolve the dilemma inherent in their role as colonial agriculturalists in a mercantilist empire.

But to underscore the uniqueness both of slavery and the wealthy slaveowners' way of life on the large, self-contained plantations it is necessary to digress momentarily to consider the great majority of planters on small, inland farms, who were wholly dependent on outside sources for even the most essential household goods, manufactures, and services.

One rare but fairly complete account of a small plantation described a 690-acre farm in St. Thomas' Parish, Orange County. John Mallory put his estate together slowly. In 1742 he paid quitrents on 249 acres; in the mid-1750's he made payments of £1.15.11½ on 690 acres, and two slaves (all slaves over 16 years of age were taxed). How many slaves he owned at this time is impossible to discover; but in his estate (attested in 1772) there was a costly imbalance between men and women, productive and non-productive slaves. Eight of his 11 slaves were women and 2 were "girls"; Dick, who was rated at £70 and the only male laborer, went to Mallory's eldest son. Two women, who were evidently expected to produce additional slaves, were valued at £70 and £60. The remainder were children, assessed at about one-half of the adult's value. These 11 slaves were worth less than £500.

Planters like John Mallory often required services, usually of the most menial, but not necessarily inexpensive, variety, that were provided by either the large planters' slave-artisans or an occasional itinerant white craftsman. A fragment of an account for household expenses from June through May 1760–61, included charges from 2 pence to 8 shillings for pointing a plow, sharpening a hoe, and "laying" [making] three hoes, a plow, and 2 horseshoes.

The Pocket plantation's critical dependence on outside support was even greater. John Smith, Jr., purchased this Pittsylvania County plantation of 713 acres from Peter Jefferson in 1755. Smith, who sold tobacco and hemp to Scottish factors in New London, Bedford County, was a larger and more politically active planter than Mallory. He served as a sub-surveyor and sub-sheriff for Albemarle County in the 1750's, and as sub-surveyor for Goochland County in the 1760's.

Smith's expenses, upkeep, and repairs were also more varied and extensive than Mallory's. In 1772 he paid £25.5 alone for work performed by a carpenter and joiner. Earlier accounts with the county handyman recorded payments for a pair of "negro shoes"; the construction of a twelve-foot-square meat house; two 50-gallon "Cyder Cases," £3.10; for "your [the white jobber's] wife Laying [midwifing] two negro Wenches", £1; and, for "sundry sort of Work, 18/6." Evidently, Smith's slaves were only field laborers, because in 1757 he contracted for such simple tasks as the construction of a kitchen and a slave quarter, "mending an old Tobo [hogshead]." In June of that year he paid Thomas Allbrittain £2.5 for "getin & Nailing on 1500 bords." He also had to hire blacksmiths for such piddling jobs as pointing a plow, and mending a teakettle and padlock. Last, a James Faniken was paid for supplying the plantation with 309 pounds of beef, for 3 days' work in the "Cellar shelters," and for "riding 8 days in Search of horses." This odd-jobber's wife was also given a small recompense for weaving 15 yards of cloth.

These plantation accounts illustrate a problem of insufficient urbanization and home manufactures so severe one planter commented that "we have no merchants, tradesmen or artificers of any sort here but what become planters in a short time"—few of the larger slaveowners, he should have added, were not also merchants and tradesmen.

Small planters like Mallory and Smith were the gentry's regular customers for retail goods and repairs as well as for slaves and home manufactures. They sold their crops to the large slaveowners who used them to increase their own credit purchases of European manufactured goods. As a type of resident factor, the great planter retailed these goods in "merchant stores," one of which is described in "King" Carter's estate inventory:

Sundry goods in the Brick House Store, under the care of Captain thomas Carter: Gartrix, Kenting, blew linnen, Patterbons, Dowals, brown oz., ticking, fine chince, fine broad falls, fine Devon. Kersey, Shalloon, men's roll, knit hose, short hose, women's wash gloves, men's gloves, blankets, boots, shoes, men's & women's; men's new woodheeled shoes, round red heels do.; spectacles in case, men's felts, men's casters, pr. scales' weights, money scales, thread, cloves, drop shot, mould shot, brass kettles, bell metal skillets, double slint decanters, tape, gunpowder, mohair, tie buttons, other buttons, brads, broad hoes, brass chaffing dishes, brass & iron candlesticks, paddlocks, hasps & staples, pewter basin, lead inkstand, knives and forks, ivory combs, horse combs, sheep shead lines, drum hooks, perch hooks; sifters, lawn searches, 1 grammer, 2 testaments, chests, trunk, leather chair.

Wealthy and powerful men like "King" Carter also supplied additional urban services based on their iron foundries, flour mills, textile weaving centers, and blacksmith shops. John Tayloe's Neabsco Ironworks in Prince William County, for example, did a thriving business in cutting new tools, repairing old ones, and in blacksmithing and locksmithing.

Even the physical appearance and layout of the large plantations made abundantly clear why a few slaveowners excelled while so many others struggled. Robert "Councillor" Carter's Nomini Hall in Westmoreland County was surrounded by 33 outbuildings, including a mill, brewery, spinning center, wheat silo, and ironworks. Extensive outbuildings such as these prompted the German traveler, Dr. Johann Schoepf, to observe that "a plantation in Virginia has often more the appearance of a small village by reason of [its] many small buildings."

Augustus John Foster, a British visitor to James Madison's Montpelier, remarked that the neighboring piedmont towns were so critically lacking in skills and services that it was necessary for Madison's slaves to be "able to do all kinds of handiwork." Accordingly, he discovered in his walks a forge, a turner's shop, a carpenter, and a wheelwright. While inspecting a very well-made wagon that "had just been completed," he noted that "all" of the farm implements were also "made on the spot." The Duc de La Rochefoucauld-Liancourt found the same thriving workshops close by at Monticello. Since Jefferson could not "expect any assistance from the two small neighboring towns, every article [was] made on his farm." His slaves were cabinetmakers, carpenters, masons, bricklayers, smiths, "&c." Although nearly all planters who recorded their views of slave children agreed that they were economic liabilities, Jefferson's young slaves manufactured nails. This small-scale household industry "yield[ed] a considerable profit"; his other unproductive slaves, the older women, spun clothing.

In addition to archaeological remains and these narrative sources, accounts and inventories often illustrate the abundance of home manufactures on the great plantations. John Page's informal inventory for his beautiful estate, Rosewell, listed:

Emanual (Shoemaker), Oliver (Blacksmith) Sam (Carpenter), Jemmey (Cooper), Sharp (Waiter), Mary (Dairy Maid), Rachel (Cook), Kate (Laundress), and Edy, Jenny, Molly, and Kate (Maids).

totals   10 in the Crop

12 Tradesmen & H[ouse] S[ervan]ts
 8 Children
 4 old
——
35

On Philip Ludwell's plantation, Green Spring, the proportion of field to non-field workers was slightly higher. He owned 81 slaves, three-fourths of whom worked "in the crop." Twelve were house "servants" (a term preferred by slaveowners when they referred to house slaves); and there were 3 gardeners and hostlers, 4 carpenters, 2 shoemakers, and a wheelwright. Coachman Nat, a "governor," presided over this plantation "family."

Great planters kept large and specialized staffs of "servants" and artisans on their home plantations; but their up-country, staple-growing quarters were comprised of tobacco fields, crop slaves, and little else. One of George Washington's periodic inventories listed 216 slaves: 67 of whom lived at Mount Vernon, and included 2 "val de Chambre," 2 waiters, 2 cooks, 3 drivers and stablers, 3 seamstresses, 2 house maids, 2 washers, 4 spinners, and (their numbers not indicated) knitters, blacksmiths and carpenters, a wagoner, a carter, and a stock keeper. He also had 2 women "almost past service," lame Peter, who had been taught to knit, and 26 children. At his mill adjacent to the home quarter, he kept a slave miller and 3 coopers to pack the meal. Thompson Mason had 50 slaves on his home plantation, 20 of whom were house "servants" alone, and many of the others were artisans.

The most complete description of a virtually self-dependent plantation is George Mason's. Describing his father's economic diversification at Gunston Hall, Mason wrote:

My father had among his slaves carpenters, coopers, sawyers, blacksmiths, tanners, curriers, shoemakers, spinners, weavers and knitters, and even a distiller. His woods furnish timber and plank for the carpenters and coopers, and charcoal for the blacksmith; his cattle killed for his own consumption and for sale supplied skins for the tanners, curriers, and shoemakers, and his sheep gave wool and his fields produced cotton and flax for the weavers and spinners, and his orchards fruit for the distiller. His carpenters and sawyers built and kept in repair all the dwelling-houses, barns, stables, ploughs, barrows, gates &c., on the plantations and the out-houses at the home house. His coopers made the hogsheads the tobacco was prised in and the tight casks to hold the cider and other liquors. The tanners and curriers with the proper vats &c., tanned and dressed the skins as well for upper as for lowere leather to the full amount of the consumption of the estate, and the shoemakers made them into shoes for the negroes. . . . The blacksmiths did all the iron work required by the establishment, as making and repairing ploughs, harrow, teeth chains, bolts &c., &c. The spinners, weavers and knitters made all the coarse cloths and stockings used by the negroes, and some of finer texture worn by the white family, nearly all worn by the children of it. The distiller made every fall a good deal of apple, peach and persimmon brandy. . . . All these operations were carried on at the home house, and their results distributed as occasion required to the different plantations. Moreover all the beeves and hogs for consumption or sale were driven up and slaughtered there at the proper seasons, and whatever was to be preserved was salted and packed away for after distribution.

Although these accounts shed light on the most essential difference between eighteenth- and nineteenth-century plantations—namely, the considerable degree of occupational specialization of the former—they do not tell us much about the slaves who were the basis for plantation self-sufficiency. Bernard Moore's advertisement for a lottery helps complete the portrait of the great slaveowner's plantation.

In 1768 Moore, a well-to-do planter and land speculator, faced economic ruin. To pay his debts he published a lottery scheme that laid bare the most essential economic and social arrangements in his extended "family." Moore's first prize, valued at £5,000, was a gristmill and forge on 1,800 acres, astride a "plentiful and constant stream." Billy (£280), a Negro man about 22, and "a very trusty good forge-man, as well at the finery as under the hammer, and understands putting up his fire," was listed with "his wife Lucy, a young wench, who works exceeding well both in the house and field." Sam (£250) about 26, and "a fine chaffery man," was also listed with his wife, Daphne, "a very good hand at the hoe, or in the house." Abraham, like most of the other men, was in his late 20's; he was an "exceeding good forge carpenter, cooper and clapboard carpenter." Bob (£150) was a master collier. Peter was 18 and a wagoner; Dick was a blacksmith, and Sampson, 32, a skipper of Moore's flat. Rachel was listed with her "very fine" children, Daniel and Thompson. Hannah, 16, and Ben, 25, a good house "servant" and carter "&c." were also listed together. Pat, "with child," lame on one side, and a "fine breeding woman," was to be sold with her 3 children. Another family Moore recognized included Casear, 30, a very good blacksmith, his wife Nanny, and their 2 children, Tab and Jane (all valued at £280). Other families included Moses, a "planter," his wife Phebe, "a very fine wench," "her" child Nell; and Robin, a sawyer, and his wife Bella and their two little girls. Sukey, about 12, and Betty, about 7, completed this list of American-born slaves. Last, native African slaves as usual were carefully indicated as "outlandish" and without skills or training. Tom (£50), "an outlandish fellow," and Lucy (£20) also "outlandish," completed Moore's "family."

"Outlandish" slaves like Tom and Lucy, strangers to the English language and seldom trained as artisans, were comparatively inexpensive. Thus they were usually purchased by smaller planters from the large slaveowners, who were slave traders as well as retailers and manufacturers. As middlemen in the trade, the great planters were indispensable to the ship captains and the companies they represented since they conducted all aspects of the sale in the colony. They evaluated the prospective buyer's credit, obtained a return cargo, provided for the maintenance of unsalable slaves (those too old, young, or ill), and sometimes they leased out Africans on a trial basis. Their commission for these services, usually 10 per cent, was evidently not sufficient; many gentlemen sold only a cargo or two before they quit the business.

"King" Carter, the wealthiest planter of his generation, has left one of the more complete descriptions of a sale which he conducted in the late 1720's. During the first half of the century, sales took place, not on the great planters' docks or at the tobacco inspection stations, but aboard the slaver. Thus, punctually at 1:00 p.m. each afternoon Carter got up from a hearty meal and several glasses of port, and rowed out from Corotoman to Captain Denton's slaver. He usually stayed until dusk; but one rainy evening kept him aboard overnight. During the three-week sale he was without customers on only two occasions. Carter usually sold between 4 and 6 Africans (most often in pairs, for between £25 to £40 per pair). The most critical part of this, or any slave sale, from Carter's vantage point was his expertise in the delicate job of appraising his neighbor's credit. Carter described his financial arrangements with Denton in this way:

I went abord Captain Denton, agreed to sell his negroes . . . I am to draw 10 per cent on the sale of commission to make good all debts in this manner, if any of exchange will not be paid, the protest to be mine. He is to run into Corotoman, there to lye for the sale, I am to be at no manner of charge, all to be charged to the owner.

This transaction was unusually smooth, for in the early part of the century, the trade was so unorganized that slave captains stopped at a number of great houses along the rivers before they made the best deal for themselves and the firms they represented. On one contract examined by Carter, the captain's list of prospective slave dealers included his own name at the top of the list but crossed out, and "Tom Nelson['s] interlined," then Carter's again, "Thomas Lee, Potomac," and one Mr. Bennet in Maryland. On another occasion Captain Haynes of the *Leopard* sailed into the York River in mid-September. He first stopped off Yorktown at Nelson's, but "finding no Orders for him there," he went north around the peninsula to Corotoman on the Rappahannock. Carter took one look at the captain's orders, and "upon Seeing [their] Strictness," said he would "not meddle with his Slaves." The season was late, the terms "preemptory," so Carter "let him go." The captain "immediately" went up the river to Carter's neighbor, John Tayloe of Mount Airy.

The slave trading season was short, from late spring to the end of the summer. Convinced that cold, chilling climate was often lethal for Africans, the buyers watched the weather carefully, come mid-September, "when the mornings & Evenings are cool," they stopped buying slaves for the season. When Governor Jenings explained to the Board of Trade why the separate traders were more successful than the Royal African Company, he wrote:

when Negroes come in about the begin[n]ing of the Summer, the planters are abundantly more fond of them, and will give greater price for them, because they are sure of the advantage of their labour in that years Crop, whereas Negroes bought at the Latter end of the year, are of little Service till the next Spring, and this is the true reason of that difference of price.

"Outlandish" Africans were not systematically broken-in or "seasoned." But rather they were put immediately to work in the last harvest of the year. One prominent Norfolk merchant and slave trader, Charles Steuart, corroborated Jenings's report, when in March 1752 he wrote: "slaves will continue in great demand for at least two months, the planters having left room in their Crops for them."

Most important, smaller slaveowners, according to one county study, provided the market for Africans. In Caroline, the county with the largest slave population, the wealthiest families (the Baylors, Corbins, and Beverleys) did not register a single African with the county court after 1732. (The age of young Africans had to be adjudged so they could be taxable at age 16.) The only wealthy families that purchased Africans were those who had numerous sons and many new homesteads. Thus, in addition to small planters, the chief registrants of young and taxable Africans were tavernkeepers, sailors, horse traders, small-time speculators, and such minor officeholders as constables and road supervisors.

In 1671 there were only about 2,000 slaves in the colony; but twenty-nine years later—when the economy had achieved the critical mass necessary to give it a market capable of absorbing a cargo from Africa—the number had tripled. At this time only about 40 per cent of the whites owned any slaves, and the great majority who did, owned one or two. The white population in 1700 was about 70,000, and from 1698 to 1708 the number of slaves doubled to about 12,000, and then increased another two-thirds by 1730. After the 1730's blacks consistently made up between 40 and 50 per cent of the colony's population. By 1763 there were equal numbers of slaves and whites in a population of approximately 340,000, or about 170,000 of each, according to Governor Francis Fauquier. In 1770 on the eve of the Revolution and the end of the slave trade, the blacks had increased another 18,000 to 188,000. In arriving at these figures, Governor Robert Dinwiddie said that he counted 3 Negro children per 2 blacks of taxable age.

Population growth, dramatized by the slaves' ability to greatly increase in number by natural means, was the demographic reality behind the establishment of the great families' economically diversified plantations in the 1720's. Since 1710, Hugh Jones noted, "our Country may be said to be altered & improved in wealth . . . more than in all the scores of years before, that from its first discovery." Jones's contemporary, William Byrd II, viewed this growth more pessimistically: the colony "will some time or other be confirm'd by [the] Name of New Guinea." Although the population figures are fragmentary, there were indications that the increase of the Africans' children was phenomenal. Elizabeth Donnan estimates that the slave trade brought about 55,000 slaves to Virginia between 1710 and 1769. Philip Curtin's estimate of a total importation to all British continental colonies to 1790, moreover, is approximately 250,000 to 300,000 Africans—a figure that could scarcely account for the size of the slave population in Virginia alone, which according to the Federal census in 1790 was 292,627. The Virginia slave population, unlike that of the British island colonies, experienced a rapid natural growth, a critical factor—so important to comparative studies of slavery in the Americas—which historians, Curtin reminds us, have neglected almost completely.

"MY BOND-MEN AND BOND-WOMEN"

"Outlandish" Africans were absolutely essential to the aristocratic planters who would be "independent on Every one but Providence." Ironically, the Christian culture that supported that Faustian wish also sanctioned the view of newly arrived Africans as godless savages. This attitude and the whites' appraisal of a slave's comprehension of English and the colonial culture were the most important realities for slaves of all kinds. A slave's birthplace and the pace and level of his socialization were the basis for the most important decisions forced upon him: his sale, task assignment, and distribution in estates. At these times there were only two kinds of blacks: those who were "outlandish"—born in Africa—and those born in America.

Colonists and travelers alike clearly understood the critical importance of an African's background and his later adjustment to slavery. Hugh Jones, an early eighteenth-century historian, for example, made the usual references to the blacks' ugly bodies, slavish natures, and "delight" for his country's "violent Heat," before stating that among "New Negroes," the best slaves were those who had been servants in their own country. But "they that have been Kings and great Men are generally lazy, haughty, and obstinate." Visitors to the colony, who at first saw few differences among slaves, soon realized that the African's origin as well as his color was the basis for the colonists' hostile evaluation of his alien culture. "The more we observe the Negroes, the more must we be persuaded that the difference distinguishing them from us does not consist in color alone," the Marquis de Chastellux observed, and he soon came to understand his hosts' standards. When comparing Virginia and Jamaica slaves he reported: "most of the Negroes are born in this country [Virginia], and it is a known fact that they are generally less depraved than those imported directly from Africa."

Virginians made similar distinctions between Africans and native American slaves when it came time to allot tasks—to decide which slaves remained in the fields and which ones came into the flourishing workshops on the home plantation to acquire the literate and technical skills that were the basis for the great plantation's self-sufficiency. This issue was viewed in a religious context, and since Christianity was at the heart of colonial culture, the African's apparent paganism was his greatest liability. Hugh Jones, for example, observed that most slaveowners believed that while baptism made slaves proud and unmanageable, this applied only to "Infidels," that is, to "wild Indians and New Negroes," who possessed neither the knowledge nor the inclination to "know and mind" our "Religion, Language, & Customs." Education and training (which he equated with conversion and baptism), on the other hand, were acceptable for American-born slaves, who were by nature "sensible, good and underst[oo]d English." Drawing attention to the fact that the source of the essential differences among slaves was traceable to their origin, Jones wrote that "Africans would obstinately persist in their own barbarous Ways." Thus he wondered "whether Baptism of such (till they be a little weaned of their savage Barbarity) be not Prostitution of a Thing so sacred." But, he concluded, the Africans' children, "those who are to live among Christians, undoubtedly they ought to be baptized."

The Bishop of London concurred: it was the Church's duty to uplift and civilize the benighted Africans. In 1727, the same year that Jones published his history, the Bishop sent an inquiry to his ministers in Virginia. Their replies underscore the extent to which colonial churches reflected the ethos of the aristocratic slaveowning families they served. "Are there any Infidels, bond or free, within your Parish; and what means are used for their conversion?" "My Lord," began a typical reply, "our Negroe Slaves imported daily, are altogether ignorant of God & Religion, and in truth have so little Docility in them that they scarce ever become capable of Instructtion; but my Lord, I have examined and improved several Negroes, Natives of Virginia." Almost invariably white ministers pointed to the relevance of the Africans' distinctive language patterns for religious instruction.

The owners are generally careful to instruct those that are capable of instruction and to bring them to Baptism, but it is impossible to instruct those that are grown up before they are carried out of their own Country, they never being able either to speak or understand our Language perfectly.

A few ministers did report that they had made significant gains in the number of slaves converted and educated. One man taught catechism classes for black youngsters every Saturday afternoon in the chapter house; another, an Eastern Shore minister, said he had baptized about 200 slaves, whom from time to time he instructed on their own plantations. But those educated were nearly always the Virginia-born, so the planters' and ministers' efforts to ameliorate their slaves' condition—to use their term—further widened the cultural gap between African and native American slaves.

By 1750 these attitudes were sharply focused by important demographic and economic developments: the leveling off of the importations of Africans, the remarkable natural increase of American-born slaves (nearly always referred to as "country-born"), and the wealthy planters' determination to offset the effects of both the severe depression of the tobacco market and their notorious debts to British merchants, by training slave-artisans and further diversifying their plantations. This required them to base their lives as well as their livelihoods on the rhythms of the plantation's intricate workings. Thus, in the final analysis, the great planter had to be the accomplished head of an extended plantation "family."

"LIKE ONE OF THE PATRIARCHS"

The large slaveowner served his plantation in essentially two ways: as an estate manager and as a patriarch. The first role was a function of his direction of the plantation's complex and demanding economic processes; it required a shrewd, calculating, and systematic regard for expenses, the delegation of authority, and the direction of slaves. The second role, defined by the master's relations to the members of a plantation "family"—composed of his kin as well as the overseer, servants white and black, field slaves, and artisans—required that the good patriarch maintain two positions, one in the neighborhood, by sumptuous living and feats of hospitality, and the other among his slaves on the plantation, by a benevolent, indulgent, and understanding view of their performance. Planters were usually more accomplished as patriarchs than estate managers, though this certainly was often not in their best interest. But their failure to achieve economic, political, and cultural self-determination in the Empire sharpened the view that the father was the source of authority on the plantation, and that this authority was indivisible. At this point particularly, the planter's two roles conflicted: it was absolutely essential to good estate management that the planter divide his authority in a rational way, so that those directly responsible for the slaves' work could supervise effectively.

To see the great slaveowner as a patriarch and estate manager is to begin to understand what it meant for him to be a product of a slave society, in which "nothing, nothing and no one escaped"; to understand, too, the nature of the "command experience"—that familiar notion historians have used to discuss the exceptional background of the famous Virginians who served the national government with such distinction during the Revolutionary and early National periods.

"A Continual Exercise of Our Patience & Economy"

Planters revealed themselves and the most intimate details of their plantation duties in accounts of their daily rounds. Poking into stores and shops, watching their slaves plant, hoe, and irrigate, persistently counting rows of corn, tobacco, and heads of cattle, they relentlessly pursued wealth and competence. "Made a Visit to my Plantations this day," Landon Carter, "King" Carter's son, noted, "that is, looked into every hole and corner of them." "I walk much about the family business," wrote a Huguenot minister and planter "and ride constantly every morning all over my plantation, giving my servants their several employments." Landon Carter's account of the estate manager's "continual exercise" preserves the mood of this way of life:

Rode out this day. Corn except where the land is very stiff is coming up, and with a broad blade.

Mill dam in tolerable good order but a little wanting to make things there very strong, and troughs to let the ponds from the runs into the canals run off into the meadow which is to be.

Making tobacco hills. Potatoes come up, want weeding.

Fork Corn not quite done in the Peach orchard. Therefore Cotton can't be planted there before next Monday, the old May day.

Wheat looks tolerable, only a trespass from the Cowpen last monday night.

No item of production, no man, beast, or building was beyond the assiduous planter's purview, as this excerpt from "Councillor" Carter's papers will illustrate:

To Richard Dozier, orders for the following summer crops: 64 acres Indian Corn; 2 acres peas, 2 acres Irish potatoes, 2 acres Turnips, 2 acres pumpkins, 1 in flax, 3 in cotton, 32 in tobacco.

"Councillor" Carter's concreteness became obsession with detail for estate managers like George Washington and Landon Carter.

Notwithstanding all Lawson's boast [one of Carter's overseers] I shall not do more than fill the Mangorike 60 foot double Shedded house with corn in the Shucks up to the Joice.

Item counts of seedlings, stores, and crops took up much of each in-spection tour because so many planters believed that their slaves and overseers took advantage of them at every opportunity. Landon Car-ter's way was to begin where even the most scrupulous planters left off. His counts involved each plant, literally tens of thousands of them:

I find it wondered at how any hand can tend 28,000 corn hills planted at any distance. But surely it cannot be reasonable to do so, when it is con-sidered that at 2 feet and 7 an acre holds 3,111 corn hills and at 6 and 5 it holds only 1,452; for it is in such a case evident, that at 7 and 2 the acre contains more than double to what it does when planted at 6 and 5 by 202 hills. Allow then that at 6 and 5 ten thousand hills only are tended; it will amount to near 7 acres that are worked each hand. Now at 7 and 2, 7 acres will contain 21,777 so that there only wants 6,223 to make up 28,000. Now that is Exactly 4 hill[s] short of 2 acres, So that the hand that tends 28,000 is only to tend 9 acres. And cannot a hand tend 9 acres of ground?

The continuous assessment of the plantation's components, of course, also included the slaves. Even their peculiarities of appear-ance and grooming habits were scrutinized and became part of the planter's lore. One slaveowner advertised for a runaway whose lips were not thick, "but seem[ed] a little longer than common." Another described an African who had run off four years earlier: he had red-dish eyes and a "remarkable loose jostling Way of walking." Sancho's master knew that his slave ran away in new shoes, "one tied with a leather thong, the other with an old black ribbon"; and another owner said that his slave's shoe heels "were pegged and nailed with 3d nails and 2d nails drove through the edges at the soles and clinched."

During their long hours among crops, slaves, and shops, planters sought to make intelligible the larger world beyond the plantation. Richard Henry Lee, the Revolutionary War general and leader of the Virginia anti-Federalists, carried a memorandum book on his rides. It is small, hand-sized, and its leather cover is gently rounded, smoothed, and polished by the action of Lee's rear pocket, saddle, and the swaying of his horse. It is a distillation of his reminders, accounts, and reading notes over a few years, which included comments on the whereabouts of two slaves (his jobber Congo and a "yellow negro girl" named Grace); the disposition of iron bars sent from Stratford to various quarters; how much pork he cut from a hog sent in pay-ment for the hire of Abraham; and plants in his window garden. Lee, like so many Virginians then and now, lavished attention on his kitchen garden: it was the plantation in microcosm, but with boundaries sufficiently restricted that control, always a problem elsewhere, was readily achieved. "Sowed [s]quare next [to the] dining room with peas, the 6 rows next [to] the dining room window are Lawsons Hotspur & the 6 rows furthest off are the Greenspring May pea." A few lines further he recorded having "counted the Sheep carefully & there were 32 head including the sic[k] one in the Cow house & the two in the fattening sheep pen. . . . Not one young Lamb yet." The planter's reading notes were scattered throughout in this manner: "Dissertations historical and political on the Ancient Republics of Italy" by Carol Denina, led to musings on standing armies in republics. Notes on the Reverend William Stith's *History of Virginia* (1747), included a reference to "Sir George Somers [who] paid [laid?] his ship's bottom seams with Lime and Turtle oil which made a fine cement for stopping the Seams of the Vesels." These observations were followed by a recipe for potato pone.

Even while he was President, George Washington was also never too far from his plantation operations. In 1793, for example—a critical year for him—the cold war with the French and English navies and the bank bill were demanding realities. But in the midst of these crises, he pored over his steward's weekly reports from Mount Vernon and sent off revealing directives. His devotion to order carried his attention to a particular group of workers: the sewers "who made only Six Shirts a Week." Then his concern was narrowed to one worker: "and the last week Caroline (without being sick) made only five"; and finally penetrated to the very items of production, and the intricacies of how they were made:

Mrs. Washington says their usual task was to make nine with Shoulder straps & good sewing:—tell them therefore from me, that what *has* been done *shall* be done by fair or foul means; & they had better make a choice of the first, for their own reputation, & for the sake of peace and quietness.

Then Washington, who after 1775 aptly called his diary "where, & how my time is Spent," concluded: "Their work ought to be well examined. The same attention ought to be given to Peter (& I supposed to Sarah likewise) or the Stockings will be knit too small."

"*I have a large Family of my own*"

Washington's familiarity with his slaves and their routines stemmed from his patriarchal role as head of a large and varied plantation "family." The correspondence of several types of colonist indicates that the plantation slaves' status as family members was assumed. John Harrower, an indentured servant and tutor, wrote home to Scotland: "our Family consists of the Col[onel], his Lady & four Children, a housekeeper, an overseer and myself, all white. But how many blacks young and old, the Lord only knows." Robert Beverley, the historian, gently chided his father-in-law, Landon Carter, for his notoriety as a stern parent, while observing that Carter had not been "sufficiently indulgent" about allowing his 22-year-old daughter to visit a woman companion. He concluded: "My familey [sic] are all well now some few Negroes excepted."

Accounts of the great planters as their peoples' doctors and judges clarify the patriarchal role and the familial, domestic character of eighteenth-century plantation slavery. In the first few days of the new year 1711, Byrd, for example, spent long hours during a fierce epidemic administering to his slaves:

I spent most of my time in looking after my sick. . . . My sick people were some worse and some well enough to go home to the quarters. . . . In the afternoon I did nothing but mind them. . . . At night I look over all my people. . . . I tended them diligently and went to the quarters to see the negroes there and gave the necessary orders about them. . . . I visited my people again.

The patriarchal role sometimes had an insidious influence on the master's behavior. Landon Carter's paternalistic care of his slave children changed his normally embittered outlook. Carter knew himself well enough to seek out situations that brought out his generous, humane qualities. He was especially gentle to those whom he perceived as weaker than himself, including "my negro children," whom he sometimes doctored. "How wonderfully has [God] blessed me both with skill and inclination to assist my poor fellow creatures." Or, "killed a fine mutton this day; ordered some broth for the sick, Nassau tells me they are all mending. I hope in God they are . . . they are human creatures and my soul I hope delighteth in relieving them." This from a man who said slaves were devils and should never be free. In momentarily drawing upon his own humanity, the old man discovered that of his slaves.

But planters were more in character as their slaves' judges. Meting out punishment, they readily lost sight of the slave's individuality. At these times one important facet of the patriarchal role, his kindness and indulgence, gave way to another, his stern righteousness.

"I must take care to keep all my people to their Duty."

The tone and phrases masters used while punishing slaves indicate that they viewed slave rebelliousness in the context of the Fifth Commandment—Honour thy father and thy mother—assuming that both slaves and free had certain rights, duties, and responsibilities toward one another. "I must again desire you will keep Tommy strictly to his Duty & obedience." Or, "cruelty to the poor slaves is a thing I always Abhored. I would think myself happy could I keep them to there [sic] duty without being Obliged to correct them." "Began this morning," Landon Carter noted, "to enforce my resolution of correcting the drunkenes[s] in my family by an example on Nassau." Washington's order preserved the same tone: "As for Waggoner Jack, a misbehaving fellow, try further correction, accompanied by admonition and advice." When two runaways sent word to their master, John Tayloe, that they would not return unless he either hired them out or sold them, his response was typical of the elite of the era he represented: "I will do neither until they return to a sense of duty."

Patriarchs also preferred to call slaves (house and field) on the home plantation "servants," and to view physical beatings as "correction" and "discipline." At the same time a few sensational and well-publicized whippings should not obscure our view of the masters' sharply equivocal feelings about beating their "people." In the era of the Revolution, which produced a mild effort to ameliorate slavery by prohibiting the trade, encouraging manumission, and discouraging sales that separated children from their mothers, some whites became openly defensive and apologetic about physically "correcting" slaves. Those who advertised runaways who had been whipped, occasionally felt compelled to explain away their slaves' wounds and scars. "His thefts were certainly the Cause of his Flight." Sam ran away "to avoid the Gallows; for he was never punished whilst with me," his master reported, "nor ever complained, neither had he any Cause to be dissatisfied at his Treatment." The manager of an ironworks said that his mulatto runaway had scars on his back, "which he got several Years before I had him"; and another advertiser simply noted: he has been "pretty much subject to the Lash by his former Master."

As a substitute for physical beatings, planters used job placement to reward some and punish others because it simply was not feasible to attempt to contain the plantation slaves' clever "trifling about" in any other way. "Councillor" Carter's order for task assignments illustrates the extent of the master's control of this important method of expressing authority on the plantation.

Negro Ralph Sawyer has committed so many offences lately that I propose to remove him from that Employment—Ralph to work as a Labourer in the crop at Colespoint.

Frank lately of Taurus & now at Colespoint he to be delivered up to Oliver [an overseer] & to be a sawyer this Exchange to be made immediately.

"To Set all the Springs in Motion"

Assigning tasks—deciding who remained on the distant quarters and who came into the plantation or household, and which young slaves were to be apprenticed—was one of the most important prerogatives of ownership, as well as a very effective way of controlling slaves. Masters seldom shared this responsibility, because "set[ting] all the Springs in Motion" allowed them to demonstrate their paternalistic concern for their "people's" welfare and best interests.

For some slaveowners, job assignment was also a way of establishing order in a more personal sense. "I would not live with too disorderly souls about me for no consideration in this life," wrote Battaile Muse, George Washington's rental agent and a distinguished Northern Neck steward. "If I cannot Keep order with Slaves I cannot do it with free men and where their is no regulations their must be much confusion—which will always be the Case unless Proper decorum is kept up." This conception of "order"—of inculcating in slaves "a sense of duty and responsibility" in order to make a confusing world more manageable—was apparently realized at Thompson Mason's plantation below Fredericksburg. The Colonel's New England tutor wrote that there were about 50 slaves on Mason's home quarter, among whom were "his weaver, his blacksmith, his carpenter, his shoemaker, as is the general practice with very independent planters." He concluded: "each one knows his place and business and every thing is conducted with the greatest order."

The patriarch's knowledge of virtually every slave was, in the final analysis, a function of the colony's terrain, economic setting, land inheritance patterns, and a brief historical phenomenon. Usually at least once in their career wealthy slaveowners were forced to relocate much of their property. The use of reserve lands and partible inheritances to establish cadet lines, soil exhaustion, and population pressures in the tidewater prompted them to develop up-country quarters as new home plantations. Moving up-river and west was a perilous venture that required shrewd and rational planning, if the planter was to avoid a crippling setback from losses of slaves and livestock.

Thus it was imperative that he attempt to extend family status even to slaves on the farthest perimeters of his holdings, that he know each slave as an individual, and that slave's idiosyncrasies and special skills.

Although for all these reasons patriarchs exercised almost exclusive control over task assignment, their stewards and overseers were charged with implementing as best they could the establishment of new quarters. The directives they received indicated that the patriarch often placed his people's well-being above economic considerations. James Mercer wrote Muse in 1777:

I send 2 Negroe Wenches Amy & Sall, Daughters of Scipio. They are fine winches but I suspect [they are] too sick to thrive here. Amy has had a three months Spell & Sall has been sick two months. . . . [Sall] shou'd live on milk, butter milk is best, & use exercise every day on horse back . . . in particular she must not work 'till she is quite well.

And Hugh Nelson, scion of the wealthy Yorktown merchant family, also wrote to Muse in 1789:

The old Woman may serve to take Care of all the Children, and Grace may be employed any Way you please. Give Nanny 4 Pieces of Bacon . . . The little Girl, Dinah, you may keep in Fauquier as a Spinner. Nanny who has one of her Eyes very much hurt, which makes it necessary to keep her here till it is well. . . . I shall be up in May.

When in 1779 John H. Norton, a member of another merchant family, established new quarters in the Valley, he carefully listed his resources, which included the abilities that enhanced the individuality of particular slaves.

I have an old fellow called Charles & his Son Anthony who have been employed always at the Carpenters business & will be very useful, his Wife Betty, a favor'd house Servant assists in our Cooking.
Mulatto Milly is the principal Spinner, she has several Children, one of which can spin & work at the Needle.

He then indicated which men he wanted in the fields (which he called "working out"), and designated Jemmy "a plowboy." Also "there is a fellow named Jack who has had a bad Complaint in his Eyes but maybe useful in looking after Stock, or plowing occasionally."

Families figured prominently in these moves, because patriarchs like James Mercer were often intent on keeping them intact:

As Lot's Boy Harry (I believe that is his name) is now deprived of all his Friends & Connections & is of a size & sort to be usefull in a factory he must come down with them & so must Bet's Husband rather than part them unless they mutually agree to part.

In many ways planters actively intervened in the slaves' fragmented family lives. Sometimes the desire to keep remnants of families together was a practical one: "as Dick is likely be troublesome I have wrote down to Mrs Burwell for his Wife even at the enormous price of £6. . . . Indeed the maintenance of her [the slave's wife] & Children is considerable more than the Hire of a Negro Fellow." At other times, masters seemed to be genuinely concerned about slave marriages, although one can never discount the strong probability that they wanted to encourage couples to produce as many children as possible. "May I beg the favour of you," one wrote his overseer, "to send Beck & her Child & purchase a likely young Virga. born Fellow between the Age of 18 & 22 or 23 Years."

"Councillor" Carter who owned about 10 plantations in several counties, and more than 400 slaves (whose "correction" he personally directed), wrote a remarkable order which read in part:

Sir, Child Negroe Molley—about two years old, [the] Daughter of Sukey of Cancer [Quarter] wants a Nurse. I understand that Negroe Payne, 71 years old of the Forest Plantation, is the father of said child—if it be agreeable to you . . . I now direct that Payne be ordered to go to Cancer Plantation & live at Sukey's house he to have the Care of both his grand Children.

This same planter once exchanged men between two quarters because he said "the Distance from Coles Point to Dicks Quarter is rather far for a Walker"; so he asked that Dennis be moved nearer to his wife, and that a slave be found to replace him.

Patriarchs also directly intervened in their slaves' domestic affairs. Byrd wrote that he "threatened Anaka with a whipping if she did not confess the intrigue between Daniel and Nurse." And when James Gordon, a Northern Neck planter, was "alarmed" by news that Cumberland was "abusing" his wife, he had him whipped the following morning. "Councillor" Carter, who was so well informed about his slaves' liaisons and marriages, reported to an overseer: "Sir, Dennis of Colespoint Quarter has Negro Frankey for a Wife, she living at Mr. Fleet Cox's Quarter. . . . I hope that Dennis & Frankey Are Constant to each other."

Wise, concerned but detached, and very understanding, the master on some occasions could have it both ways: as owner and estate manager, on the one hand, and as father for all members of the plantation "family," on the other. Robert Wormeley Carter, 41 years of age, dutifully reported to his father in Williamsburg about his arbitration between an outraged overseer and a slave woman. Jackson, the Sabine Hall overseer, recaptured a runaway on the road to Williamsburg and "turned up her cloathes and whiped her Breach." But, the son assured the old man, he "check[e]d" Jackson "for this mode of correction," and "made the matter up between them."

More often though, masters were caught in the inherent contradiction of their two roles. James Mercer in his role as patriarch wrote to his steward in 1778: "I shall direct George to be well hunted after, we must break the habit of runing away by severe example." But a year later Mercer, the estate manager and entrepreneur, no longer the kind patriarch, advised: "as to Negroes, Indulgence Spoils them, either make them do their Duty or let them run away, when we save their Corn & Cloathes & if idle at home they wont earn it." The master's ambivalence about his roles, slaves, and slavery also directly contributed to the abusive, exploitative relations between plantation slaves and their supervisors. Norton by his own admission worsened the arrangements on one of his plantations. He mentioned to his steward: "I have told Payne [an overseer] & the People that I must have large Crops made & ordered that the people in any instance to do their Duty otherwise they should suffere for discharging him."

Patriarchs, characteristically refusing to divide their authority, insisting on making the most trivial decisions, and demanding bumper crops while berating overseers for driving slaves, undermined their representatives' confidence in their own judgment. Thus absenteeism inevitably provoked widespread non-cooperation among the slaves. When the owner left the plantation in the hands of the demoralized overseer the situation rapidly deteriorated. "My spinners," wrote Landon Carter, "imagining I was gone yesterday instead of their usual day's work spun but 2 ounces a piece." While visiting another quarter he noted: "I must declare I saw no care on my whole plantation, but everybody did as they pleased, Came, Went, Slept or Worked as they would."

The master's insensitivity to the overseer's position was even more remarkable in light of his own recognition that his slaves were tough, clever, and troublesome and that his representatives on the quarters must therefore be strong, talented men. Mercer directed his steward to hire an overseer who "must be what is called tight in order to learn my lazy Negroes how to work." Washington sized up one prospective overseer as "a tolerably good looking man and [he] has the appearance of an active one—but how far any man, unacquainted with Negroes is capable of managing them, is questionable." The President realized that slaves were quick to exploit weaknesses in an overseer's character. An old man who handled the "house People" and ditchers was honest, sober, well-meaning, and "something knowing," in Washington's estimation. Unfortunately, he was also "not accustomed to Negroes," who since they were in "no sort of awe of him— of course do as they please." Because they were not given the means to do their job, overseers were a convenient target for the persistently non-cooperative plantation and quarter slaves. Landon Carter understood the process of attrition that steadily wore them down. Overseers, he said, "tire as cornfields do."

Overseers and their employers argued repeatedly about the question of payment in crop shares or salary; about problems of supplies for both slaves and overseer; about pasturage for the overseer's horse, milk cows, reports of untended fences and stray cattle and serving "wenches" for his wife and family. But the basic and most divisive issue was based upon the related problems of delegating authority in the master's absence and the use of slave informers.

Overseers who tried to imitate their employers' paternalism by using persuasion and incentives were moderately successful. They used what little authority they had at their disposal to manipulate and cajole slaves, occasionally overlooking a young pig cut out of season, discreetly keeping unlocked a corn or cider store, or simply allowing slaves to visit adjoining quarters or plantations during the evening and on Sundays. But when these privileges were cut off, the field workers balked. A familiar note of exasperation is heard in a report to John Hatley Norton from his York County overseer. The planter's quarter was about to be abandoned and the laborers, evidently satisfied with the arrangements thereon, were in no mood to cooperate. Faced with this situation, the overseer reported that he had "to hurrey to get [his] Corn of hand as fast as posable tho the negroes Seem verey Dul and Sloath full Sense they have heared that the Plantation wase to be Broke up." He could, he noted apologetically, accomplish very little to date, and then "onley when [he was] Driveing and Storming at them and verey often [he was] a bliged to whipe." Charles Dabney, an estate steward, accounted for the problems on a Louisa County plantation in this way: his previous overseer "was so good natured to the Negroes under him [that] he suffered them to impose on him very much." Dabney complained that under the present overseer "the Negroes are very unwilling to give up the privileges they were allowed."

Overseers were seldom "good natured." Unlike masters, they were sometimes sadistic. "There are very few of the common Overseers that have the least feeling of humanity for Slaves," Hugh Washington, the President's relative, reported, "they treat them in general (when left to themselves) as if they were not of the same species." George Washington concurred: "I expect little of this from McKoy [an overseer]—or indeed from most of his class; for they seem to consider a Negro much in the same light as they do the brute beasts on the farms; and often times treat them as inhumanely." In another letter to his steward, Hugh Washington wrote:

I once wrote to You on the Subject of the Negroes ill treatment by the common Overseers; who in general have not the least humanity in regard to the Slaves under them, & I know that they require much looking after to prevent their using them ill.

I know from experience, that Negroes are in general an ungrateful set of beings that there is no such thing as satisfying them in regard to their Overseers; but indeed Sir the common run of Overseers if left to themselves, woud be cruel to them.

When Joseph Ball was notified of the loss of several of his slaves' children he replied: "You [his steward and nephew] let unmerciful overseers beat and abuse them Inhumanely and Break their hearts."

The planter's source of information of this type was often a "trusted servant." This practice, which further weakened the overseer's position, was defended in a letter from James Mercer to his steward:

I have allmost constantly found Nigroes tell Truth enough of distant overseers & I am now told that Moore has sold every grain of his own Corn yet Suds his own horse three times a day out of mine, that he has now seven Hoggs raised in my Estate that the Nigroes can't get a drop of Milk tho' there is a plenty even to spare Old Buidine & his [Moore's] Pigs every day. . . . I remember all the Bacon I laid in for Mill Wrights, Carpenters &c was also expended. . . .

Jefferson also used informers: "Stanley [his overseer] has killed by his own confession 12 hogs, but as Jupiter sais [sic] 16. . . . The negroes say he has sold a great deal of corn."

Muse, an exceptionally fine steward, was adamantly against this delicate question of the patriarch's right to know personally each slave as an expression of his authority. The relationship between a master and his field slaves should be only proprietary. Planters who made themselves the counsellors and advisors of slaves contributed to their dissatisfaction. His letter to Thomas Fairfax (whose family had once owned the entire Northern Neck as a vast proprietary grant) warned of the consequences of moderation and reasonableness with quarter "hands":

I wish the two observations you make respecting the meadow & hogs was the only injury the Estate was to sustain from the last six months carrying on the business. I think the loss of 100 Acres land usually fallowed; Grain badly put in; Stock neglected; meadow rooten up with hogs; Creature[s] [be]ing in the orchard; Fences burnt; corn not gather'd at Christma[s] will prove in a few years no small loss to the owner of the Estate. This Conduct has arose greatly from the authority taken from the overseer by hearing every tale that deceitful negroes will advance.

"Your last letter," Fairfax replied angrily, "seems to Contain a tacit charge against me, I must not let it pass unnoticed. . . . You Say (in fact) that I have been in part the Cause of it, by giving ear to the tales of negroes which has lessened the overseers authority. No man," he continued, "who possessed the principles of Justice and humanity would ever deny those who are dependent on him (whether Slave or freemen) the privilege of making known their grievances to him." This enlightened patriarch sensed that his view was unique: "as to humanity toward Slaves, it appears to be an indefinite term in this Country and there are very few masters perhaps whose sentiments and mine would agree upon this point. What I might Call a want of humanity, others might call a necessary Coercion."

Fairfax's argument, as idealistic as his conception of slavery, is the more remarkable because it is addressed to a man who dealt directly with plantation slaves. It is also an eloquent argument and a fine example of the idealism of some patriarchs who, imbued with the natural rights philosophy of the Revolution, were determined to apply it to their relationships with slaves.

But the whites and blacks on the quarters saw the issue differently. One steward reported: "It gives me great concern to think a report of this Negro who is prejudiced to the highest degree that you should conclude the Negroes in Louisa have not been treated with the humanity that the *Brutes* are Intitled." Those who considered slaves as "brutes," as objects, were most likely to be the men who worked with them as their supervisors. Freemen who worked with those in bondage were convinced of the slaves' discontented, rebellious nature.

The eighteenth-century Virginia planter was caught between his desire for self-sufficiency and his ultimate dependence on Great Britain. He was also forced to confront and forced to socialize a strange

and threatening people, the Africans whom he imported and enslaved to support his way of life. The presence of these "outlandish"
men, themselves soon caught between their old ways and the new
colonial culture, created for owners another paradox. As an estate
manager, the planter had to be a shrewd and calculating business-
man who was able to rationally divide his authority among his supervisors on the plantations and quarters. But since the master's concept
of authority was paternalistic, he felt that to be a good patriarch—
wise, tolerant, and benevolent—he must retain complete control over
all members of his extended plantation family. This situation left the
overseer with little real power, the planter trapped between the contradictions inherent in his roles as estate manager and patriarch, and
the plantation an especially vulnerable target for the field slaves'
persistent rebelliousness and acts of sabotage.

III
THE STRUCTURE
OF PLANTER SOCIETY
COHESION and CONFLICT

The structure of white society changed dramatically over the colonial period. In each of the major plantation colonies a small group of interrelated families achieved a position of political and social dominance. The rise to power of these families began late in the seventeenth century, and by the mid-eighteenth century the process was virtually complete. All four essays in this section are concerned with this important social development. The authors examine not only the origins and character of the plantation gentry but also the relation of that gentry to the rest of white colonial society.

William Stith (1705–55), an eighteenth-century Anglican clergyman, provides us with an excellent description of the gentry's cultural dominance over what he called the "Generality of the People." Stith is remembered today primarily as a president of the College of William and Mary and as one of Virginia's first historians, but in 1752 he delivered a remarkable sermon before the colony's General Assembly entitled *The Sinfulness . . . of Gaming*. Stith claimed that "high Gaming" had grown precipitously within recent years, and asserted that "it has seized, without Exception, upon all Ranks and Conditions of our People; and hath equally infected the *high and low, rich and poor, one with another*."

After cataloguing the many evils associated with gambling, Stith made a surprisingly frank admission. No single minister, not even one selected to preach before the General Assembly, could begin to remove this or any other vice without the full support of "Persons of Fortune and Distinction." It was they who provided the cultural norms for other Virginians. "For I have long observed by a melancholy Experience," Stith concluded, "that the best written Discourse, nay even the plainest and most important Instances of Duty, will lose all their Weight and Influence with the Generality of the People, if they are contradicted by the Lives and Conversations, or even by the unmannerly Scoffs and irreverent Gibes of their rich and powerful Neighbours."

Virginians of "Fortune and Distinction" may not have appreciated Reverend Stith's forthright discussion of their activities at the race track and gaming tables, but most of them undoubtedly agreed that a handful of wealthy planters exercised a cultural influence disproportionate to their numbers in society. Indeed, so great was their power over all aspects of colonial life that historians sometimes refer to them as an aristocracy. But this term is misleading, for the members of the plantation elites that had fully developed in the Chesapeake area by 1720 and in South Carolina by 1740 did not owe their social status to noble titles acquired at birth. The foundation of their dominance lay in the aggressive, single-minded acquisition of land and slaves, a process that for many gentry families began unspec-

tacularly with the arrival of a middle-class English immigrant sometime during the seventeenth century.

In his essay, "Politics and Social Structure in Virginia," Bernard
Bailyn analyzes the formation of this cohesive, self-confident ruling
elite. Bailyn first inquires how eighteenth-century Virginians created
an atmosphere of unusual political harmony after experiencing nearly
a hundred years of civil unrest. By way of answering this question,
Bailyn proposes that political stability in seventeenth-century America required a high correlation between political and social leadership.
In other words, the more influence socially prominent persons exercised over civil affairs, the more likely it was that the state would
operate peacefully.

During Virginia's early history, no group of leaders established both
social and political pre-eminence. Some gentlemen died, others returned to England, and a few roughnecks tried unsuccessfully to
obtain social and political dominance through physical force. According to Bailyn, a crucial change in the character of Virginia society occurred at about the middle of the seventeenth century. A new
type of colonist began to arrive in Virginia. These newer arrivals possessed sufficient capital and commercial contacts to secure positions of
social prominence within a relatively short time. Since, however, the
royal governor and his favorites monopolized the most desirable offices within the colonial government, the newcomers found their
road to political leadership effectively blocked—a situation they regarded as intolerable. Their frustrations exploded in a full-scale civil
war, called Bacon's Rebellion, which gave the rising gentry political
authority commensurate with its social status.

Bailyn explains also how the more complex social conditions con-
sequent upon Bacon's Rebellion allowed a small group of powerful
Virginia families to gain lasting social and political dominance, thus
removing the systemic tensions that had earlier produced unrest.
What were these factors? What role did English administrators play
in producing such congruence between political and social status in
Virginia? How would you contrast Bailyn's explanation of Bacon's
Rebellion to that presented in my article? How do you think the
changing racial composition of Virginia's population influenced the
rise of a new social and political elite?

Throughout the colonial South the locus of the gentry's political
power was in the lower house of the legislature. This elective
bodies stubbornly resisted attempts by appointed crown officials to
encroach upon what the leading planters came to regard as their
political and economic rights. Some historians have seen the develop-

ment of the colonial assemblies as connected in some way with the growth of democracy in America, but as Jack P. Greene explains in his essay, "The Foundations of Political Power in the Virginia House of Burgesses, 1720–1776," the gentlemen who became burgesses hardly represented a cross section of eighteenth-century Virginia society. Greene discovers that the 110 most powerful lawmakers were a remarkably homogeneous group. Certainly one reason Virginia enjoyed such political harmony during most of the eighteenth century was the absence of deep-seated social divisions of the kind that often spawn political faction. Greene points out also that, even though entry into this ruling elite became progressively more difficult, new names did appear on the influential legislative committees after 1700. The political system developing in colonial Virginia did not automatically promote newcomers of wealth and ability; but, by the same token, it did not necessarily reward members of the established gentry families with high political office. How would you describe one of the top 110 political leaders? Why do you suppose the voters of Virginia regularly elected men of this type to the House of Burgesses when they might have promoted one of their humbler neighbors? In what way does Greene expand upon Bailyn's analysis of the development of the Virginia gentry?

When concentrating upon the gentry's political dominance, we may inadvertently overlook the insecurity, even fear, that was a constant aspect of colonial plantation life. The growing number of black slaves in all the Southern colonies posed an ongoing threat to internal security; and even though the blacks mounted few rebellions of consequence, the great planters were worried about maintaining control over their dependent workers. In 1736 an alarmed William Byrd II declared that the slave traders "import so many negroes hither that I fear this colony will sometime or other be confounded by the name of New Guinea." The problems of producing and marketing a staple crop such as tobacco created additional anxieties for planters like Byrd. Many of the elements determining the planter's economic well-being, such as the weather, the health of his labor force, the world consumption of his crop, were clearly beyond his control. Even William Fitzhugh, a Virginian who amassed an estate of over fifty thousand acres and who was one of the most influential men of his generation, bemoaned the uncertainties that plagued his life. In 1690 he warned an English correspondent to think twice before allowing his son to become a colonial planter, for "if either neglect carelessness or unskilfullness should happen its all brought to nought, & if the best husbandry & the greatest forecast & skill were used, yet ill luck at Sea, a fall of a Market, or twenty other accidents may ruin & overthrow the best Industry."

The great planters never escaped the insecurities associated with slavery, but they did gradually develop ways to overcome the uncertainties of a single-crop economy. In an important essay based on the rich probate records of colonial Maryland, Aubrey C. Land describes how, over the eighteenth century, the wealthiest Chesapeake planters systematically expanded their entrepreneurial interests. They freed themselves from the hazards of tobacco production and, whenever possible, turned their capital and talents to enterprises such as manufacturing, merchandising, money-lending, legal services, and land speculation. The advantages enjoyed by these men over the undiversified planter became more apparent as time passed, and one prominent Virginia gentleman could write of his son in 1751, "I should be glad he would be fond of some business for planting alone is poor doings, but with other businesses it will answer very well." How much this economic trend altered traditional social relations is difficult to judge. It is clear, however, that by the mid-eighteenth century a few affluent entrepreneurs in the Chesapeake area were giving substantial credit to their poorer neighbors, and their growing indebtedness may well have enhanced the gentry's already considerable social and political dominance.

Land's essay also underscores the fact that marginal farmers made up the great majority of the colonial white population. These people were not the independent yeomen who figure so prominently in American mythology. The Maryland probate records reveal that, of the men who left wills during the eighteenth century, between three-quarters and one-half lived at best in what Land terms "rude sufficiency." When growing conditions were good, they managed to survive from one year to the next, but when an unexpected disaster struck, they had no resources, no savings, to protect them from falling hopelessly into debt.

The existence of such a large group of impoverished colonists raises provocative questions that carry us far beyond the scope of this article. If so many eighteenth-century freemen were so poor, why was there so little political and social unrest? Why did no Nathaniel Bacon organize these planters? Could the expanding black population in the Chesapeake colonies have caused these white farmers to think in terms of racial, rather than class divisions and thus, out of a fear of upsetting white hegemony, to accept passively their lot in Southern society? And we cannot help but wonder how such persons viewed the political process. Land suggests that their major demand of elected officials was to "hold public expenses to the barest minimum." This interpretation is plausible considering their desperate economic straits; but where then does that leave the high constitutional principles that supposedly motivated the Founding Fathers in their struggle for independence? What did it require to mobilize these poor farmers in support of the American Revolution?

The final essay in this section approaches eighteenth-century planter society from an entirely different perspective. Rhys Isaac analyzes forms of popular culture in Virginia on the eve of the American Revolution. The author's familiarity with cultural anthropology clearly enriches his understanding of what he labels Virginia's "cultural disjunction." According to Isaac, cultural divisions within this colony found expression not in politics, as we might expect, but in religion. Put simply, the Baptists rejected the culture of Virginia's ruling gentry, and refused to participate in the rituals that took place around courthouses and Anglican churches throughout the colony. On such occasions the members of the local gentry asserted their claim to cultural dominance, and before an audience of their country neighbors they swaggered and bullied, fought and drank, gambled and danced—providing what was in effect a public display of gentry values. Because the Baptists subscribed to a quite different system of values, they behaved in ways that the gentry found offensive.

Isaac traces the conflict between these two groups, noting that while the gentry successfully maintained its political control, it nevertheless felt profoundly threatened by the evangelical movement. How do you explain the gentry's response to its critics? Did the ruling planters of Virginia react more strongly than the situation justified? Could they have simply ignored the Baptists? In exactly what manner did the Baptists plan to restructure social relations within Virginia?

BERNARD BAILYN
Politics and Social Structure in Virginia

By the end of the seventeenth century the American colonists faced an array of disturbing problems in the conduct of public affairs. Settlers from England and Holland, reconstructing familiar institutions on American shores, had become participants in what would appear to have been a wave of civil disobedience. Constituted authority was confronted with repeated challenges. Indeed, a veritable anarchy seems to have prevailed at the center of colonial society, erupting in a series of insurrections that began as early as 1635 with the "thrusting out" of Governor Harvey in Virginia. Culpeper's Rebellion in Carolina, the Protestant Association in Maryland, Bacon's Rebellion in Virginia, Leisler's seizure of power in New York, the resistance to and finally the overthrow of Andros in New England—every colony was affected.

These outbursts were not merely isolated local affairs. Although their immediate causes were rooted in the particular circumstances of the separate colonies, they nevertheless had common characteristics. They were, in fact, symptomatic of a profound disorganization of European society in its American setting. Seen in a broad view, they reveal a new configuration of forces which shaped the origins of American politics.

Bernard Bailyn, "Politics and Social Structure in Virginia," reprinted by permission from J. M. Smith, ed., *Seventeenth-Century America* (Chapel Hill: University of North Carolina Press for the Institute of Early American History and Culture, Williamsburg, Virginia, 1959), pp. 90–115.

In a letter written from Virginia in 1623, George Sandys, the resident treasurer, reported despondently on the character and condition of the leading settlers. Some of the councilors were "no more then Ciphers," he wrote; others were "miserablie poore"; and the few substantial planters lived apart, taking no responsibility for public concerns. There was, in fact, among all those "worthie the mencioninge" only one person deserving of full approval. Lieutenant William Peirce "refuses no labour, nor sticks at anie expences that may aduantage the publique." Indeed, Sandys added, Peirce was "of a Capacitie that is not to bee expected in a man of his breedinge."

The afterthought was penetrating. It cut below the usual complaints of the time that many of the settlers were lazy malcontents hardly to be preferred to the Italian glassworkers, than whom, Sandys wrote, "a more damned crew hell never vomited." What lay behind Sandys' remark was not so much that wretched specimens were arriving in the shipments of servants nor even that the quality of public leadership was declining but that the social foundations of political power were being strangely altered.

All of the settlers in whatever colony presumed a fundamental relationship between social structure and political authority. Drawing on a common medieval heritage, continuing to conceive of society as a hierarchical unit, its parts justly and naturally separated into inferior and superior levels, they assumed that superiority was indivisible; there was not one hierarchy for political matters, another for social purposes. John Winthrop's famous explanation of God's intent that "in all times some must be rich some poore, some highe and eminent in power and dignitie; others meane and in subieccion" could not have been more carefully worded. Riches, dignity, and power were properly placed in apposition; they pertained to the same individuals.

So closely related were social leadership and political leadership that experience if not theory justified an identification between state and society. To the average English colonist the state was not an abstraction existing above men's lives, justifying itself in its own terms, taking occasional human embodiment. However glorified in monarchy, the state in ordinary form was indistinguishable from a more general social authority; it was woven into the texture of everyday life. It was the same squire or manorial lord who in his various capacities collated to the benefice, set the rents, and enforced the statutes of Parliament and the royal decrees. Nothing could have been more alien to the settlers than the idea that competition for political leadership should be open to all levels of society or that obscure social origins or technical skills should be considered valuable qualifications for office. The proper response to new technical demands on public servants was not to give power to the skilled but to give skills to the powerful. The English gentry and landed aristocracy remained politically adaptable and hence politically competent, assuming when necessary new public functions, eliminating the need for a professional state bureaucracy. By their amateur competence they made possible a continuing identification between political and social authority.

In the first years of settlement no one had reason to expect that this characteristic of public life would fail to transfer itself to the colonies. For at least a decade and a half after its founding there had been in the Jamestown settlement a small group of leaders drawn from the higher echelons of English society. Besides well-born soldiers of fortune like George Percy, son of the Earl of Northumberland, there were among them four sons of the West family—children of Lord de la Warr and his wife, a second cousin of Queen Elizabeth. In Virginia the West brothers held appropriately high positions; three of them served as governors. Christopher Davison, the colony's secretary, was the son of Queen Elizabeth's secretary, William Davison, M.P. and Privy Councilor. The troublesome John Martin, of Martin's Brandon, was the son of Sir Richard Martin, twice Lord Mayor of London, and also the brother-in-law of Sir Julius Caesar, Master of the Rolls and Privy Councilor. Sir Francis and Haute Wyatt were sons of substantial Kent gentry and grandsons of the Sir Thomas Wyatt who led the rebellion of 1554 against Queen Mary. George Sandys' father was the Archbishop of York; of his three older brothers, all knights and M.P.'s, two were eminent country gentlemen, and the third, Edwin, of Virginia Company fame, was a man of great influence in the city. George Thorpe was a former M.P. and Gentleman of the Privy Chamber.

More impressive than such positions and relationships was the cultural level represented. For until the very end of the Company period, Virginia remained to the literary and scientific an exotic attraction, its settlement an important moment in Christian history. Its original magnetism for those in touch with intellectual currents affected the early immigration. Of the twenty councilors of 1621, eight had been educated at Oxford, Cambridge, or the Inns of Court. Davison, like Martin trained in the law, was a poet in a family of poets. Thorpe was a "student of Indian views on religion and astronomy." Francis Wyatt wrote verses and was something of a student of political theory. Alexander Whitaker, M.A., author of *Good Newes from Virginia*, was the worthy heir "of a good part of the learning of his renowned father," the master of St. John's College and Regius Professor of Divinity at Cambridge. John Pory, known to history mainly as the speaker of the first representative assembly in America, was a Master of Arts, "protege and disciple of Hakluyt," diplomat, scholar, and traveler, whose writings from and about America have a rightful place in literary history. Above all there was George Sandys, "poet, traveller, and scholar," a member of Lord Falkland's literary circle; while in Jamestown he continued as a matter of course to work on his notable translation of Ovid's *Metamorphoses*.

There was, in other words, during the first years of settlement a direct transference to Virginia of the upper levels of the English social hierarchy as well as of the lower. If the great majority of the settlers were recruited from the yeoman class and below, there was nevertheless a reasonable representation from those upper groups acknowledged to be the rightful rulers of society.

It is a fact of some importance, however, that this governing elite did not survive a single generation, at least in its original form. By the thirties their number had declined to insignificance. Percy, for example, left in 1612. Whitaker drowned in 1617. Sandys and Francis Wyatt arrived only in 1621, but their enthusiasm cooled quickly; they were both gone by 1626. Of the Wests, only John was alive and resident in the colony a decade after the collapse of the Company. Davison, who returned to England in 1622 after only a year's stay, was sent back in 1623 but died within a year of his return. Thorpe was one of the six councilors slain in the massacre of 1622. Pory left for England in 1622; his return as investigating commissioner in 1624 was temporary, lasting only a few months. And the cantankerous Martin graced the Virginia scene by his absence after 1625; he is last heard from in the early 1630's petitioning for release from a London debtor's prison.

To be sure, a few representatives of important English families, like John West and Edmund Scarborough, remained. There were also one or two additions from the same social level. But there were few indeed of such individuals, and the basis of their authority had changed. The group of gentlemen and illuminati that had dominated the scene during the Company era had been dispersed. Their disappearance created a political void which was filled soon enough, but from a different area of recruitment, from below, from the toughest and most fortunate of the surviving planters whose eminence by the end of the thirties had very little to do with the transplantation of social status.

The position of the new leaders rested on their ability to wring material gain from the wilderness. Some, like Samuel Mathews, started with large initial advantages, but more typical were George Menefie and John Utie, who began as independent landowners by right of transporting themselves and only one or two servants. Abraham Wood, famous for his explorations and like Menefie and Utie the future possessor of large estates and important offices, appears first as a servant boy on Mathews' plantation. Adam Thoroughgood, the son of a country vicar, also started in Virginia as a servant, aged fourteen. William Spencer is first recorded as a yeoman farmer without servants.

Such men as these—Spencer, Wood, Menefie, Utie, Mathews—were the most important figures in Virginia politics up to the Restoration, engrossing large tracts of land, dominating the Council, unseating Sir John Harvey from the governorship. But in no traditional sense were they a ruling class. They lacked the attributes of social authority, and their political dominance was a continuous achievement. Only with the greatest difficulty, if at all, could distinction be expressed in a genteel style of life, for existence in this generation was necessarily crude. Mathews may have created a flourishing estate and Menefie had splendid fruit gardens, but the great tracts of land such men claimed were almost entirely raw wilderness. They had risen to their positions, with few exceptions, by brute labor and shrewd manipulation; they had personally shared the burdens of settlement. They succeeded not because of, but despite, whatever gentility they may have had. William Claiborne may have been educated at the Middle Temple; Peirce could not sign his name; but what counted was their common capacity to survive and flourish in frontier settlements. They were tough, unsentimental, quick-tempered, crudely ambitious men concerned with profits and increased landholdings, not the grace of life. They roared curses, drank exuberantly, and gambled (at least according to deVries) for their servants when other commodities were lacking. If the worst of Governor Harvey's offenses had been to knock out the teeth of an offending councilor with a cudgel, as he did on one occasion, no one would have questioned his right to the governorship. Rank had its privileges, and these men were the first to claim them, but rank itself was unstable and the lines of class or status were fluid. There was no insulation for even the most elevated from the rude impact of frontier life.

As in style of life so in politics, these leaders of the first permanently settled generation did not re-create the characteristics of a stable gentry. They had had little opportunity to acquire the sense of public responsibility that rests on deep identification with the land and its people. They performed in some manner the duties expected of leaders, but often public office was found simply burdensome. Reports such as Sandys' that Yeardley, the councilor and former governor, was wholly absorbed in his private affairs and scarcely glanced at public matters and that Mathews "will rather hazard the payment of fforfeitures then performe our Injunctions" were echoed by Harvey throughout his tenure of office. Charles Harmar, justice of the peace on the Eastern Shore, attended the court once in eight years, and Claiborne's record was only slightly better. Attendance to public duties had to be specifically enjoined, and privileges were of necessity accorded provincial officeholders. The members of the Council were particularly favored by the gift of tax exemption.

The private interests of this group, which had assumed control of public office by virtue not of inherited status but of newly achieved and strenuously maintained economic eminence, were pursued with little interference from the traditional restraints imposed on a responsible ruling class. Engaged in an effort to establish themselves in the land, they sought as specific ends: autonomous local jurisdiction, an aggressive expansion of settlement and trading enterprises, unrestricted access to land, and, at every stage, the legal endorsement of acquisitions. Most of the major public events for thirty years after the dissolution of the Company—and especially the overthrow of Harvey—were incidents in the pursuit of these goals.

From his first appearance in Virginia, Sir John Harvey threatened the interests of this emerging planter group. While still in England he had identified himself with the faction that had successfully sought the collapse of the Company, and thus his mere presence in Virginia was a threat to the legal basis of land grants made under the Company's charter. His demands for the return as public property of goods that had once belonged to the Company specifically jeopardized the planters' holdings. His insistence that the governorship was more than a mere chairmanship of the Council tended to undermine local autonomy. His conservative Indian policy not only weakened the settlers' hand in what already seemed an irreconcilable enmity with the natives but also restricted the expansion of settlement. His opposition to Claiborne's claim to Kent Island threatened to kill off the lucrative Chesapeake Bay trade, and his attempt to ban the Dutch ships from the colony endangered commerce more generally. His support of the official policy of economic diversification, together with his endorsement of the English schemes of tobacco monopoly, alienated him finally and completely from the Council group.

Within a few months of his assuming the governorship, Harvey wrote home with indignation of the "waywardnes and oppositions" of the councilors and condemned them for factiously seeking "rather for their owne endes then either seekinge the generall good or doinge right to particuler men." Before a year was out the antagonisms had become so intense that a formal peace treaty had to be drawn up between Harvey and the Council. But both sides were adamant, and conflict was inescapable. It exploded in 1635 amid comic opera scenes of "extreame coller and passion" complete with dark references to Richard the Third and musketeers "running with their peices presented." The conclusion was Harvey's enraged arrest of George Menefie "of suspicion of Treason to his Majestie"; Utie's response, "And wee the like to you sir"; and the governor's forced return to England.

Behind these richly heroic "passings and repassings to and fro" lies not a victory of democracy or representative institutions or anything of the sort. Democracy, in fact, was identified in the Virginians' minds with the "popular and tumultuary government" that had prevailed in the old Company's quarter courts, and they wanted none of it; the Assembly as a representative institution was neither greatly sought after nor hotly resisted. The victory of 1635 was that of resolute leaders of settlement stubbornly fighting for individual establishment. With the reappointment of Sir Francis Wyatt as governor, their victory was assured and in the Commonwealth period it was completely realized. By 1658, when Mathews was elected governor, effective interference from outside had disappeared and the supreme authority had been assumed by an Assembly which was in effect a league of local magnates secure in their control of county institutions.

One might at that point have projected the situation forward into a picture of dominant county families dating from the 1620's and 1630's, growing in identification with the land and people, ruling with increasing responsibility from increasingly eminent positions. But such a projection would be false. The fact is that with a few notable exceptions like the Scarboroughs and the Wormeleys, these struggling planters of the first generation failed to perpetuate their leadership into the second generation. Such families as the Woods, the Uties, the Mathews, and the Peirces faded from dominant positions of authority after the deaths of their founders. To some extent this was the result of the general insecurity of life that created odds against the physical survival in the male line of any given family. But even if male heirs had remained in these families after the death of the first generation, undisputed eminence would not. For a new emigration had begun in the forties, continuing for close to thirty years, from which was drawn a new ruling group that had greater possibilities for permanent dominance than Harvey's opponents had had. These newcomers absorbed and subordinated the older group, forming the basis of the most celebrated oligarchy in American history.

Most of Virginia's great eighteenth-century names, such as Bland, Burwell, Byrd, Carter, Digges, Ludwell, and Mason, appear in the colony for the first time within ten years either side of 1655. These progenitors of the eighteenth-century aristocracy arrived in remarkably similar circumstances. The most important of these immigrants were younger sons of substantial families well connected in London business and governmental circles and long associated with Virginia; family claims to land in the colony or inherited shares of the original Company stock were now brought forward as a basis for establishment in the New World.

Thus the Bland family interests in Virginia date from a 1618 investment in the Virginia Company by the London merchant John Bland, supplemented in 1622 by another in Martin's Hundred. The merchant never touched foot in America, but three of his sons did come to Virginia in the forties and fifties to exploit these investments. The Burwell fortunes derive from the early subscription to the Company of Edward Burwell, which was inherited in the late forties by his son, Lewis I. The first William Byrd arrived about 1670 to assume the Virginia properties of his mother's family, the Steggs, which dated back to the early days of the Company. The Digges's interests in Virginia stem from the original investments of Sir Dudley Digges and two of his sons in the Company, but it was a third son, Edward, who emigrated in 1650 and established the American branch of the family. Similarly, the Masons had been financially interested in Virginia thirty-two years before 1652, when the first immigrant of that family appeared in the colony. The Culpeper clan, whose private affairs enclose much of the history of the South in the second half of the seventeenth century, was first represented in Virginia by Thomas Culpeper, who arrived in 1649; but the family interests in Virginia had been established a full generation earlier: Thomas' father, uncle, and cousin had all been members of the original Virginia Company and their shares had descended in the family. Even Governor Berkeley fits the pattern. There is no mystery about his sudden exchange in 1642 of the life of a dilettante courtier for that of a colonial administrator and estate manager. He was a younger son without prospects, and his family's interests in Virginia, dating from investments in the Company made twenty years earlier, as well as his appointment held out the promise of an independent establishment in America.

Claims on the colony such as these were only one, though the most important, of a variety of forms of capital that might provide the basis for secure family fortunes. One might simply bring over enough of a merchant family's resources to begin immediately building up an imposing estate, as, presumably, did that ambitious draper's son, William Fitzhugh. The benefits that accrued from such advantages were quickly translated into landholdings in the development of which these settlers were favored by the chronology of their arrival. For though they extended the area of cultivation in developing their landholdings, they were not obliged to initiate settlement. They fell heirs to large areas of the tidewater region that had already been brought under cultivation. "Westover" was not the creation of William Byrd; it had originally been part of the De la Warr estate, passing, with improvements, to Captain Thomas Pawlett, thence to Theodorick Bland, and finally to Byrd. Lewis Burwell inherited not only his father's land, but also the developed estate of his stepfather, Wingate. Some of the Carters' lands may be traced back through John Utie to a John Jefferson, who left Virginia as early as 1628. Abraham Wood's entire Fort Henry property ended in the hands of the Jones family. The Blands' estate in Charles City County, which later became the Harrisons' "Berkeley" plantation, was cleared for settlement in 1619 by servants of the "particular" plantation of Berkeley's Hundred.

Favored thus by circumstance, a small group within the second generation migration moved toward setting itself off in a permanent way as a ruling landed gentry. That they succeeded was due not only to their material advantages but also to the force of their motivation. For these individuals were in social origins just close enough to establishment in gentility to feel the pangs of deprivation most acutely. It is not the totally but the partially dispossessed who build up the most propulsive aspirations, and behind the zestful lunging at propriety and status of a William Fitzhugh lay not the narcotic yearnings of the disinherited but the pent-up ambitions of the gentleman *manqué*. These were neither hardhanded pioneers nor dilettante romantics, but ambitious younger sons of middle-class families who knew well enough what gentility was and sought it as a specific objective.

The establishment of this group was rapid. Within a decade of their arrival they could claim, together with a fortunate few of the first generation, a marked social eminence and full political authority at the county level. But their rise was not uniform. Indeed, by the seventies a new circumstance had introduced an effective principle of social differentiation among the colony's leader. A hierarchy of position within the newly risen gentry was created by the Restoration government's efforts to extend its control more effectively over its mercantile empire. Demanding of its colonial executives and their advisors closer supervision over the external aspects of the economy, it offered a measure of patronage necessary for enforcement. Public offices dealing with matters that profoundly affected the basis of economic life—tax collection, customs regulation, and the bestowal of land grants—fell within the gift of the governor and tended to form an inner circle of privilege. One can note in Berkeley's administration the growing importance of this barrier of officialdom. Around its privileges there formed the "Green Spring" faction, named after Berkeley's plantation near Jamestown, a group bound to the governor not by royalist sympathies so much as by ties of kinship and patronage.

Thus Colonel Henry Norwood, related to Berkeley by a "near affinity in blood," was given the treasurership of the colony in 1650, which he held for more than two decades. During this time Thomas Ludwell, a cousin and Somerset neighbor of the governor, was secretary of state, in which post he was succeeded in 1678 by his brother Philip, who shortly thereafter married Berkeley's widow. This Lady Berkeley, it should be noted, was the daughter of Thomas Culpeper, the immigrant of 1649 and a cousin of Thomas Lord Culpeper who became governor in 1680. Immediately after her marriage to Berkeley, her brother Alexander requested and received from the governor the nomination to the surveyor-generalship of Virginia, a post he filled for twenty-three years while resident in England, appointing as successive deputies the brothers Ludwell, to whom by 1680 he was twice related by marriage. Lady Berkeley was also related through her mother to William Byrd's wife, a fact that explains much about Byrd's prolific office-holding.

The growing distinctiveness of provincial officialdom within the landed gentry may also be traced in the transformation of the Council. Originally, this body had been expected to comprise the entire effective government, central and local; councilors were to serve, individually or in committees, as local magistrates. But the spread of settlement upset this expectation, and at the same time as the local offices were falling into the hands of autonomous local powers representing leading county families, the Council, appointed by the governor and hence associated with official patronage, increasingly realized the separate, lucrative privileges available to it.

As the distinction between local and central authority became clear, the county magistrates sought their own distinct voice in the management of the colony, and they found it in developing the possibilities of burgess representation. In the beginning there was no House of Burgesses; representation from the burghs and hundreds was conceived of not as a branch of government separate from the Council but as a periodic supplement to it. Until the fifties the burgesses, meeting in the Assemblies with the councilors, felt little need to form themselves into a separate house, for until that decade there was little evidence of a conflict of interests between the two groups. But when, after the Restoration, the privileged status of the Council became unmistakable and the county magnates found control of the increasingly important provincial administration preempted by this body, the burgess part of the Assembly took on a new meaning in contrast to that of the Council. Burgess representation now became vital to the county leaders if they were to share in any consistent way in affairs larger than those of the counties. They looked to the franchise, hitherto broad not by design but by neglect, introducing qualifications that would ensure their control of the Assembly. Their interest in provincial government could not longer be expressed in the conglomerate Assembly, and at least by 1663 the House of Burgesses began to meet separately as a distinct body voicing interests potentially in conflict with those of the Council.

Thus by the eighth decade the ruling class in Virginia was broadly based on leading county families and dominated at the provincial level by a privileged officialdom. But this social and political structure was too new, too lacking in the sanctions of time and custom, its leaders too close to humbler origins and as yet too undistinguished in style of life, to be accepted without a struggle. A period of adjustment was necessary, of which Bacon's Rebellion was the climactic episode.

Bacon's Rebellion began as an unauthorized frontier war against the Indians and ended as an upheaval that threatened the entire basis of social and political authority. Its immediate causes have to do with race relations and settlement policy, but behind these issues lay deeper elements related to resistance against the maturing shape of a new social order. These elements explain the dimensions the conflict reached.

There was, first, resistance by substantial planters to the privileges and policies of the inner provincial clique led by Berkeley and composed of those directly dependent on his patronage. These dissidents, among whom were the leaders of the Rebellion, represented neither the downtrodden masses nor a principle of opposition to privilege as such. Their discontent stemmed to a large extent from their own exclusion from privileges they sought. Most often their grievances were based on personal rebuffs they had received as they reached for entry into provincial officialdom. Thus—to speak of the leaders of the Rebellion—Giles Bland arrived in Virginia in 1671 to take over the agency of his late uncle in the management of his father's extensive landholdings, assuming at the same time the lucrative position of customs collector which he had obtained in London. But, amid angry cries of *"pittyfull fellow, puppy* and *Sonn of a Whore,"* he fell out first with Berkeley's cousin and favorite, Thomas Ludwell, and finally with the governor himself; for his "Barbarous and Insolent Behaviors" Bland was fined, arrested, and finally removed from the collectorship. Of the two "chiefe Incendiarys," William Drummond and Richard Lawrence, the former had been quarreling with Berkeley since 1664, first over land claims in Carolina, then over a contract for building a fort near James City, and repeatedly over lesser issues in the General Court; Lawrence "some Years before . . . had been partially treated at Law, for a considerable Estate on behalfe of a Corrupt favorite." Giles Brent, for his depredations against the Indians in violation of official policy, had not only been severely fined but barred from public office. Bacon himself could not have appeared under more favorable circumstances. A cousin both of Lady Berkeley and of the councilor Nathaniel Bacon, Sr., and by general agreement "a Gent:man of a Liberall education" if of a somewhat tarnished reputation, he had quickly staked out land for himself and had been elevated, for reasons "best known to the Governour," to the Council. But being "of a most imperious and dangerous hidden Pride of heart . . . very ambitious and arrogant," he wanted more, and quickly. His alienation from and violent opposition to Berkeley were wound in among the animosities created by the Indian problem and were further complicated by his own unstable personality; they were related also to the fact that Berkeley finally turned down the secret offer Bacon and Byrd made in 1675 for the purchase from the governor of a monopoly of the Indian trade.

These specific disputes have a more general aspect. It was three decades since Berkeley had assumed the governorship and begun rallying a favored group, and it was over a decade since the Restoration had given this group unconfined sway over the provincial government. In those years much of the choice tidewater land as well as the choice offices had been spoken for, and the tendency of the highly placed was to hold firm. Berkeley's Indian policy—one of stabilizing the borders between Indians and whites and protecting the natives from depredation by land-hungry settlers—although a sincere attempt to deal with an extremely difficult problem, was also conservative, favoring the established. Newcomers like Bacon and Bland and particularly landholders on the frontiers felt victimized by a stabilization of the situation or by a controlled expansion that maintained on an extended basis the existing power structure. They were logically drawn to aggressive positions. In an atmosphere charged with violence, their interests constituted a challenge to provincial authority. Bacon's primary appeal in his "Manifesto" played up the threat of this challenge:

Let us trace these men in Authority and Favour to whose hands the dispensation of the Countries wealth has been commited; let us observe the sudden Rise of their Estates [compared] with the Quality in wch they first entered this Country. . . . And lett us see wither their extractions and Education have not bin vile, And by what pretence of learning and vertue they could [enter] soe soon into Imployments of so great Trust and consequence, let us . . . see what spounges have suckt up the Publique Treasure and wither it hath not bin privately contrived away by unworthy Favourites and juggling Parasites whose tottering Fortunes have bin repaired and supported at the Publique chardg.

Such a threat to the basis of authority was not lost on Berkeley or his followers. Bacon's merits, a contemporary wrote, "thretned an eclips to there riseing gloryes. . . . (if he should continue in the Governours favour) of Seniours they might becom juniours, while there younger Brother . . . might steale away that blessing, which they accounted there owne by birthright."

But these challengers were themselves challenged, for another main element in the upheaval was the discontent among the ordinary settlers at the local privileges of the same newly risen county magnates who assailed the privileges of the Green Spring faction. The specific Charles City County grievances were directed as much at the locally dominant family, the Hills, as they were at Berkeley and his clique. Similarly, Surry County complained of its county court's highhanded and secretive manner of levying taxes on "the poore people" and of setting the sheriffs' and clerks' fees; they petitioned for the removal of these abuses and for the right to elect the vestry and to limit the tenure of the sheriffs. At all levels the Rebellion challenged the stability of newly secured authority.

It is this double aspect of discontent behind the violence of the Rebellion that explains the legislation passed in June, 1676, by the so-called "Bacon's Assembly." At first glance these laws seem difficult to interpret because they express disparate if not contradictory interests. But they yield readily to analysis if they are seen not as the reforms of a single group but as efforts to express the desires of two levels of discontent with the way the political and social hierarchy was becoming stabilized. On the one hand, the laws include measures designed by the numerically predominant ordinary settlers throughout the colony as protests against the recently acquired superiority of the leading county families. These were popular protests and they relate not to provincial affairs but to the situation within the local areas of jurisdiction. Thus the statute restricting the franchise to freeholders was repealed; freemen were given the right to elect the parish vestrymen; and the county courts were supplemented by elected freemen to serve with the regularly appointed county magistrates.

On the other hand, there was a large number of measures expressing the dissatisfactions not so much of the ordinary planter but of the local leaders against the prerogatives recently acquired by the provincial elite, prerogatives linked to officialdom and centered in the Council. Thus the law barring office-holding to newcomers of less than three years' residence struck at the arbitrary elevation of the governor's favorites, including Bacon; and the acts forbidding councilors to join the county courts, outlawing the governor's appointment of sheriffs and tax collectors, and nullifying tax exemption for councilors all voiced objections of the local chieftains to privileges enjoyed by others. From both levels there was objection to profiteering in public office.

Thus the wave of rebellion broke and spread. But why did it subside? One might have expected that the momentary flood would have become a steady tide, its rhythms governed by a fixed political constellation. But in fact it did not; stable political alignments did not result. The conclusion to this controversy was characteristic of all the insurrections. The attempted purges and counterpurges by the leaders of the two sides were followed by a rapid submerging of factional identity. Occasional references were later made to the episode, and there were individuals who found an interest in keeping its memory alive. Also, the specific grievances behind certain of the attempted legal reforms of 1676 were later revived. But of stable parties or factions around these issues there were none.

It was not merely that in the late years of the century no more than in the early was there to be found a justification for permanently organized political opposition or party machinery, that persistent, organized dissent was still indistinguishable from sedition; more important was the fact that at the end of the century as in 1630 there was agreement that some must be "highe and eminent in power and dignitie; others meane and in subieccion." Protests and upheaval had resulted from the discomforts of discovering who was, in fact, which, and what the particular consequences of "power and dignitie" were.

But by the end of the century the most difficult period of adjustment had passed and there was an acceptance of the fact that certain families were distinguished from others in riches, in dignity, and in access to political authority. The establishment of these families marks the emergence of Virginia's colonial aristocracy.

It was a remarkable governing group. Its members were soberly responsible, alive to the implications of power; they performed their public obligations with notable skill. Indeed, the glare of their accomplishments is so bright as occasionally to blind us to the conditions that limited them. As a ruling class the Virginian aristocracy of the eighteenth century was unlike other contemporary nobilities or aristocracies, including the English. The differences, bound up with the special characteristics of the society it ruled, had become clear at the turn of the seventeenth century.

Certain of these characteristics are elusive, difficult to grasp and analyze. The leaders of early eighteenth-century Virginia were, for example, in a particular sense, cultural provincials. They were provincial not in the way of Polish *szlachta* isolated on their estates by poverty and impassable roads, nor in the way of sunken *seigneurs* grown rustic and old-fashioned in lonely Norman chateaux. The Virginians were far from uninformed or unaware of the greater world; they were in fact deeply and continuously involved in the cultural life of the Atlantic community. But they knew themselves to be provincials in the sense that their culture was not self-contained; its sources and superior expressions were to be found elsewhere than in their own land. They must seek it from afar; it must be acquired, and once acquired be maintained according to standards externally imposed, in the creation of which they had not participated. The most cultivated of them read much, purposefully, with a diligence the opposite of that essential requisite of aristocracy, uncontending ease. William Byrd's diary with its daily records of stints of study is a stolid testimonial to the virtues of regularity and effort in maintaining standards of civilization set abroad.

In more evident ways also the Virginia planters were denied an uncontending ease of life. They were not *rentiers*. Tenancy, when it appeared late in the colonial period, was useful to the landowners mainly as a cheap way of improving lands held in reserve for future development. The Virginia aristocrat was an active manager of his estate, drawn continuously into the most intimate contacts with the soil and its cultivation. This circumstance limited his ease, one might even say bound him to the soil, but it also strengthened his identity with the land and its problems and saved him from the temptation to create of his privileges an artificial world of self-indulgence.

But more important in distinguishing the emerging aristocracy of Virginia from other contemporary social and political elites were two very specific circumstances. The first concerns the relationship between the integrity of the family unit and the descent of real property. "The English political family," Sir Lewis Namier writes with particular reference to the eighteenth-century aristocracy,

is a compound of "blood," name, and estate, this last . . . being the most important of the three. . . . The name is a weighty symbol, but liable to variations. . . . the estate . . . is, in the long run, the most potent factor in securing continuity through identification. . . . Primogeniture and entails psychically preserve the family in that they tend to fix its position through the successive generations, and thereby favour conscious identification.

The descent of landed estates in eighteenth-century England was controlled by the complicated device known as the strict settlement which provided that the heir at his marriage received the estate as a life tenant, entailing its descent to his unborn eldest son and specifying the limitations of the encumbrances upon the land that might be made in behalf of his daughters and younger sons.

It was the strict settlement, in which in the eighteenth century perhaps half the land of England was bound, that provided continuity over generations for the landed aristocracy. This permanent identification of the family with a specific estate and with the status and offices that pertained to it was achieved at the cost of sacrificing the younger sons. It was a single stem of the family only that retained its superiority; it alone controlled the material basis for political dominance.

This basic condition of aristocratic governance in England was never present in the American colonies, and not for lack of familiarity with legal forms. The economic necessity that had prompted the widespread adoption of the strict settlement in England was absent in the colonies. Land was cheap and easily available, the more so as one rose on the social and political ladder. There was no need to deprive the younger sons or even daughters of landed inheritances in order to keep the original family estate intact. Provision could be made for endowing each of them with plantations, and they in turn could provide similarly for their children. Moreover, to confine the stem family's fortune to a single plot of land, however extensive, was in the Virginia economy to condemn it to swift decline. Since the land was quickly worn out and since it was cheaper to acquire new land than to rejuvenate the worked soil by careful husbandry, geographical mobility, not stability, was the key to prosperity. Finally, since land was only as valuable as the labor available to work it, a great estate was worth passing intact from generation to generation only if it had annexed to it a sufficient population of slaves. Yet this condition imposed severe rigidities in a plantation's economy—for a labor force bound to a particular plot was immobilized—besides creating bewildering confusions in law.

The result, evident before the end of the seventeenth century, was a particular relationship between the family and the descent of property. There was in the beginning no intent on the part of the Virginians to alter the traditional forms; the continued vitality of the ancient statutes specifying primogeniture in certain cases was assumed. The first clear indication of a new trend came in the third quarter of the century, when the leading gentry, rapidly accumulating large estates, faced for the first time the problem of the transfer of property. The result was the subdivision of the great holdings and the multiplication of smaller plots while the net amount of land held by the leading families continued to rise.

This trend continued. Primogeniture neither at the end of the seventeenth century nor after prevailed in Virginia. It was never popular even among the most heavily endowed of the tidewater families. The most common form of bequest was a grant to the eldest son of the undivided home plantation and gifts of other tracts outside the home county to the younger sons and daughters. Thus by his will of 1686 Robert Beverley, Sr., bequeathed to his eldest son, Peter, all his land in Gloucester County lying between "Chiescake" and "Hoccadey's" creeks (an unspecified acreage); to Robert, the second son, another portion of the Gloucester lands amounting to 920 acres; to Harry, 1,600 acres in Rappahannock County; to John, 3,000 acres in the same county; to William, two plantations in Middlesex County; to Thomas, 3,000 acres in Rappahannock and New Kent counties; to his wife, three plantations including those "whereon I now live" for use during her lifetime, after which they were to descend to his daughter Catherine, who was also to receive £200 sterling; to his daughter Mary, £150 sterling; to "the childe that my wife goeth with, be it male or female," all the rest of his real property; and the residue of his personal property was "to be divided and disposed in equall part & portion betwix my wife and children." Among the bequests of Ralph Wormeley, Jr., in 1700 was an estate of 1,500 acres to his daughter Judith as well as separate plantations to his two sons.

Entail proved no more popular than primogeniture. Only a small minority of estates, even in the tidewater region, were ever entailed. In fact, despite the extension of developed land in the course of the eighteenth century, more tidewater estates were docked of entails than were newly entailed.

Every indication points to continuous and increasing difficulty in reproducing even pale replicas of the strict settlement. In 1705 a law was passed requiring a special act of the Assembly to break an entail; the law stood, but between 1711 and 1776 no fewer than 125 such private acts were passed, and in 1734 estates of under £200 were exempted from the law altogether. The labor problem alone was an insuperable barrier to perpetuating the traditional forms. A statute of 1727, clarifying the confused legislation of earlier years, had attempted to ensure a labor force on entailed land by classifying slaves as real property and permitting them to be bound together with land into bequests. But by 1748 this stipulation had resulted in such bewildering "doubts, variety of opinions, and confusions" that it was repealed. The repeal was disallowed in London, and in the course of a defense of its action the Assembly made vividly clear the utter impracticality of entailment in Virginia's economy. Slaves, the Assembly explained, were essential to the success of a plantation, but "slaves could not be kept on the lands to which they were annexed without manifest prejudice to the tenant in tail. . . . often the tenant was the proprietor of fee simple land and much fitter for cultivation than his intailed lands, where he could work his slaves to a much greater advantage." On the other hand, if a plantation owner did send entailed slaves where they might be employed most economically the result was equally disastrous:

the frequent removing and settling them on other lands in other counties and parts of the colony far distant from the county court where the deeds or wills which annexed them were recorded and the intail lands lay; the confusion occasioned by their mixture with fee simple slaves of the same name and sex and belonging to the same owner; the uncertainty of distinguishing one from another after several generations, no register of their genealogy being kept and none of them having surnames, were great mischiefs to purchasers, strangers, and creditors, who were often unavoidably deceived in their purchases and hindered in the recovery of their just debts. It also lessened the credit of the country; it being dangerous for the merchants of Great Britain to trust possessors of many slaves for fear the slaves might be intailed.

A mobile labor force free from legal entanglements and a rapid turnover of lands, not a permanent hereditary estate, were prerequisites of family prosperity. This condition greatly influenced social and political life. Since younger sons and even daughters inherited extensive landed properties, equal often to those of the eldest son, concentration of authority in the stem family was precluded. Third generation collateral descendants of the original immigrant were as important in their own right as the eldest son's eldest son. Great clans like the Carters and the Lees, though they may have acknowledged a central family seat, were scattered throughout the province on estates of equal influence. The four male Carters of the third generation were identified by contemporaries by the names of their separate estates, and, indistinguishable in style of life, they had an equal access to political power.

Since material wealth was the basis of the status which made one eligible for public office, there was a notable diffusion of political influence throughout a broadening group of leading families. No one son was predestined to represent the family interest in politics, but as many as birth and temperament might provide. In the 1750's there were no fewer than seven Lees of the same generation sitting together in the Virginia Assembly; in the Burgesses they spoke for five separate counties. To the eldest, Philip Ludwell Lee, they conceded a certain social superiority that made it natural for him to sit in the Council. But he did not speak alone for the family; by virtue of inheritance he had no unique authority over his brothers and cousins.

The leveling at the top of the social and political hierarchy, creating an evenness of status and influence, was intensified by continuous intermarriage within the group. The unpruned branches of these flourishing family trees, growing freely, met and intertwined until by the Revolution the aristocracy appeared to be one great tangled cousinry.

As political power became increasingly diffused throughout the upper stratum of society, the Council, still at the end of the seventeenth century a repository of unique privileges, lost its effective superiority. Increasingly through the successive decades its authority had to be exerted through alignments with the Burgesses—alignments made easier as well as more necessary by the criss-crossing network of kinship that united the two houses. Increasingly the Council's distinctions became social and ceremonial.

The contours of Virginia's political hierarchy were also affected by a second main conditioning element, besides the manner of descent of family property. Not only was the structure unusually level and broad at the top, but it was incomplete in itself. Its apex, the ultimate source of legal decision and control, lay in the quite different society of England, amid the distant embroilments of London, the court, and Parliament. The levers of control in that realm were for the most part hidden from the planters; yet the powers that ruled this remote region could impose an arbitrary authority directly into the midst of Virginia's affairs.

One consequence was the introduction of instabilities in the tenure and transfer of the highest offices. Tenure could be arbitrarily interrupted, and the transfer to kin of such positions at death or resignation—uncertain in any case because of the diffusion of family authority—could be quite difficult or even impossible. Thus William Byrd II returned from England at the death of his father in 1704 to take over the family properties, but though he was the sole heir he did not automatically or completely succeed to the elder Byrd's provincial offices. He did, indeed, become auditor of Virginia after his father, but only because he had carefully arranged for the succession while still in London; his father's Council seat went to someone else, and it took three years of patient maneuvering through his main London contact, Micajah Perry, to secure another; he never did take over the receivership. Even such a power as "King" Carter, the reputed owner at his death of 300,000 acres and 1,000 slaves, was rebuffed by the resident deputy governor and had to deploy forces in England in order to transfer a Virginia naval office post from one of his sons to another. There was family continuity in public office, but at the highest level it was uncertain, the result of place-hunting rather than of the absolute prerogative of birth.

Instability resulted not only from the difficulty of securing and transferring high appointive positions but also and more immediately from the presence in Virginia of total strangers to the scene, particularly governors and their deputies, armed with extensive jurisdiction and powers of enforcement. The dangers of this element in public life became clear only after Berkeley's return to England in 1677, for after thirty-five years of residence in the colony Sir William had become a leader in the land independent of his royal authority. But

Howard, Andros, and Nicholson were governors with full legal powers but with at best only slight connections with local society. In them, social leadership and political leadership had ceased to be identical.

In the generation that followed Berkeley's departure, this separation between the two spheres created the bitterest of political controversies. Firmly entrenched behind their control of the colony's government, the leading families battled with every weapon available to reduce the power of the executives and thus to eliminate what appeared to be an external and arbitrary authority. Repeated complaints by the governors of the intractable opposition of a league of local oligarchs marked the Virginians' success. Efforts by the executives to discipline the indigenous leaders could only be mildly successful. Patronage was a useful weapon, but its effectiveness diminished steadily, ground down between a resistant Assembly and an office-hungry bureaucracy in England. The possibility of exploiting divisions among the resident powers also declined as kinship lines bound the leading families closer together and as group interests became clearer with the passage of time. No faction built around the gubernatorial power could survive independently; ultimately its adherents would fall away and it would weaken. It was a clear logic of the situation that led the same individuals who had promoted Nicholson as a replacement for Andros to work against him once he assumed office.

Stability could be reached only by the complete identification of external and internal authority through permanent commitment by the appointees to local interests. Commissary Blair's extraordinary success in Virginia politics was based not only on his excellent connections in England but also on his marriage into the Harrison family, which gave him the support of an influential kinship faction. There was more than hurt pride and thwarted affection behind Nicholson's reported insane rage at being spurned by the highly marriageable Lucy Burwell; and later the astute Spotswood, for all his success in imposing official policy, fully quieted the controversies of his administration only by succumbing completely and joining as a resident Virginia landowner the powers aligned against him.

But there was more involved than instability and conflict in the discontinuity between social and political organization at the topmost level. The state itself had changed its meaning. To a Virginia planter of the early eighteenth century the highest public authority was no longer merely one expression of a general social authority. It had become something abstract, external to his life and society, an ultimate power whose purposes were obscure, whose direction could neither be consistently influenced nor accurately plotted, and whose human embodiments were alien and antagonistic.

The native gentry of the early eighteenth century had neither the need nor the ability to fashion a new political theory to comprehend their experience, but their successors would find in the writings of John Locke on state and society not merely a reasonable theoretical position but a statement of self-evident fact.

I have spoken exclusively of Virginia, but though the histories of each of the colonies in the seventeenth century are different, they exhibit common characteristics. These features one might least have expected to find present in Virginia, and their presence there is, consequently, most worth indicating.

In all of the colonies the original transference of an ordered European society was succeeded by the rise to authority of resident settlers whose influence was rooted in their ability to deal with the problems of life in wilderness settlements. These individuals attempted to stabilize their positions, but in each case they were challenged by others arriving after the initial settlements, seeking to exploit certain advantages of position, wealth, or influence. These newcomers, securing after the Restoration governmental appointments in the colonies and drawn together by personal ties, especially those of kinship and patronage, came to constitute colonial officialdom. This group introduced a new principle of social organization; it also gave rise to new instabilities in a society in which the traditional forms of authority were already being subjected to severe pressures. By the eighth decade of the seventeenth century the social basis of public life had become uncertain and insecure, its stability delicate and sensitive to disturbance. Indian warfare, personal quarrels, and particularly the temporary confusion in external control caused by the Glorious Revolution became the occasions for violent challenges to constituted authority.

By the end of the century a degree of harmony had been achieved, but the divergence between political and social leadership at the topmost level created an area of permanent conflict. The political and social structures that emerged were by European standards strangely shaped. Everywhere as the bonds of empire drew tighter the meaning of the state was changing. Herein lay the origins of a new political system.

JACK P. GREENE
Foundations of Political Power in the Virginia House of Burgesses, 1720-1776

Historians have devoted more attention to the Virginia House of Burgesses than to any other lower house in the continental colonies. They have treated its internal development, its part in royal government, its procedure, and its personnel. They have assessed its role in developing the leaders of the Revolutionary generation and traced its part in the "struggle for liberty." Yet, no one has attempted to analyze the structure of power within the Burgesses in the half century before the American Revolution.

The first question to be asked in such an analysis is how was power distributed in the house? Was it spread more or less equally among all members, or was it generally concentrated in the hands of a few? The answer to this question lies in the committees where the work of the house was done and where the real decisions were made. The only way one can hope to determine the pattern of the distribution of power in the eighteenth-century house is by a qualitative analysis of committee posts—that is, by a study which takes into account not only the number of committee posts held by each member but also the varying degrees of importance of the committees themselves. [See Note on Method and Sources.]

I have undertaken such an analysis and used my findings as a yardstick to measure the influence or power of individual burgesses. The

Jack P. Greene, "Foundations of Political Power in the Virginia House of Burgesses, 1720–1776," *William and Mary Quarterly*, 3rd ser., 16 (1959): 485–506. Copyright © 1959 by Jack P. Greene; reprinted by permission.

results indicate that relatively few members played significant roles in the proceedings of the house: of the 630 men who sat in that body between 1720 and 1776, some 520 can safely be eliminated from consideration, because only 110 members belonged at one time or another to the select few who dominated the proceedings of the house. Of these few, some, of course, were more powerful than others. In fact, the leaders as a whole may be divided into two groups, those of the first rank and those of the second. In any given session, the top level was composed of the speaker, who made appointments to all committees, and from two to perhaps seven or eight others, including, as a rule, the chairmen of the standing committees. Men of somewhat less importance, usually five to ten in number, constituted the second level. For example, in the 1736 session five men at the top level handled about a third of the committee assignments while seven others at the second level handled another fourth. Altogether these twelve burgesses—one-sixth of the total membership—occupied more than half of the committee seats. Until 1742 it was not uncommon for as many as one-third to one-half of the burgesses to serve on no committees at all; then, for reasons that are not now entirely clear, the size of the standing committees was enlarged and nearly three-fourths of the members were given assignments on these committees. Beginning in 1748, the speaker adopted the practice of giving each member at least one post on a standing committee, but this diffusion of assignments does not appear to have affected the structure of power in the house; in 1752 somewhat less than one-fifth of the members handled over half of the business of the house, with the six most powerful men occupying a fourth of the committee posts and eleven others holding another fourth. This pattern did not change significantly for the rest of the colonial period. It was modified slightly after 1766, when Peyton Randolph succeeded John Robinson as speaker. Randolph further increased the size of the standing committees and, more important, sprinkled the major assignments among a greater number of members, with the result that the number of men at both levels of power increased slightly.

These men of power provided the house with a certain continuity of leadership from 1720 until well after the Declaration of Independence. Some of them died, some retired, some were defeated at the polls, but never at any time was there any wholesale turnover in leadership. This continuity plus the lack of evidence of any major dissatisfaction with the leadership or of the existence of any group intent upon challenging it emphasizes the fact that organized political parties did not exist in colonial Virginia. There was often disagreement on specific issues, but, as St. George Tucker later suggested to William Wirt when the latter was preparing his biography of Patrick Henry, the disagreements were "only such as different men, coming from different parts of our extensive Country might well be expected to entertain." Tucker had never witnessed anything in the House of Burgesses "that bore the appearance of *party spirit.*"

The discovery of the fact that the House of Burgesses was dominated by the few rather than the many immediately raises some important questions about the leaders. What were their professional and economic interests, their social and family backgrounds and connections, their political experience and education, their national origins and religious affiliations, and their geographical distribution?

Most of these men were comparatively wealthy. Unfortunately, it is usually impossible to determine the extent of a man's wealth at any given time, but at least a general idea of the land and slave holdings of most of the 110 may be culled from existing wills, inventories, tithable and tax lists, and personal records. Information on land holdings is available for all but ten. Slightly less than three-fourths of them had large holdings—that is, holdings in excess of ten thousand acres. Seven of the 110, and perhaps three others, owned more than forty thousand acres; and the holdings of forty-six, certainly, and perhaps as many as sixty-four, exceeded ten thousand acres. A dozen possessed from one to five thousand acres. Only one man is thought to have owned fewer than five hundred acres. Records of slaveholdings are more difficult to find, but reasonably exact information is available for over half of the 110, and most of the others are known to have possessed some slaves. Quite naturally, the larger landowners—men like John Robinson, Charles and Landon Carter, Benjamin Harrison, and Archibald Cary—also owned the greater number of slaves. Eleven of those for whom records are available owned more than three hundred slaves—a staggering number for the times. Twenty-five possessed from fifty to three hundred slaves; twenty-two others had more than ten. Land and slaves were, of course, not the only assets of these burgesses. Livestock, plantation dwellings and outbuildings, farm equipment, and town houses must be added to their riches. Some men, like the Nelsons and Richard Adams, had large mercantile establishments; and a few dabbled in mining and manufacturing.

Most of the 110 leaders of the house were, of course, planters. Indeed, at least ninety-one were directly involved in planting and raising tobacco, although a third of these engaged in planting only as a secondary occupation. The lawyers—most of whom were planters on the side—were the next most numerous professional or occupational group. Thirty-nine of the 110 were practicing lawyers, but they were far more significant than their number would indicate. The services of trained lawyers were invaluable to the house. They had precisely those talents required in framing legislation and carrying on the business of the Burgesses; and throughout the period under consideration, they were conspicuous by their presence at the top level of power. Of the four men who served as speaker, three—John Holloway, Sir John Randolph, and Peyton Randolph—were lawyers. Other occupational groups were less prominent. Of the thirteen men not accounted for above, ten were merchants, two were physicians, and one was a teacher.

Nearly all of the leaders of the house had secondary economic interests. It has already been pointed out that the majority of the lawyers were planters too. So also were the merchants, one of the physicians, and the teacher. Similarly, most of those who were primarily planters had other interests. Their most important secondary occupation was land speculation. Over two-fifths, and perhaps more, speculated in Western lands—a profitable avocation. A dozen participated in some form of mercantile activity. Three were engaged in mining; four were part-time surveyors; four were part-time soldiers; and one was a part-time teacher. Archibald Cary might even be classed a manufacturer, for one of his many secondary interests was an iron works.

Historians from the time of William Wirt to the present have considered family an important ingredient of political power in eighteenth-century Virginia. Bernard Bailyn has recently put forward the provocative thesis that a new ruling class emerged out of an immigration to Virginia that began in the late 1630's or early 1640's and continued through the 1660's. According to Bailyn, this ruling class supplanted the leaders of the earlier immigrants, secured more or less permanent control first of the county institutions and then of the House of Burgesses, and supplied much of the political leadership of the eighteenth century. My own investigations of the family backgrounds of the Burgesses' leaders indicate that this thesis is only partly valid. Certainly, the generation that came to Virginia between 1635 and 1670 contributed more leaders than any other generation. Forty-nine of the 110 were descendants of that generation. Only seven derived from the pre-1635 immigrants. However, fifty others—nearly half of the leaders who dominated the Burgesses from 1720 to 1776—descended from the several generations that came to the colony after 1670. This fact is significant, for it indicates that the earlier immigrants did not have a monopoly on political power or a very tight control over the House of Burgesses. In fact, families still comparatively new on the Virginia scene in 1720 supplied a significant proportion of the Burgesses' leadership during the fifty years preceding the Revolution. Nearly one-fifth of the 110 were drawn from families that arrived in Virginia between 1690 and 1720, and another tenth from those that came after 1720. Some of the newcomers, of course, found marriage into an established family a convenient avenue to social and political power, but many, like Speaker John Holloway, John Clayton, and James Power, acquired wealth, position, and political power without the advantages of connections with older families—an indication that social lines were still fluid and that political power was still attainable for the ambitious and gifted among the newly arrived.

It should not be inferred, however, that family connections were unimportant. Over half of the leaders were connected either through blood or marriage to one of the great eighteenth-century families, and only a conspicuous few reached the top level of power without such a connection. Indeed, certain families—notably the Randolphs, Carters, Beverleys, and Lees—supplied an unusually large proportion of the leaders of the house. Including descendants through both male and female lines, the Randolphs provided eleven, the Carters nine, the Beverleys eight, and the Lees six. The Blands, Burwells, and Corbins each furnished four, and the Blairs, Harrisons, Ludwells, and Nelsons three; these families were connected through marriage with other leading burgesses: six had marriage ties with the Carters, five with the Randolphs, and four with the Beverleys. Membership in, or alliance with, one of these families was certainly an important political asset, although, to keep the matter in proper perspective, from one-third to one-half of the leaders were not related to any of these families and not every member so related attained political power.

In religion and nationality the leaders were remarkably homogeneous. Of the 80 per cent ascertainable, all were Anglicans. It seems likely that those about whom information is not available were also Anglican, although it is entirely possible that several adhered to other Protestant faiths. In national origins the vast majority were English, and, if there were a few Scots, some Welsh, and even an occasional Irishman, still they all were Britons.

The educational level of the 110 leading burgesses appears to have been remarkably high. At least fifty had some education at the college or university level. Some forty attended the College of William and Mary, but others journeyed to England for at least a part of their formal schooling. Richard Henry Lee and Robert Munford studied at Wakefield Academy in Leeds; Charles and Landon Carter at Solomon Low's School, near London; Gabriel Jones at the Blue Coat School in Christ's Hospital, London; and four others at unknown schools in the British Isles. Ten others read law at the Inns of Court—for whatever that may or may not have been worth. A few matriculated at the universities; two at Oxford, another at Cambridge, and one, possibly two, at Edinburgh. Of those who had neither the benefits of an English education nor study at William and Mary, many, like Francis Lightfoot Lee, were taught at home by a private tutor. Others, like George Washington, got their education in parish schools conducted by local clergymen. No fewer than seventeen of those without university training successfully undertook the study of law; they proceeded either, like Edmund Pendleton and Paul Carrington, under the watchful eye of a practicing attorney or, like Patrick Henry, on their own. From the records at hand it is impossible to determine if the educational attainments of the leaders were higher than those of their fellow burgesses or just how much higher their educational level was than the general level in Virginia. In all likelihood, however, they were at least as well educated as any men in the colony.

The leaders' formal education was supplemented by practical experience at the county and parish levels. In fact, a record of active county and parish service was in the background of almost every burgess. The late Charles S. Sydnor, in his study of eighteenth-century Virginia politics, found that posts on the county courts, the parish vestry, and the county militia were important milestones on the pathway to political power. My own investigation amply supports his findings. Either before or during their service in the house, well over four-fifths of the Burgesses' men of power between 1720 and 1776 served as gentlemen justices of the peace. Over half were vestrymen, and nearly two-fifths were officers of the county militia. A few had also been clerks, king's attorneys, sheriffs, surveyors, and coroners in the counties. Some had served as town officials; no fewer than five had been mayors of Williamsburg. Five others combined burgessing with the colony's attorney generalship. Each of these posts—military, judicial, civil, and ecclesiastical—gave the prospective burgess an opportunity to develop the sort of leadership that would prove useful in the house, to gain an intimate knowledge of his future constituents, and to learn something of the obligations and responsibilities of political office and political power.

An analysis of the geographical distribution of the leaders shows that no one section had a monopoly on political power within the house. Neither does there appear to have been any attempt by representatives from the older counties in the Tidewater to exclude from places of importance those burgesses who came from the newer areas. On the other hand, it appears that leadership and geographical origins were not unrelated, for leaders were rarely drawn from sections settled for less than a generation. During the period under consideration, more leaders came from the Tidewater, in particular from the region extending from the south side of the James River northward to the Rappahannock and from the western rim of Chesapeake Bay westward to the fall line, than from any other section; in fact, until 1730 most of the leaders were Tidewater men. However, from 1705 on, representatives from the Northern Neck, that area lying between the Rappahannock and Potomac Rivers and stretching westward to the mountains, played an increasingly important role in the affairs of the house and by 1730 equaled the Tidewater in supplying the house with leaders. In the 1730's, the counties around the fall line also began to contribute a significant number of leaders. This development was, after all, a logical one, especially since the social and economic patterns of the Tidewater were extended not only to the Northern Neck and the fall line area but also into the Piedmont, and since family ties cut across geographical lines. From 1689 to the end of the colonial period, there appears to have been an almost continuous shift of the geographical center of power northward and westward, following the frontier by about a generation. Thus, the house did not draw leaders from the Piedmont until the late 1740's, nearly twenty-five years after the first settlement of that region. Similarly, although the occupation of the Shenandoah Valley and mountain area further west began in the 1740's, none of its representatives rose to positions of power until the late 1760's.

Why these particular 110 rose to positions of power rather than their colleagues is a question of fundamental importance. As individuals they exhibit most of the "qualifications" I have discussed. They were wealthy, derived part of their income from planting, were often related to the great Virginia families, were Anglicans, were of English (or at least of British) origin, had attained a high educational level for the time and place, were experienced in local politics, and came from areas settled for at least a generation. These were the tangibles upon which political power was based, although the lack of any one, two, or even three of these qualifications might not necessarily bar a man from a position of power. The more essential ele-

ments were wealth, family, and education; but even a generous helping of all three would not guarantee a position among the leaders of
the house. Otherwise William Byrd III, Robert Wormeley Carter,
Charles Carter, Jr., Richard Bland, Jr., and others would have been
assured of such a place. In the long run the capacity to put these elements to effective use—call it political acumen, sagacity, the quality
of political leadership—was probably decisive, although it is not sus-
ceptible of analysis in a study of this nature. But to secure the support of the electorate and the confidence of his colleagues and to exercise leadership in the Virginia House of Burgesses, 1720–76, a man
had to have some measure of the tangible "qualifications" as well as
the capacity to use them.

THE 110 LEADERS OF THE VIRGINIA HOUSE OF BURGESSES 1720–1776

The 110 were selected on the basis of the quantitative analysis described
in the Note on Method and Sources below and include any member who
performed a significant portion of the Burgesses' committee business at
any one session between 1720 and 1776. I have treated several short sessions as single sessions. The three between February 20, 1746, and April
18, 1747, are referred to as 1746–47; the three between February 14 and
November 2, 1754, as 1754; the three between May 1 and November 8,
1755, as 1755; the two between March 25 and September 8, 1756, as
1756; the two between April 14, 1757, and April 12, 1758, as 1757–58;
the two between September 14 and November 11, 1758, as 1758; the
two between February 22 and November 21, 1759, as 1759; the three between March 4, 1760, and April 1, 1761, as 1760–61; the three between
November 3, 1761, and April 7, 1762, as 1761–62; the two between
October 30, 1764, and June 1, 1765, as 1764–65; the two between November 6, 1766, and April 11, 1767, as 1766–67; and the two between
November 7, 1769, and June 28, 1770, as 1769–70.

Name and Primary Occupation	Service and Constituency	Sessions in First Rank	Sessions in Second Rank
Acrill, William (lawyer)	1736: Charles City	1736	
Adams, Richard (merchant)	1752–65: New Kent 1769–76: Henrico		1769–70
Alexander, John (planter)	1766–75: Stafford		1772

Name and Primary Occupation	Service and Constituency	Sessions in First Rank	Sessions in Second Rank
Aylett, William (planter)	1736–40: Westmoreland		1738
Baker, Richard (lawyer)	1768–71: Isle of Wight		1769–70
Banister, John (lawyer)	1766–68, 1769–76: Dinwiddie		1769–70; 1772; 1775
Barradall, Edward (lawyer)	1738–42: College of William and Mary	1740; 1742	1738
Beverley, William (planter)	1734–40: Orange 1742–49: Essex	1744; 1746–47; 1748–49	1736; 1738; 1740; 1742
Blair, Archibald (physician)	1718, 1727–34: Jamestown 1720–26: James City		May, 1718; 1720; 1722; 1730; 1732
Blair, John, Sr. (merchant)	1734: Jamestown 1736–40: Williamsburg		1736; 1738
Blair, John, Jr. (lawyer)	1766–70: College of William and Mary	1766–67; 1769–70	1768; 1769
Bland, Richard (lawyer)	1742–76: Prince George	1746–47; 1748–49; 1752; 1753; 1754; 1755; 1756; 1757–58; 1758; 1759; 1760–61; 1762; 1763; 1764–65; 1766–67; 1768; 1769–70; 1771; 1772; 1773; 1774; 1775	1761–62; 1769
Bolling, Robert (merchant)	1723–34: Prince George	1732	1734
Braxton, Carter (planter)	1761–71, 1775–76: King William	1775	1766–67
Braxton, George, Jr. (planter)	1742–49, 1758–61: King & Queen	1746–47; 1748–49	1742
Burwell, Carter (planter)	1742–55: James City	1754; 1755	1746–47; 1748–49; 1752; 1753
Burwell, Lewis of Kingsmill (planter)	1758–74: James City		1764–65; 1766–67; 1769–70

Name and Primary Occupation	Service and Constituency	Sessions in First Rank	Sessions in Second Rank
Burwell, Nathaniel (planter)	1710–12: Jamestown 1720: Gloucester		1720
Carrington, Paul (lawyer)	1765–76: Charlotte		1769–70; 1772; 1775
Carter, Charles of Cleve (planter)	1734–64: King George	1742; 1744; 1746–47; 1748–49; 1752; 1753; 1754; 1755; 1756; 1757–58; 1759; 1760–61	1736; 1758; 1761–62
Carter, Charles of Corotoman (planter)	1758–76: Lancaster		1769–70
Carter, Landon (planter)	1752–68: Richmond	1752; 1754; 1755; 1756; 1757–58; 1759; 1766–67	1758; 1760–61; 1762; 1764–65
Cary, Archibald (planter)	1748–49: Goochland 1756–76: Chesterfield	1762; 1764–65; 1766–67; 1769–70; 1772; 1775	1757–58; 1758; 1760–61; 1768; 1769; 1773; 1774
Chiswell, John (planter)	1742–55: Hanover 1756–58: Williamsburg		1755
Claiborne, Augustine (lawyer)	1748–53: Surry		1753
Clayton, John (lawyer)	1715: Jamestown 1720–26: James City 1727–34: Williamsburg	1720; 1722; 1728; 1730; 1732; 1734	1715
Conway, Edwin (planter)	1710–18, 1723–55: Lancaster	1736; 1738; 1740; 1742; 1744; 1746–47	1712; 1715; 1730; 1732; 1734; 1752
Corbin, Gawin, Sr. (planter)	1698–1705, 1718–22: Middlesex 1715: King & Queen	1715; May, 1718; 1720	1703; 1704; 1705; Nov., 1718; 1722
Corbin, Gawin, Jr. (planter)	1734–40: King & Queen 1742–47: Middlesex	1736	1738; 1744; 1746–47
Corbin, Richard (planter)	1748–49: Middlesex		1748–49
Dandridge, Bartholomew (planter)	1772–76: New Kent		1775

Name and Primary Occupation	Service and Constituency	Sessions in First Rank	Sessions in Second Rank
Digges, Dudley (lawyer)	1752–76: York	1775	1754; 1755; 1756; 1757–58; 1769–70; 1772
Digges, William (planter)	1752–71: Warwick		1754; 1755; 1757–58; 1760–61
Eskridge, George (lawyer)	1705–14, 1718–34: Westmoreland	1728; 1730; 1732	1710; 1712; 1713; May, 1718; Nov., 1718; 1734
Eyre, Littleton (merchant)	1742–61: Northampton		1752
Eyre, Severn (lawyer)	1766–73: Northampton	1769–70	1766–67; 1772
Fitzhugh, Henry (planter)	1734–42: Stafford	1736; 1738; 1740; 1742	1734
Fitzhugh, William (planter)	1772–76: King George		1772
Fleming, John (lawyer)	1756–67: Cumberland		1764–65; 1766–67
Fry, Joshua (teacher)	1746–54: Albemarle	1753	1748–49; 1752
Gray, Edwin (planter)	1769–76: Southampton		1774
Grymes, John (planter)	1718–22: Middlesex		May, 1718; Nov., 1718; 1720
Harmar, John (merchant)	1742–47: Williamsburg		1742
Harrison, Benjamin, Sr. (planter)	1736–45: Charles City	1744	1738; 1740; 1742
Harrison, Benjamin, Jr. (planter)	1748–76: Charles City	1769–70; 1772	1753; 1755; 1757–58; 1759; 1760–61; 1762; 1764–65; 1766–67; 1768; 1769; 1773; 1774
Harrison, Henry (planter)	1715–30: Surry	May, 1718	1722; 1723; 1728; 1730
Harwood, William (planter)	1742–76: Warwick		1774

Name and Primary Occupation	Service and Constituency	Sessions in First Rank	Sessions in Second Rank
Hedgman, Peter (planter)	1732–40: Prince William 1742–58: Stafford		1748–49
Henry, Patrick (lawyer)	1765–68: Louisa 1769–76: Hanover	1769–70	1766–67; 1772
Holloway, John (lawyer)	1710–14: King & Queen 1720–22, 1727–34: York 1723–26: Williamsburg	1710; 1712; 1713; 1714; 1720; 1722; 1723; 1726; 1728; 1730; 1732	1711–12
Holt, James (lawyer)	1772–76: Norfolk County		1772
Jefferson, Thomas (lawyer)	1769–76: Albemarle		1775
Johnson, Philip (planter)	1752–58: King & Queen 1761–65: James City		1753; 1755; 1757–58
Johnston, George (lawyer)	1758–65: Fairfax		1759; 1762
Jones, Gabriel (lawyer)	1748–53: Frederick 1756–58, 1769–71: Augusta 1758–61: Hampshire		1757–58; 1769–70
Jones, Joseph (lawyer)	1772–76: King George	1775	1772
Jones, Robert (lawyer)	1748–55: Surry		1748–49; 1752; 1753
Kemp, Matthew (lawyer)	1723–30: Middlesex	1730	1728
Lee, Francis Lightfoot (planter)	1758–68: Loudoun 1769–76: Richmond		1766–67; 1775
Lee, Henry (lawyer)	1758–76: Prince William	1775	1766–67; 1769–70; 1772
Lee, Richard of Lee Hall (planter)	1757–76: Westmoreland		1769; 1769–70; 1774
Lee, Richard Henry (planter)	1758–76: Westmoreland	1762; 1766–67; 1769–70; 1772; 1774	1759; 1760–61; 1761–62; 1764–65; 1769; 1771; 1773
Lee, Thomas (planter)	1726–33: Westmoreland	1732	

Name and Primary Occupation	Service and Constituency	Sessions in First Rank	Sessions in Second Rank
Lomax, Lunsford (planter)	1742–55: Caroline		1744; 1746–47; 1752; 1754; 1755
Ludwell, Philip (planter)	1742–49: Jamestown	1748–49	1744; 1746–47
McCarty, Daniel, Sr. (planter)	1705–06, 1715–23: Westmoreland	1715; May, 1718; Nov., 1718	1705; 1722; 1723
McCarty, Daniel, Jr. (planter)	1734–44: Westmoreland		1738
Martin, John (merchant)	1730–34, 1738–40: Caroline 1752–56: King William		1734; 1740; 1752; 1753; 1754; 1755
Mason, David (planter)	1758–76: Sussex		1774
Mason, Thomson (lawyer)	1766–71: Stafford 1772–74: Loudoun		1766–67
Mercer, George (planter)	1761–65: Frederick		1762
Mercer, James (lawyer)	1762–76: Hampshire	1775	1766–67; 1769–70
Meriwether, Nicholas (planter)	1705–20: New Kent 1722–34: Hanover	1712	1710; 1714; 1715; 1730; 1732; 1734
Munford, Robert (planter)	1765–76: Mecklenburg	1775	
Nelson, Thomas (1716–87) (lawyer)	1745–49: York	1746–47	1748–49
Nelson, Thomas (1738–89) (merchant)	1761–76: York	1775	1769–70; 1772
Nelson, William (merchant)	1742–45: York	1744	1742
Norton, John (merchant)	1749–55: York		1755
Nicholas, Robert Carter (lawyer)	1756–61: York 1766–76: James City	1756; 1757–58; 1760–61; 1769–70; 1772; 1774; 1775	1758; 1759; 1766–67; 1768; 1773
Page, John (lawyer)	1752–68: Gloucester		1754; 1755; 1756; 1757–58

Name and Primary Occupation	Service and Constituency	Sessions in First Rank	Sessions in Second Rank
Pendleton, Edmund (lawyer)	1752–76: Caroline	1754; 1755; 1756; 1757–58; 1760–61; 1764–65; 1766–67; 1768; 1769–70; 1772	1752; 1753; 1758; 1759; 1761–62; 1762; 1769; 1773; 1774
Power, James (lawyer)	1742–47: King William 1752–58: New Kent	1754; 1755; 1756	1746–47; 1752
Randolph, Beverley (planter)	1744–49: College of William and Mary		1746–47
Randolph, Isham (planter)	1738–40: Goochland		1740
Randolph, Sir John (lawyer)	1734–36: College of William and Mary	1734; 1736	
Randolph, John, Jr. (lawyer)	1769: Lunenburg 1775–76: College of William and Mary		1775
Randolph, Peter (planter)	1749: Henrico		1748–49
Randolph, Peyton (lawyer)	1748–49, 1761–75: Williamsburg 1752–61: College of William and Mary	1748–49; 1752; 1753; 1755; 1756; 1757–58; 1758; 1759; 1760–61; 1761–62; 1762; 1764; 1764–65; 1766–67; 1768; 1769; 1769–70; 1771; 1772; 1773; 1774; 1775	
Randolph, Richard (planter)	1727–48: Henrico	1734; 1742; 1746–47	1730; 1732; 1736; 1740; 1744
Randolph, William, Sr. (planter)	1715–26: Henrico	1726	May, 1718; 1720; 1723
Randolph, William, Jr. (planter)	1752–61: Henrico	1757–58	1753; 1754; 1756; 1759
Reade, Clement (lawyer)	1748–54, 1758–63: Lunenburg		1752; 1753; 1759

Name and Primary Occupation	Service and Constituency	Sessions in First Rank	Sessions in Second Rank
Riddick, Lemuel (planter)	1736–68, 1769–75: Nansemond		1742; 1744; 1748–49; 1752; 1755; 1764–65; 1769–70; 1772
Robinson, Christopher (planter)	1752–58: Middlesex		1753
Robinson, John (planter)	1727–65: King & Queen	1732; 1734; 1736; 1738; 1740; 1742; 1744; 1746–47; 1748–49; 1752; 1753; 1754; 1755; 1756; 1757–58; 1758; 1759; 1760–61; 1761–62; 1762; 1763; 1764; 1764–65	
Ruffin, John (planter)	1754–55: Surry		1755
Starke, Bolling (lawyer)	1769–72: Dinwiddie		1769; 1769–70
Tabb, Thomas (merchant)	1748–58, 1761–69: Amelia		1766–67
Tayloe, John (planter)	1727–32: Richmond		1730; 1732
Walker, Thomas (physician)	1752–54: Louisa 1756–61: Hampshire 1761–76: Albemarle		1757–58; 1764–65; 1769–70
Waller, Benjamin (lawyer)	1744–61: James City	1746–47; 1748–49; 1752; 1754; 1755; 1756; 1757–58; 1760–61	1744; 1753; 1758; 1759
Waller, William (lawyer)	1742–53, 1756–60: Spotsylvania		1748–49; 1752
Washington, George (planter)	1758–65: Frederick 1766–76: Fairfax		1769–70; 1772
Whiting, Beverley (lawyer)	1738–55: Gloucester	1746–47; 1748–49; 1752; 1753	1744

Name and Primary Occupation	Service and Constituency	Sessions in First Rank	Sessions in Second Rank
Whiting, Thomas (planter)	1755–76: Gloucester		1775
Willis, Francis (planter)	1727–40, 1745–49: Gloucester		1732; 1734; 1738
Wood, James (planter)	1766, 1769–76: Frederick		1775
Woodson, John (planter)	1768–76: Goochland		1772; 1774
Wormeley, Ralph (planter)	1742–64: Middlesex		1748–49
Wythe, George (lawyer)	1754–55: Williamsburg 1758–61: College of William and Mary 1761–68: Elizabeth City	1764–65; 1766–67	1754; 1755; 1759; 1760–61; 1761–62; 1762

NOTE ON METHOD AND SOURCES

In preparing the above article and table, I have established seven categories of committees according to their relative importance and the nature of their work and, for lack of a better device, assigned numerical values to each. Five categories apply to committees appointed to handle the regular work of the legislative session. They are, in descending order of importance, standing committees, extraordinary committees, committees of the whole house, major committees, and routine committees. The standing committees and the committees of the whole house were so designated by the Burgesses. By the end of the colonial period there were six standing committees: privileges and elections, propositions and grievances, public claims, courts of justice, trade, and religion. They handled the bulk of house business and for that reason were certainly the most important. Chairmanships of the standing committees were, next to the speakership, the most honored posts in the house. I considered as extraordinary committees all those involved in determining matters of broad policy both in regard to internal affairs in Virginia and to Virginia's relations with the mother country, particularly during the years of crisis after 1763. The remaining committees I divided into two groups, those handling purely routine business and those concerned with matters of somewhat greater importance. The latter group I called major committees; the former, routine committees. In addition, the Burgesses occasionally appointed what might be called extrasessionary committees—that is, committees created to perform legislative or sometimes even executive tasks when the Burgesses was not in session. They included those to correspond with the London agent and those to supervise military expenditures during the French and Indian War. I divided them into major and minor committees.

To differentiate between the relative importance of these seven categories, I have assigned the following numerical values to the memberships and chairmanships of each: chairman, standing committee—15; member, standing committee—5; member, major extrasessionary committee—8; member, minor extrasessionary committee—6; chairman, extraordinary committee—7; member, extraordinary committee—4; chairman, committee of the whole—3; chairman, major committee—5; member, major committee—3; chairman, routine committee—3; member, routine committee—2.

I have ranked the individual burgesses for each session between 1720 and 1776 by counting up their total number of committee posts in each category, assigning them the stated values for each post, and in turn adding up those values. Obviously, this system is not entirely satisfactory, but it seems to me to reflect more accurately the value of each man's committee work than would a simple quantitative tabulation of the total number of his assignments.

AUBREY C. LAND

Economic Base and Social Structure: The Northern Chesapeake in the Eighteenth Century

The *Maryland Gazette* for 18 October 1749 carried an obituary of more than common interest:

On the Eleventh Instant Died, at his Seat on Wye River in Queen Anne's County, Richard Bennett, Esq. in the Eighty-third Year of his Age, generally lamented by all that knew him. As his great fortune enabled him to do much good, so (happily for many) his Inclination was equal to his Ability, to relieve the indigent and distressed, which he did very liberally, without regarding of what Party, Religion or Country, they were. As he was the greatest Trader in this Province, so great Numbers fell in his Debt, and a more merciful Creditor could not be, having never deprived the Widows or Orphans of his Debtors of a Support; and when what the Debtors left, was not sufficient for that purpose, frequently supply'd the deficiency. His long Experience and great Knowledge in Business, as well as his known Candor and generosity, occasion'd many to apply to him for Advice and Assistance, and none were ever disappointed of what was in his Power, and several by his means, extricated out of great Difficulties . . . .

A later issue adds some particulars:

On Wednesday last was solemnized the Funeral of Richard Bennett, Esq. of Wye River, in a very handsome and decent Manner, by the Direction

Aubrey C. Land, "Economic Base and Social Structure: The Northern Chesapeake in the Eighteenth Century," *Journal of Economic History*, 25 (1965): 639–54. Reprinted by permission of Aubrey C. Land and the Economic History Association.

of his sole executor, the Hon. Col. Edward Lloyd. Mr. Bennett, by his Will, has forgiven above one hundred and fifty of his poor Debtors, and has made Provision for the Maintainance of many of his Overseers, and other poor Dependents, and settled a Sum of Money to be paid annually to the Poor of a Parish in Virginia: and done many other Acts of Charity and Munificence. He was supposed to be the Richest Man on the Continent . . . .

Bennett's obvious virtues as a Christian gentleman need no underscoring, but two comments of the eulogist should be noted: his great wealth and his calling as a "trader." Perhaps the enthusiastic editor went beyond the exact truth in estimating Bennett's fortune, though probably not much. The field certainly included a few other candidates for the richest man. A neighbor across the Bay, Charles Carroll, counted his total worth at something like a hundred thousand pounds sterling, including £30,000 loaned at 6 per cent interest. Robert Carter, south of the Potomac in Virginia, could reckon himself worth nearly as much. The second William Byrd had left an impressive heritage which his son of the same name had already begun to dissipate. Even by the standards of London these were wealthy men.

All three alternate possibilities for the title of richest man are better known than Bennett, because they have had biographers, or because they played important political roles, or both. They belong to what has been variously called the aristocracy, the ruling oligarchy, or the squirearchy. The pejorative connotations of all three terms incline me toward a label suggested by a profound student of early American social and cultural history [Louis B. Wright], "the southern agrarian leaders." We can understand them in a sense as leaders of an agrarian area. But when we inquire about the economic milieu in which they flourished or seek the mechanisms by which they acquired their dominant positions, we are faced with some difficulties.

The traditional historiography has leaned heavily on literary evidence, and when it does not ignore these questions often gives impressions that are positively misleading. As sources, personal letters, travel accounts, and memoirs have the great merit of being relatively easy to put into context and ideal to paraphrase. A few dozen up to a few thousand items of this kind can be quilted into interesting and convincing patterns. The procedure has the limitations of the sources. Even the most acute observer focuses on objects of high visibility. The high tor eclipses the molehill in the landscape until the king falls to his death because of the "little gentleman in black velvet."

In the eighteenth-century Chesapeake, the "great planters" were the element of high visibility. They held slaves, owned vast estates, and built magnificent houses that have survived as showpieces. Visitors came under the spell of these gracious livers and left charming accounts of their balls, their tables, and their luxury. Planters themselves contributed to the effect. They wrote letters and a few left diaries that have survived along with their great houses. Viewed through these sources they cut large figures and play the star roles in the arrangements that the people of the Chesapeake made for themselves in that period. These personages are accurately enough drawn, but they are a detail, though an important one, in the total production. Unfortunately the supporting cast and stage hands that made the production possible receive next to no attention, sometimes not even the courtesy of a billing. Just as *Hamlet* cannot be successfully staged without Hamlet, there can hardly be a play with Hamlet alone.

Not much literary evidence for the minor figures has come down; but another kind does exist and, even though bristling with difficulties and overawing in bulk, it can be compelled to yield some data for a fuller view. This body of material has been brought together in two despositories, the Maryland Hall of Records and the Virginia State Archives, and properly canvassed will fill in some gaps in our knowledge of Chesapeake affairs. It consists of inventories and accounts of the estates in personalty of all free men at the time of their death. The argument in this paper applies only to Maryland, for which a statistical analysis has been completed. The Virginia counties that have been analyzed give me the clear impression that differences between the areas north and south of the Potomac are not very great in respect of the basic contention here. Both were a part of a single economic region which political boundaries could not split asunder and were treated as a unit in contemporary British commercial records.

To obtain from the voluminous Maryland records a sample that faithfully reflects conditions in the northern Chesapeake, some of the usual economies are not possible. Geographical sampling by selected counties is ruled out. The process of carving new counties out of large older counties went on continuously from 1690 to the Revolution. Consequently the county of one decade is not necessarily the same unit in a later decade. Accordingly, all counties of the province are included. Over the entire eighty-year period 1690–1770 for which the records are reasonably complete the alternate decades from 1690–1699 to 1750–1759 have been tabulated. If it can be assumed that these sizable samples reflect with reasonable accuracy the spectrum of planters' estates, then we have some basis for understanding an otherwise shadowy aspect of the Chesapeake economy.

The profile of estates in the decade January 1, 1690, to December

31, 1699, shows an unexpected imbalance. Three quarters of these estates (74.6 per cent, to be precise) are of the magnitude £100 sterling or less. In the next bracket, £100 to £200, the percentage drops to 12.1, and in succeeding hundred-pound brackets to 5.5 per cent, 2.7 per cent, 1.4 per cent, 1.3 per cent, 0.6 per cent, and 0.3 per cent. After a break in the distribution, a meager 1.5 per cent at the top are valued at £1,000 sterling or greater.

Beyond the obvious fact that the less affluent far outnumber the better off, this analysis tells us little. The estates, small or great, are all those of planters—a handful of physicians, mariners, and clergymen specifically excepted. "Planter," then, simply describes an occupation without indicating economic status of the individual. To get at what this distribution means in terms of worldly goods, standard of living, and possibly social status, it is necessary to look at particulars in the inventories themselves. Here impressions become vivid.

The planters at the bottom of the scale, those with estates of £100 or less, have at best a "country living": a saddle horse or two, half a dozen or fewer cows, a few swine to furnish fresh or salt meat for the table according to the season, a modest assortment of household utensils—sometimes nothing more than a cooking pot or skillet, a few tools and agricultural implements. Many essentials of a household—for instance, plates and cups—are missing in fully half the inventories, an omission indicating that makeshifts such as wooden bowls and gourds took the place of these articles. The appraisers of estates overlooked no article, not even a cracked cup without a handle or a single glass bottle. In brief the standard of living might be described as rude sufficiency. The self-styled poet laureate of Maryland, Eben Cooke, calls planters at this level "cockerouses."

The inventories also speak to the productivity of these small planters. In those inventories made during the autumn and winter after the tobacco had been cut the appraisers carefully estimated the size of the deceased's crop. Crop entries range from twelve hundred pounds, a trifle over two hogsheads, up to three thousand pounds, or about six hogsheads. This represented the producer's cash crop, almost his entire annual income, excepting possibly the occasional sale of a heifer, a pig, or a few bushels of corn to a neighbor or local trader. Reckoning the price of tobacco at ten shillings a hundred, these small producers could count their disposable incomes at a figure between £6 and £15 a year.

Even taking into account the small planter's self-sufficiency in fresh vegetables from the kitchen garden, cereals from whatever field crops he grew besides tobacco, and meat from his own farm animals, an income of this size imposed iron limitations on him. Between investment and consumption he had no choice. Such necessities as thread, needles, powder and shot, coarse fabrics for clothing or featherbeds, and an occasional tool or a household utensil strained his credit at the country store until his crop was sold. For the small planter, provincial quitrents, church tithes, and taxes represented a a real burden. He cast his ballot for a representative who could resist the blandishments of governors and hold public expenses to the barest minimum. In good part the pressures from men of his kind kept investment in the public sector to lowest dimensions, whether the object was a county courthouse, a lighthouse, or a governor's mansion. As a private person he could not invest from savings because he had none. With tobacco crops barely sufficient to cover his debt to the country merchant, a disastrous year could prostrate him. A lawsuit, the death of cattle in a winter freeze, or a fire in house or barn forced him to contract debts which had often not been paid at the time of his death and which ate up his entire personal estate, leaving his heirs without a penny. Not infrequently his administrator actually overpaid his estate in order to save trifling family heirlooms more precious than their valuation in the inventory. Investment in a slave or indentured servant to increase his productivity, though not completely out of the question, was very difficult.

The small planter clearly was not the beneficiary of the planting society of the Chesapeake. He bred his increase and added to the growing population that filled up vacant land from the shoreline to the mountains before the Revolution. In the language of the courts he qualified as a planter. Considering the circumstances of his life, it would stretch the usual meaning of the term to call him a yeoman, particularly if he fell in the lower half of his group.

In the brackets above £100, different characteristics of the estates immediately strike the eye. Sumptuary standards of planters above this line were obviously higher. Kitchens had ampler stocks of utensils; and for dining, earthenware and china replaced the gourds and wooden makeshifts that apparently were the rule on tables of families in the lowest economic bracket. Ticking stuffed with flock gave way to bedsteads and bedding. Even more striking is the prevalence of bond labor, both indentured servants and slaves, in this higher stratum. The transition comes abruptly. In estates below £100, servants or slaves rarely appear and then only in those within a few pounds of the line. In the estates at £100 to £200, the inventories of eight out of ten estates list bond labor—a higher percentage, actually, than in any of the succeeding £100 brackets up to £500.

In fact, these estates falling between £100 and £500 form a relatively homogeneous group. Altogether they comprise 21.7 per cent of all estates. Though existence for the planter is less frugal, his worldly goods show few signs of real luxury. Not a single estate was debt free, though fewer than a tenth had debts amounting to more than half the value of the inventory. The number of slaves in single estates does not run high: from one to five in 90 per cent of the estates that had them at all. Yet even this small number represented between half and two thirds of the appraised valuation. Reflecting the additional hands for husbandry, tobacco crops ran higher roughly in proportion to the number of slaves or indentured servants. Crops ranged from twelve hundred pounds (planters with no bond labor) up to nearly twenty thousand pounds, or from a little over two up to forty hogsheads. Again using ten shillings per hundred for transforming tobacco values to sterling, we can put the incomes from tobacco production alone between £6 and £100 a year. Other sources of income for families with bond labor should not be ruled out. Doubtless off-season occupations such as riving staves or shingles, sawing plank, and making cereal crops occupied some productive time. Unfortunately only occasional data on this type of product appear, enough to call for acknowledgment but insufficient for measurement.

Nevertheless, with annual incomes of these dimensions from their tobacco crops, planters in this group had alternatives not open to the lowest income group. As respectable citizens with community obligations to act as overseers of roads, appraisers of estates and similar duties, they might choose to lay by something to see their sons and daughters decently started in turn as planters or wives of planters. Or they might within the limitations of their estates live the good life, balancing consumption against income. Social pressure must have urged them in this direction, to a round of activities that included local politics and such country entertainments as dances, horseracing, and cockfights, occasionally punctuated with drinking brawls complete with eye-gougings and other practices not usually associated with the genteel life of the planter. Whatever the choice it is difficult to see how the planter in these circumstances could add appreciably to his estate in a short period of years, or even in a lifetime.

Still further up the scale, the estates appraised at sums above £500 form an even smaller percentage of the total. The five £100 brackets between £500 and £1,000 include altogether 2.2 per cent of all estates. At first glance this small group appears to be a plusher version of the preceding: somewhat more slaves, larger tobacco crops, more personal goods including some luxury items. These are planters of substance, much closer to the stereotype, as the character and contents of their inventories show. And in their activities they moved on a higher plane. One had represented his county for a term in the General Assembly and another had served on the county court as a justice of the peace. In the matter of indebtedness, however, some interesting differences appear. Just over half the inventories list debts owed to the estate among the major assets. In a few cases the portion of total assets in the form of debts owed the estate runs to half or more.

What I think we see here is an emerging business or entrepreneurial element, a small group of planters with sources of income other than planting alone. All were planters in the sense that they, or their bond labor, produced tobacco crops. But the appreciable number in the creditor category have other concerns. The nature of these concerns appears more clearly in the most affluent element, whose members can be studied individually as cases.

This element includes all persons with estates inventoried at more than £1,000 sterling. In the decade 1690–1699, they represent 1.6 per cent of the total. They were the "great planters" of the day.

The smallest estate in personalty, that of Nicholas Gassaway of Anne Arundel County, was inventoried at £1,017 14s. 11½d. sterling; the largest, that of Henry Coursey of Talbot County, at £1,667 17s. 1¼d. Perhaps estates of this size would have cut a mean figure beside those of the sugar planters of the West Indies. In the northern Chesapeake of the closing years of the seventeenth century, they loom high.

The composition of these largest estates varies a bit from what we might expect of the great planter's holdings. Slaves comprise less than a quarter of the assets and, in several, less than a fifth. It should be remembered that this decade lies in the transition period when slaves were displacing indentured servants as field labor. Even so, the numbers seem unimpressive—often no greater than slave holdings in estates a third as large. By contrast, the number and the amount of assets in the form of debts owed the estate are striking. Altogether they comprised between a quarter and a half of the assets in individual estates. In one of the largest estates, debts owed the deceased came to 78 per cent of the total assets.

The inventories themselves give some clues as to how these large planters had become creditors. Occasionally an industrious appraiser included information on how the debtor had incurred his obligation: for a pipe of wine, for a parcel of steers, for corn, for rent of a certain property, for goods. In short, the great planter had also become a "trader." Frequently a portion of the inventory is simply labeled "in the store" and the contents of that room or building listed under this heading. Then the origin of the debts becomes clear. Sometimes they ran well over a hundred major items and were carefully listed under captions "sperate debts" and "desperate debts."

Putting this cross section or sample against the general outlines of the Chesapeake economy, I suggest the hypothesis that the men of first fortune belonged functionally to a class whose success stemmed from entrepreneurial activities as much as, or even more than, from their direct operations as producers of tobacco. The Chesapeake closely resembles pioneer economies of other times and places. It was a region with a relatively low ratio of population to resources and an equally low ratio of capital to resources. External commerce was characterized by heavy staple exports and high capital imports. Internally this flow created a current of high capital investment, full employment, profit inflation, and rising property values. The tobacco staple did not lend itself to bonanza agriculture, as did sugar in the West India islands where fortunes could be made in a decade. Consequently the Chesapeake planters did not go "back home" to dazzle the populace with their wealth. Their returns derived in the first instance from tobacco production, which afforded a competence, and secondly from enterprise, which gave greater rewards. As entrepreneurs, they gave the Chesapeake economy both organization and direction. They took the risks, made the decisions, and reaped the rewards or paid the penalties. And they worked unremittingly at these tasks, which could not be performed in their absence by the small planter or by overseers.

It is not easy to analyze the activities of this economic elite into neat categories. They were at once planters, political leaders, and businessmen. The first two roles tend to obscure the last. Their role in politics is a textbook commonplace. As planters they lived in the great tradition, some even ostentatiously. On this point testimony is abundant and unambiguous. Had they depended solely on the produce of their tobacco fields, they doubtless would have lived up to or beyond current income. And some did. But in fact many among them increased their fortunes substantially and a few spectacularly, while still maintaining their reputations as good livers. During the early years of the eighteenth century, when the tobacco trade was far from booming, some of the first families of the Chesapeake established themselves as permanent fixtures. Several had come to the first rank, or very near it, both in politics and wealth, by 1700: the Taskers, the Catholic Carrolls, the Lloyds, and the Trumans. Others, less well known but eventually architects of equal or greater fortunes, were rising in the scale within another decade: the Bordleys, the Chews, the Garretts, the Dulanys, the Bennetts, and the Protestant Carrolls. The secret of their success was business enterprise, though almost to a man they lived as planters separated from the kind of urban community in which their more conspicuously entrepreneurial counterparts to the north had their residences and places of business. An examination of the chief forms of enterprise discloses the mechanisms by which they came to the top of the heap.

One of the most profitable enterprises and one most commonly associated with the great planters of the Chesapeake, land speculation, appears early in the eighteenth century in both Virginia and Maryland. The Virginia Rent Roll of 1704, admitted as imperfect but the best that could be done at the time, shows half a dozen holdings that suggest speculative intent. After these tentative beginnings, speculators moved quite aggressively during the administration of Spotswood and his successors, when hugh grants in the vacant back country became commonplace events for privileged insiders, with the governors themselves sharing the spoils of His Majesty's bounty. In the more carefully regulated land system of Maryland, agents of the Lords Baltimore made a few large grants to favored persons like Charles Carroll the Settler in the first two decades of the century. During these same decades other wary speculators took up occasional large grants. The Maryland system compelled speculators to be cautious, because it exacted some money for the patents and made evasion of quitrents nearly impossible. But by the 1730's, eager speculators had glimpsed a vision of the possible returns and kept the land office busy issuing warrants for unpatented areas. For a relatively modest outlay a small number of Marylanders obtained assets with which they experimented for years before discovering the last trick in turning them to account.

Speculators capitalized their assets in two chief ways, both enormously profitable. First, as landlords of the wild lands, they leased to tenants who paid rents and at the same time improved their leaseholds by clearing, planting orchards, and erecting houses, barns, and fences. Almost exclusively long-term leases, either for years (commonly twenty-one) or for lives, these instruments specified the improvements to be made. Tenants who could not save from current income thus under compulsion contributed their bit to capital formation to the ultimate benefit of the landlord. Literary sources give the impression that tenancy was not very widespread, but the records tell another story. Something over a third of the planters in the lowest £100 bracket in Maryland leased their land. Secondly, the large landholder sold off plantation-size parcels as settlement enveloped his holdings and brought values to the desired level. Not content to leave this movement to chance, many speculators hastened the process by encouraging immigration and by directing the movement of settlers toward their own properties. Jonathan Hagar in Maryland and William Byrd in Virginia are two among many who attempted to enhance the value of their properties in this way. It is difficult to determine profits even for single speculators except for short periods. Experience must have varied widely, and undoubtedly some speculators failed. But some of the successful ones made incredible gains in a relatively short span of years.

Even more ubiquitous than the planter-speculator was the planter-merchant. The inventories and accounts contain much evidence on the organization of commerce in the tobacco counties of the Chesapeake. Hardly a parish lacked one or more country stores, often no more than a tiny hut or part of a building on the grounds of a planter who could supply, usually on credit, the basic needs of neighboring small producers—drygoods, hoes and other small implements, salt, sugar, spices, tea, and almost always liquor. Inventories show some small stores with a mere handful of those articles in constant demand. Others had elaborate stocks of women's hats, mirrors, mourning gloves, ribbons, patent medicines, and luxury goods. The names of several great families are associated with country stores, particularly in the earlier generations of the line. Frequently, store-keeping duties fell to a trusted servant or to a younger member of the family as a part of his training. Occasionally, an apprentice from one of the county families came to learn the mysteries of trade by measuring out fabrics or liquors and keeping the accounts.

As with land speculation, determining profits of merchants is next to impossible. Consumers complained bitterly of high markups, and a few storekeepers boasted of them. Even so, the country merchant's profits were not limited to sale of goods alone. He stood to gain on another transaction. He took his payment in tobacco, the crops of the two- to six-hogshead producers. The small planter participated directly in the consignment system of the early eighteenth century only to a limited extent. His petty wants and his small crop hardly justified the London merchant's time and trouble in maintaining him as a separate account. His nexus to the overseas market was the provincial merchant, who took tobacco at prices that allowed at least a small profit to himself on every hogshead.

Closely allied to merchandising, moneylending presents almost as great problems of analysis. The Chesapeake economy operated on an

elaborate network of credit arrangements. Jefferson's famous remark
that Virginia planters were a species of property attached to certain
great British merchant houses may have been true of some planters, as
it was of Jefferson himself. But the observation has created a mis-
chievous view of credit relations between England and the tobacco
colonies and does not describe the debt pattern within the area at all
accurately. A full account awaits the onslaught of an industrious
graduate student armed with electronic tapes and computers. Meanwhile the accounts can tell us something. Country merchants had to
be prepared to extend credit beyond that for goods purchased by their
customers. They paid for some of their customers at least the church
tithes, the tax levies, and the freedom dues of indentured servants
who had served their terms. These petty book debts could be collected
with interest in any county court. Loans to artisans—the shoemakers,
tanners, and blacksmiths who multiplied in number toward mid century—were of a different order. For working capital, the artisan in
need of £5 to £20 and upward turned to men of means, the "traders."
Far from abating, the demand for capital increased as the century
wore on.

Investment opportunities were never lacking for planters with
ready money or with credit in England. As lenders, they squarely
faced the conflict of the law and the profits. By law they could take
interest at 6 per cent for money loans and 8 per cent for tobacco
loans. One wonders why the Carrolls chose to loan their £30,000
sterling at 6 per cent, even on impeccable securities. Could the answer be in part that returns at this rate equaled those from further
investment in planting? At any rate they did choose to lend, following the example of Bennett and a dozen or so others.

Far more profitable as an investment opportunity, manufacturing
exercised an enduring fascination on imaginative men of the Chesapeake. During Virginia Company days, before the first settlement of
Maryland, glass and iron had figured among the projects launched
under Company stimulus. Although these had come to ruin in the
massacre of 1622, Virginians never gave up hope of producing iron.

Their success was limited; but in the upper reaches of the Bay a
combination of easily worked ore, limitless forests for charcoal, oyster
shell, and water transportation from the furnace site invited exploitation. British syndicates moved first to establish the Principio Works
and later the Nottingham and Lancashire works. These remained in
British hands until the Revolutionary confiscations. Last of the big
four, the Baltimore Iron Works (1733) became the largest producer

and the biggest money-maker. Five Maryland investors subscribed the initial capital of £3,500 sterling. The Baltimore enterprise was a triumph for native capital, though technicians and technology were both imported from Britain. After the first three years of operation the partners received handsome dividends but always plowed a substantial part of the profits back into the enterprise. By the early 1760's the share of each partner was valued at £6,000 sterling. The five partners were among the first fortunes in Maryland.

Beyond iron making, other forms of enterprise (mostly small-scale manufacturing or processing) attracted investment capital. In nearly all areas of the Chesapeake some shipbuilding, cooperage, and milling establishments provided essential local services or commodities. None of these required either the capital outlay or the organization of an ironworks. Consequently, as enterprises they were attractive to investors with modest capital but large ambitions. In the area of Baltimore, flour milling developed major proportions after mid century, as the upper counties of Maryland found grain more profitable than tobacco as a field crop.

An astonishing percentage of the personal fortunes of the northern Chesapeake had their roots in law practice. While not entrepreneurial in a technical sense, the rewards went to the enterprising. During the seventeenth century lawyers were neither numerous nor always in good odor. Private persons attended to their own legal business in the courts. By 1700, the fashion had changed as the courts insisted on greater formality in pleading and as the cumbersome machinery of the common law compelled the uninstructed to turn to the professional. Pleading "by his attorney" swiftly replaced appearances *in propria persona*. Still the legal profession remained trammeled. Laws strictly regulated fees attorneys could take and kept these at levels low enough that the ablest members of the Maryland bar went on strike in the 1720's. What lawyers lacked in size of fees they made up in number of cases. An attorney might, and frequently did, bring thirty or forty cases to trial in a three- or four-day session of a county court. Had these been litigation over land, an impression widely held by students who use the *Virginia Reports* and the *Maryland Reports*, attorneys might have spent their entire time in title searches, examining witnesses, and preparing their cases. The court proceedings at large, however, show fifty cases of debt collection for every case over land; and sometimes the ratio runs as high as a hundred to one. One traveler to the Chesapeake, remarking on the "litigious spirit," wryly concluded that this spectacle of everybody suing everybody else was a kind of sport peculiar to the area. In fact, the numbers of suits grew out of the very arrangements—a tissue of book debts, bills of exchange, and promissory notes—that kept the mechanism operating.

In this milieu the lawyer had an enviable position. From his practice he derived a steady income freed from direct dependence on returns from the annual tobacco fleet. In a phrase, he had ready money the year 'round. Furthermore, he had an intimate knowledge of the resources and dependability of the planters in the county—and, indeed, throughout the province if he also practiced at the bar of the superior courts. Consequently he could take advantage of opportunities on the spot, whether they were bargains in land, sales of goods or produce, or tenants seeking leases. He could besides avoid the costs of litigation that inevitably arose as he involved himself in land speculation, lending, or merchandising, as many did. As a rule the lawyers did well, and the most enterprising moved into the highest brackets of wealth. Perhaps the most spectacular example, Thomas Bordley, a younger son of a Yorkshire schoolmaster, came from an impecunious immigrant apprentice in a Maryland law office to distinction in the law, in politics, and in Maryland society within the span of a short lifetime. After his premature death in 1726 his executors brought to probate the largest estate in the history of the province to that time.

Quite commonly, lawyers added a minor dimension to their income from office holding. A fair percentage of Maryland offices were sinecures that could be executed by deputies for a fraction of the fees. Most carried modest stipends, but a few eagerly-sought prizes paid handsomely. Baltimore's provincial secretary received £1,000 per annum.

This is not the place to argue the returns from planting, pure and simple. Many planters did well without other sources of income. But impressive fortunes went to those who, in addition, put their talents to work in some of the ways described above. A few engaged in all. The list is finite, for we are referring here to a small percentage of planters, those with estates above £1,000: in that decade 1690–1699 to 1.6 per cent, in 1710–1719 to 2.2 per cent, in 1730–1739 to 3.6 per cent, and in 1750–1759 to 3.9 per cent. When tabulated and examined for group characteristics, they resemble functionally a type that could easily come under that comprehensive eighteenth-century term, merchant. They look very unlike the planter of the moonlight-and-magnolias variety. It is a commentary on the prosperity of the northern Chesapeake that, as this favored category increased in percentage and in absolute numbers, so did the magnitude of its members' individual fortunes. The sample taken just before the turn of the century shows top fortunes between £1,000 and £2,000, with none above. The sample decade 1730–1739 includes an appreciable number over £2,000. The two largest were those of Samuel Chew (£9,937) and Amos Garrett (£11,508), both merchants. Even these did not match the fortunes left by Dr. Charles Carroll and Daniel Dulany the Elder in the decade 1750–1759, nor that of Benjamin Tasker in the next.

The poor were not excluded, individually or as a group, from the general prosperity of the Chesapeake. Four individuals—Thomas Macnemara, Thomas Bordley, Daniel Dulany, and Dr. Charles Carroll—moved up the scale from nothing to the top bracket of wealth, two of them from indentured servitude. These were extraordinary men, but their careers indicate the avenues open to their combination of talents for the law, land speculation, moneylending, merchandising, and manufacturing in which they engaged. Of course all were planters as well.

But for the mass, advance was by comparison glacial. The composition of the base on which such performances took place changed more slowly. In the fourth decade of the eighteenth century the percentage of planters in the lowest economic group, those with estates of £100 or less, had fallen to 54.7 per cent, in marked contrast to the 74.6 per cent of the decade 1690–1699. Between the same two sample decades the percentage in the next higher category of estates (£100 to £500) had increased to 35.7 per cent from 21.7 per cent. If this means that the poor were getting richer, it also means for the great majority that they were doing so by short and slow steps. Together, these two lowest categories still made up 90.4 per cent of the planting families in 1730–1739, as compared with 96.3 per cent in the last decade of the seventeenth century. Nonetheless, the shift toward a higher standard of living within this huge mass of lesser planters is quite as important a commentary on the economic well-being of the Chesapeake as is the growth in numbers and magnitude of the great fortunes.

It is never easy to know just how much to claim for statistical evidence. Perhaps there is enough here to raise doubts about the descriptive accuracy of reports from Chesapeake planters themselves. These sound like a protracted wail of hard times, rising occasionally in crescendo to prophecies of impending ruin. Yet even during the early and least prosperous decades, the northern Chesapeake experienced some growth. During the second quarter of the century and on into the following decades the samples made for this study indicate a quickened rate. The results worked no magic change in the way of life or economic station for the small planter, the mass of Maryland. These were always the overwhelming percentage of the producers. As a social group they come in for little notice. Their lives lack the glitter and incident that has made the great planter the focus of all eyes. By the standards of the affluent society theirs was a drab, rather humdrum, existence bound to the annual rhythm of the field crop. The highest rewards were for those who could transcend the routine of producing tobacco and develop the gainful activities that kept the economy functioning.

RHYS ISAAC

Evangelical Revolt:
The Nature of the Baptists' Challenge to the Traditional Order in Virginia, 1765 to 1775

An intense struggle for allegiance had developed in the Virginia countryside during the decade before the Revolution. Two eyewitness accounts may open to us the nature of the conflict.

First, a scene vividly remembered and described by the Reverend James Ireland etches in sharp profile the postures of the forces in contest. As a young man Ireland, who was a propertyless schoolmaster of genteel origin, had cut a considerable figure in Frederick County society. His success had arisen largely from his prowess at dancing and his gay facility as a satiric wit. Then, like many other young men at this time (*ca.* 1768), he came deeply "under conviction of sin" and withdrew from the convivialities of gentry society. When an older friend and patron of Ireland heard that his young protégé could not be expected at a forthcoming assembly, this gentleman, a leader in county society, sensed the challenge to his way of life that was implicit in Ireland's withdrawal. He swore instantly that "there could not be a dance in the settlement without [Ireland] being there, and if they would leave it to him, he would convert [him], and that to the dance, on Monday; and they would see [Ireland] lead the ball that day." Frederick County, for all its geographical spread, was a

Rhys Isaac, "Evangelical Revolt: The Nature of the Baptists' Challenge to the Traditional Order in Virginia, 1765 to 1775," *William and Mary Quarterly*, 3rd ser., 31 (1974):345–68. Copyright © 1974 by Rhys Isaac; reprinted by permission.

close community. Young James learned that his patron would call, and dreaded the coming test of strength:

When I viewed him riding up, I never beheld such a display of pride arising from his deportment, attitude and jesture; he rode a lofty elegant horse, . . . his countenance appeared to me as bold and daring as satan himself, and with a commanding authority [he] called upon me, if I were there to come out, which I accordingly did, with a fearful and timorous heart. But O! how quickly can God level pride. . . . For no sooner did he behold my disconsolate looks, emaciated countenance and solemn aspect, than he . . . was riveted to the beast he rode on. . . . As soon as he could articulate a little his eyes fixed upon me, and his first address was this; "In the name of the Lord, what is the matter with you?"

The evident overdramatization in this account is its most revealing feature for it is eloquent concerning the tormented convert's heightened awareness of the contrast between this social world he was leaving and the one he was entering.

The struggle for allegiance between these social worlds had begun with the Great Awakening in the 1740s, but entered into its most fierce and bitter phase with the incursions of the "New Light" Separate Baptists into the older parts of Virginia in the years after 1765. The social conflict was not over the distribution of political power or of economic wealth, but over the ways of men and the ways of God. By the figures in the encounter described we may begin to know the sides drawn: on the one hand, a mounted gentleman of the world with "commanding authority" responding to challenge; on the other, a guilt-humbled, God-possessed youth with "disconsolate looks . . . and solemn aspect."

A second scene—this time in the Tidewater—reveals through actions some characteristic responses of the forces arrayed. From a diary entry of 1771 we have a description of the disruption of a Baptist meeting by some gentlemen and their followers, intent on upholding the cause of the established Church:

Brother Waller informed us . . . [that] about two weeks ago on the Sabbath Day down in Caroline County he introduced the worship of God by singing. . . . The Parson of the Parish [who had ridden up with his clerk, the sheriff, and some others] would keep running the end of his horsewhip in [Waller's] mouth, laying his whip across the hymn book, etc. When done singing [Waller] proceeded to prayer. In it he was violently jerked off the stage; they caught him by the back part of his neck, beat his head against the ground, sometimes up, sometimes down, they carried him through a gate that stood some considerable distance, where a gentleman [the sheriff] gave him . . . twenty lashes with his horsewhip. . . . Then Bro. Waller was released, went back singing praise to God, mounted the stage and preached with a great deal of liberty.

Violence of this kind had become a recurrent feature of social-religious life in Tidewater and Piedmont. We must ask: What kind of conflict was this? What was it that aroused such antagonism? What manner of man, what manner of movement, was it that found liberty in endurance under the lash?

The continuation of the account gives fuller understanding of the meaning of this "liberty" and of the true character of this encounter. Asked "if his nature did not interfere in the time of violent persecution, when whipped, etc.," Waller "answered that the Lord stood by him . . . and poured his love into his soul without measure, and the brethren and sisters about him singing praises . . . so that he could scarcely feel the stripes . . . rejoicing . . . that he was worthy to suffer for his dear Lord and Master.

Again we see contrasted postures: on the one hand, a forceful, indeed brutal, response to the implicit challenge of religious dissidence; on the other, an acceptance of suffering sustained by shared emotions that gave release—"liberty." Both sides were, of course, engaged in combat, yet their modes of conducting themselves were diametrically opposite. If we are to understand the struggle that had developed, we must look as deeply as possible into the divergent styles of life, at the conflicting visions of what life should be like, that are reflected in this episode.

Opposites are intimately linked not only by the societal context in which they occur but also by the very antagonism that orients them to each other. The strength of the fascination that existed in this case is evident from the recurrent accounts of men drawn to Baptist meetings to make violent opposition, who, at the time or later, came "under conviction" and experienced conversion. The study of a polarity such as we find in the Virginia pre-Revolutionary religious scene should illuminate not only the conflict but also some of the fundamental structures of the society in which it occurred. A profile of the style of the gentry, and of those for whom they were a pattern, must be attempted. Their values, and the system by which these values were maintained, must be sketched. A somewhat fuller contrasting picture of the less familiar Virginia Baptist culture must then be offered, so that its character as a radical social movement is indicated.

The gentry style, of which we have seen glimpses in the confrontation with Baptists, is best understood in relation to the concept of honor—the proving of prowess. A formality of manners barely concealed adversary relationships; the essence of social exchange was overt self-assertion.

Display and bearing were important aspects of this system. We can best get a sense of the self-images that underlay it from the symbolic importance of horses. The figure of the gentleman who came to call Ireland back to society was etched on his memory as mounted on a "lofty . . . elegant horse." It was noted repeatedly in the eighteenth century that Virginians would "go five miles to catch a horse, to ride only one mile upon afterwards." This apparent absurdity had its logic in the necessity of being mounted when making an entrance on the social scene. The role of the steed as a valuable part of proud self-presentation is suggested by the intimate identification of the gentry with their horses that was constantly manifested through their conversation. Philip Fithian, the New Jersey tutor, sometimes felt that he heard nothing but "Loud disputes concerning the Excellence of each others Colts . . . their Fathers, Mothers (for so they call the Dams) Brothers, Sisters, Uncles, Aunts, Nephews, Nieces, and Cousins to the fourth Degree!"

Where did the essential display and self-assertion take place? There were few towns in Virginia; the outstanding characteristic of settlement was its diffuseness. Population was rather thinly scattered in very small groupings throughout a forested, river-dissected landscape. If there is to be larger community in such circumstances, there must be centers of action and communication. Insofar as cohesion is important in such an agrarian society, considerable significance must attach to the occasions when, coming together for certain purposes, the community realizes itself. The principal public centers in traditional Virginia were the parish churches and the county courthouses, with lesser foci established in a scatter of inns or "ordinaries." The principal general gatherings apart from these centers were for gala events such as horse race meetings and cockfights. Although lacking a specifically community character, the great estate house was also undoubtedly a very significant locus of action. By the operation of mimetic process and by the reinforcement of expectations concerning conduct and relationships, such centers and occasions were integral parts of the system of social control.

The most frequently held public gatherings at generally distributed centers were those for Sunday worship in the Anglican churches and chapels. An ideal identification of parish and community had been expressed in the law, making persistent absence from church punishable. The continuance of this ideal is indicated by the fact that prosecutions under the law occurred right up to the time of the Revolution.

Philip Fithian has left us a number of vivid sketches of the typical Sunday scene at a parish church, sketches that illuminate the social nature and function of this institution. It was an important center of communication, especially among the elite, for it was "a general custom on Sundays here, with Gentlemen to invite one another home to dine, after Church; and to consult about, determine their common business, either before or after Service," when they would engage in discussing "the price of Tobacco, Grain etc. and settling either the lineage, Age, or qualities of favourite Horses." The occasion also served to demonstrate to the community, by visual representation, the rank structure of society. Fithian's further description evokes a dramatic image of haughty squires trampling past seated hoi polloi to their pews in the front. He noted that it was "not the Custom for Gentlemen to go into Church til Service is beginning, when they enter in a Body, in the same manner as they come out."

Similarly, vestry records show that fifty miles to the south of Fithian's Westmoreland County the front pews of a King and Queen County church were allocated to the gentry, but the pressure for place and precedence was such that only the greatest dignitaries (like the Corbins) could be accommodated together with their families; lesser gentlemen represented the honor of their houses in single places while their wives were seated farther back.

The size and composition of the ordinary congregations in the midst of which these representations of social style and status took place is as yet uncertain, but Fithian's description of a high festival is very suggestive on two counts: "This being Easter-Sunday, all the Parish seem'd to meet together High, Low, black, White all come out." We learn both that such general attendance was unusual, and that at least once a year full expression of ritual community was achieved. The whole society was then led to see itself in order.

The county courthouse was a most important center of social action. Monthly court days were attended by great numbers, for these were also the times for markets and fairs. The facts of social dominance were there visibly represented by the bearing of the "gentlemen justices" and the respect they commanded. On court days economic exchange was openly merged with social exchange (both plentifully sealed by the taking of liquor) and also expressed in conventional forms of aggression—in banter, swearing, and fighting.

The ruling gentry, who set the tone in this society, lived scattered across broad counties in the midst of concentrations of slaves that often amounted to black villages. Clearly the great houses that they erected in these settings were important statements: they expressed a style, they asserted a claim to dominance. The lavish entertainments, often lasting days, which were held in these houses performed equally important social functions in maintaining this claim, and in establishing communication and control within the elite itself. Here the convivial contests that were so essential to traditional Virginia social culture would issue in their most elaborate and stylish performances.

The importance of sporting occasions such as horse racing meets and cockfights for the maintenance of the values of self-assertion, in challenge and response, is strongly suggested by the comments of the marquis de Chastellux concerning cockfighting. His observations, dating from 1782, were that "when the principal promoters of this diversion [who were certainly gentry] propose to [match] their champions, they take great care to announce it to the public; and although there are neither posts, nor regular conveyances, this important news spreads with such facility, that the planters for thirty or forty miles round, attend, some with cocks, but all with money for betting, which is sometimes very considerable." An intensely shared interest of this kind, crossing but not leveling social distinctions, has powerful effects in transmitting style and reinforcing the leadership of the elite that controls proceedings and excels in the display.

Discussion so far has focused on the gentry, for *there* was established in dominant form the way of life the Baptists appeared to challenge. Yet this way was diffused throughout the society. All the forms of communication and exchange noted already had their popular acceptances with variations appropriate to the context, as can be seen in the recollections of the young Devereux Jarratt. The son of a middling farmer-artisan, Jarratt grew up totally intimidated by the proximity of gentlemen, yet his marked preference for engagement "in keeping and exercising race-horses for the turf . . . in taking care of and preparing game-cocks for a match and main" served to bind him nonetheless into the gentry social world, and would, had he persisted, have brought him into contact—gratifying contact—with gentlemen. The remembered images of his upbringing among the small farmers of Tidewater New Kent County are strongly evocative of the cultural continuum between his humble social world and that of the gentry. In addition to the absorbing contest pastimes mentioned, there were the card play, the gathering at farmhouses for drinking (cider not wine), violin playing, and dancing.

The importance of pastime as a channel of communication, and even as a bond, between the ranks of a society such as this can hardly be too much stressed. People were drawn together by occasions such as horse races, cockfights, and dancing as by no other, because here men would become "known" to each other—"known" in the ways which the culture defined as "real." Skill and daring in that violent duel, the "quarter race"; coolness in the "deep play" of the betting that necessarily went with racing, cockfighting, and cards—these were means whereby Virginia males could prove themselves. Conviviality was an essential part of the social exchange, but through its soft coating pressed a harder structure of contest, or "emulation" as the contemporary phrase had it. Even in dancing this was so. Observers noted not only the passion for dancing—"*Virginians* are of genuine Blood—They will dance or die!"—but also the marked preference for the jig—in effect solo performances by partners of each sex, which were closely watched and were evidently competitive. In such activities, in social contexts high or low, enhanced eligibility for marriage was established by young persons who emerged as virtuosos of the dominant style. Situations where so much could happen presented powerful images of the "good life" to traditional Virginians, especially young ones. It was probably true, as alleged, that religious piety was generally considered appropriate only for the aged.

When one turns to the social world of the Baptists, the picture that emerges is so striking a negative of the one that has just been sketched that it must be considered to have been structured to an important extent by processes of reaction to the dominant culture.

Contemporaries were struck by the contrast between the challenging gaiety of traditional Virginia formal exchange and the solemn fellowship of the Baptists, who addressed each other as "Brother" and "Sister" and were perceived as "the most melancholy people in the world"—people who "cannot meet a man upon the road, but they must ram a text of Scripture down his throat." The finery of a gentleman who might ride forth in a gold-laced hat, sporting a gleaming Masonic medal, must be contrasted with the strict dress of the Separate Baptist, his hair "cut off" and such "superfluous forms and Modes of Dressing . . . as cock't hatts" explicitly renounced.

Their appearance was austere, to be sure, but we shall not understand the deep appeal of the evangelical movement, or the nature and full extent of its challenging contrast to the style and vision of the gentry-oriented social world, unless we look into the rich offerings beneath this somber exterior. The converts were proffered some escape from the harsh realities of disease, debt, overindulgence and deprivation, violence and sudden death, which were the common lot of small farmers. They could seek refuge in a close, supportive, orderly community, "a congregation of faithful persons, called out of the world by divine grace, who mutually agreed to live together, and execute gospel discipline among them." Entrance into this community was attained by the relation of a personal experience of profound importance to the candidates, who would certainly be heard with respect, however humble their station. There was a community resonance for deep feelings, since, despite their sober face to the outside world, the Baptists encouraged in their religious practice a sharing of emotion to an extent far beyond that which would elicit crushing ridicule in gentry-oriented society. Personal testimonies of the experiences of simple folk have not come down to us from that time, but the central importance of the ritual of admission and its role in renewing the common experience of ecstatic conversion is powerfully evoked by such recurrent phrases in the church books as "and a dore was opened to experience." This search for deep fellow-feeling must be set in contrast to the formal distance and rivalry in the social exchanges of the traditional system.

The warm supportive relationship that fellowship in faith and experience could engender appears to have played an important part in the spread of the movement. For example, about the year 1760 Peter Cornwell of Fauquier County sought out in the backcountry one Hays of pious repute, and settled him on his own land for the sake of godly companionship. "Interviews between these two families were frequent . . . their conversation religious . . . in so much that it began to be talked of abroad as a very strange thing. Many came to see them, to whom they related what God did for their souls . . . to the spreading of seriousness through the whole neighbourhood."

A concomitant of fellowship in deep emotions was comparative equality. Democracy is an ideal, and there are no indications that the pre-Revolutionary Baptists espoused it as such, yet there can be no doubt that these men, calling each other brothers, who believed that the only authority in their church was the meeting of those in fellowship together, conducted their affairs on a footing of equality in sharp contrast to the explicit preoccupation with rank and precedence that characterized the world from which they had been called. Important Baptist church elections generally required unanimity and might be held up by the doubts of a few. The number of preachers who were raised from obscurity to play an epic role in the Virginia of their day is a clear indication of the opportunities for fulfillment that the movement opened up to men who would have found no other avenue for public achievement. There is no reason to doubt the contemporary reputation of the early Virginia Baptist movement as one of the poor and unlearned. Only isolated converts were made among the gentry, but many among the slaves.

The tight cohesive brotherhood of the Baptists must be understood as an explicit rejection of the formalism of traditional community organization. The antithesis is apparent in the contrast between Fithian's account of a parish congregation that dispersed without any act of worship when a storm prevented the attendance of both parson and clerk, and the report of the Baptist David Thomas that "when no minister . . . is expected, our people meet notwithstanding; and spend . . . time in praying, singing, reading, and in religious conversation."

The popular style and appeal of the Baptist Church found its most powerful and visible expression in the richness of its rituals, again a total contrast to the "prayrs read over in haste" of the colonial Church of England, where even congregational singing appears to have been a rarity. The most prominent and moving rite practiced by the sect was adult baptism, in which the candidates were publicly sealed into fellowship. A scrap of Daniel Fristoe's journal for June 15–16, 1771, survives as a unique contemporary description by a participant:

(Being sunday) about 2000 people came together; after preaching [I] heard others that proposed to be baptized. . . . Then went to the water where I preached and baptized 29 persons. . . . When I had finished we went to a field and making a circle in the center, there laid hands on the persons baptized. The multitude stood round weeping, but when we sang *Come we that love the lord* and they were so affected that they lifted up their hands and faces towards heaven and discovered such chearful countenances in the midst of flowing tears as I had never seen before.

The warm emotional appeal at a popular level can even now be felt in that account, but it must be noted that the scene was also a vivid enactment of *a* community within and apart from *the* community. We must try to see that closed circle for the laying on of the hands through the eyes of those who had been raised in Tidewater or Piedmont Virginia with the expectation that they would always have a monistic parish community encompassing all the inhabitants within its measured liturgical celebrations. The antagonism and violence that the Baptists aroused then also become intelligible.

The celebration of the Lord's Supper frequently followed baptism, in which circumstances it was a further open enactment of closed community. We have some idea of the importance attached to this public display from David Thomas's justification:

. . . should we forbid even the worst of men, from viewing the solemn representation of his [the LORD JESUS CHRIST's] dying agonies? May not

the sight of this mournful tragedy, have a tendency to alarm stupid creatures . . . when GOD himself is held forth . . . trembling, falling,
bleeding, yea, expiring under the intollerable pressure of that wrath due
to [sin]. . . . And therefore, this ordinance should not be put under a
bushel, but on a candlestick, that all may enjoy the illumination.

We may see the potency attributed to the ordinances starkly through
the eyes of the abashed young John Taylor who, hanging back from
baptism, heard the professions of seven candidates surreptitiously,
judged them not saved, and then watched them go "into the water,
and from thence, as I thought, seal their own damnation at the Lord's
table. I left the meeting with awful horror of mind."

More intimate, yet evidently important for the close community,
were the rites of fellowship. The forms are elusive, but an abundance
of ritual is suggested by the simple entry of Morgan Edwards concerning Falls Creek: "In this church are admitted, Evangelists, Ruling Elders, deaconesses, laying on of hands, feasts of charity, anoint-
ing the sick, kiss of charity, washing feet, right hand of fellowship,
and devoting children." Far from being mere formal observances,
these and other rites, such as the ordaining of "apostles" to "pervade"
the churches, were keenly experimented with to determine their efficacy.

Aspects of preaching also ought to be understood as ritual rather
than as formal instruction. It was common for persons to come under
conviction or to obtain ecstatic release "under preaching," and this
established a special relationship between the neophyte and his or
her "father in the gospel." Nowhere was the ritual character of the
preaching more apparent than in the great meetings of the Virginia
Separate Baptist Association. The messengers would preach to the
people along the way to the meeting place and back; thousands
would gather for the Sunday specially set aside for worship and
preaching. There the close independent congregational communities
found themselves merged in a great and swelling collective. The
varieties of physical manifestations such as crying out and falling
down, which were frequently brought on by the ritualized emotional-
ism of such preaching, are too well known to require description.

Virginia Baptist sermons from the 1770s have not survived, perhaps
another indication that their purely verbal content was not considered of the first importance. Ireland's account of his early ministry
(he was ordained in 1769) reveals the ritual recurrence of the dominant themes expected to lead into repentance those who were not
hardened: "I began first to preach . . . our awful apostasy by the
fall; the necessity of repentance unto life, and of faith in the Lord

Jesus Christ . . . our helpless incapacity to extricate ourselves there-from I stated and urged."

As "seriousness" spread, with fear of hell-fire and concern for salvation, it was small wonder that a gentleman of Loudoun County should find to his alarm "that the *Anabaptists* . . . growing very numerous . . . seem to be increasing in affluence [influence?]; and . . . quite destroying pleasure in the Country; for they encourage ardent Pray'r; strong and constant faith, and an intire Banishment of *Gaming, Dancing,* and Sabbath-Day Diversions." That the Baptists were drawing away increasing numbers from the dominant to the insurgent culture was radical enough, but the implications of solemnity, austerity, and stern sobriety were more radical still, for they called into question the validity—indeed the propriety—of the occasions and modes of display and association so important in maintaining the bonds of Virginia's geographically diffuse society. Against the system in which proud men were joined in rivalry and convivial excess was set a reproachful model of an order in which God-humbled men would seek a deep sharing of emotion while repudiating indulgence of the flesh. Yet the Baptist movement, although it must be understood as a revolt against the traditional system, was not primarily negative. Behind it can be discerned an impulse toward a tighter, more effective system of values and of exemplary conduct to be established and maintained within the ranks of the common folk.

In this aspect evangelicalism must be seen as a popular response to mounting social disorder. It would be difficult—perhaps even impossible—to establish an objective scale for measuring disorder in Virginia. What can be established is that during the 1760s and 1770s disorder was perceived by many as increasing. This has been argued for the gentry by Jack P. Greene and Gordon S. Wood, and need not be elaborated here. What does need to be re-emphasized is that the gentry's growing perception of disorder was focused on those forms of activity which the Baptists denounced and which provided the main arenas for the challenge and response essential to the traditional "good life." It was coming to be felt that horse racing, cockfighting, and card play, with their concomitants of gambling and drinking, rather than serving to maintain the gentry's prowess, were destructive of it and of social order generally. Display might now be negatively perceived as "luxury."

Given the absence of the restraints imposed by tight village community in traditional Virginia, disorder was probably an even more acute problem in the lower than in the upper echelons of society—more acute because it was compounded by the harshness and brutality of everyday life, and most acute in the proportion to the social proximity of the lowest stratum, the enslaved. The last named sector of society, lacking sanctioned marriage and legitimated familial authority, was certainly disorderly by English Protestant standards, and must therefore have had a disturbing effect on the consciousness of the whole community.

As the conversion experience was at the heart of the popular evangelical movement, so a sense of a great burden of guilt was at the heart of the conversion experience. An explanation in terms of social process must be sought for the sudden widespread intensification and vocal expression of such feelings, especially when this is found in areas of the Virginia Piedmont and Tidewater where no cultural tradition existed as preconditioning for the communal confession, remorse, and expiation that characterized the spread of the Baptist movement. The hypothesis here advanced is that the social process was one in which popular perceptions of disorder in society—and hence by individuals in themselves—came to be expressed in the metaphor of "sin." It is clear that the movement was largely spread by revolt from within, not by "agitators" from without. Commonly the first visit of itinerant preachers to a neighborhood was made by invitation of a group of penitents already formed and actively meeting together. Thus the "spread of seriousness" and alarm at the sinful disorder of the traditional world tended to precede the creation of an emotional mass movement "under preaching." A further indication of the importance of order-disorder preoccupations for the spread of the new vision with its contrasted life style was the insistence on "works." Conversion could ultimately be validated among church members only by a radical reform of conduct. The Baptist church books reveal the close concern for the disciplinary supervision of such changes.

Drunkenness was a persistent problem in Virginia society. There were frequent cases in the Baptist records where censure, ritual excommunication, and moving penitence were unable to effect a lasting cure. Quarreling, slandering, and disputes over property were other endemic disorders that the churches sought patiently and endlessly to control within their own communities. With its base in slavery, this was a society in which contest readily turned into disorderly violence. Accounts of the occasion, manner, and frequency of wrestling furnish a horrifying testimony to the effects of combining a code of honor with the coarseness of life in the lower echelons of society. Hearing that "by appointment is to be fought this Day . . . two fist Battles between four young Fellows," Fithian noted the common causes of such conflicts, listing numbers of trivial affronts such as that one "has in a merry hour call'd [another] a *Lubber*, . . . or a *Buckskin*, or a *Scotchman*, . . . or offered him a dram without wiping the mouth of the Bottle." He noted also the savagery of the fighting, including "Kicking, Scratching, Biting, . . . Throtling, Gouging [the eyes], Dismembring [the private parts]. . . . This spectacle . . . generally is attended with a crowd of People!" Such practices prevailed throughout the province. An episode in the life of one of the great Baptist preachers, John, formerly "swearing Jack," Waller, illustrates both prevailing violence and something of the relationship between classes. Waller and some gentry companions were riding on the road when a drunken butcher addressed them in a manner they considered insolent. One of the gentlemen had a horse trained to rear and "paw what was before him," which he then had it do to frighten the butcher. The man was struck by the hooves and died soon after. Tried for manslaughter, the company of gentlemen were acquitted on a doubt as to whether the injury had indeed caused the butcher's death. The episode may have helped prepare Waller for conversion into a radically opposed social world.

Nowhere does the radicalism of the evangelical reaction to the dominant values of self-assertion, challenge, and response of the gentry-oriented society reveal itself so clearly as in the treatment of physical aggression. In the Baptist community a man might come forward by way of confession with an accusation against himself for "Geting angry Tho in Just Defence of himself in Despute." The meeting of another church was informed that its clerk, Rawley Hazard, had been approached on his own land and addressed in "Very scurrilous language" and then assaulted, and that he then "did defend himself against this sd Violence, that both the Assailant and Defendent was much hurt." The members voted that the minister "do Admonish Brother Rawley . . . in the presents of the Church . . . saying that his defence was Irregular."

A further mark of their radicalism, and without doubt the most significant aspect of the quest for a system of social control centered in the people, was the inclusion of slaves as "brothers" and "sisters" in their close community. When the Baptists sealed the slaves unto eternal life, leading them in white robes into the water and then back to receive the bread and wine, they were also laying upon them responsibility for godly conduct, demanding an internalization of strict Protestant Christian values and norms. They were seeking to create an orderly moral community where hitherto there had seemed to be none.

The slaves were members and therefore subject to church discipline. The incidence of excommunication of slaves, especially for the sin of adultery, points to the desire of the Baptists to introduce their own standards of conduct, including stable marital relationships, among slaves. A revealing indication of the perception of the problem in this area is found in the recurrent phrase that was sometimes given as the sole reason for excommunication: "walking disorderly." Discipline was also clearly directed toward inculcating a sense of duty in the slaves, who could be excommunicated for "disobedience and Aggrevation to [a] master."

The recurrent use of the words "order," "orderly," "disorderly" in the Baptist records reveals a preoccupation that lends further support to the hypothesis that concern for the establishment of a securer system of social control was a powerful impulse for the movement. "Is it orderly?" is the usual introduction to the queries concerning right conduct that were frequently brought forward for resolution at monthly meetings.

With alarm at perceived disorder must also be associated the deep concern for Sabbath-day observance that is so strongly manifested in autobiographies, apologetics, and church books. It appears that the Virginia method of keeping the Sabbath "with sport, merriment, and dissipation" readily served to symbolize the disorder perceived in society. It was his observation of this that gave Ireland his first recorded shock. Conversely, cosmic order was affirmed and held up as a model for society in the setting aside on the Lord's Day of worldly pursuits, while men expressed their reverence for their Maker and Redeemer.

When the Baptist movement is understood as a rejection of the style of life for which the gentry set the pattern and as a search for more powerful popular models of proper conduct, it can be seen why the ground on which the battle was mainly fought was not the estate or the great house, but the neighborhood, the farmstead, and the slave quarter. This was a contemporary perception, for it was generally charged that the Baptists were "continual fomenters of discord" who "not only divided good neighbours, but slaves and their masters; children and their parents . . . wives and their husbands." The only reported complaint against the first preachers to be imprisoned was of "their running into private houses and making dissensions." The struggle for allegiance in the homesteads between a style of life modeled on that of the leisured gentry and that embodied in evangelicalism was intense. In humbler, more straitened circumstances a popular culture based on the code of honor and almost hedonist values was necessarily less securely established than among the more affluent gentry. Hence the anxious aggressiveness of popular anti-New Light feeling and action.

The Baptists did not make a bid for control of the political system —still less did they seek a leveling or redistribution of worldly wealth. It was clearly a mark of the strength of gentry hegemony and of the rigidities of a social hierarchy with slavery at its base that the evangelical revolt should have been closely restricted in scope. Yet the Baptists' salvationism and sabbatarianism effectively redefined morality and human relationships; their church leaders and organization established new and more popular foci of authority, and sought to impose a radically different and more inclusive model for the maintenance of order in society. Within the context of the traditional monistic, face-to-face, deferential society such a regrouping necessarily constituted a powerful challenge.

The beginnings of a cultural disjunction between gentry and sections of the lower orders, where hitherto there had been a continuum, posed a serious threat to the traditional leaders of the community; their response was characteristic. The popular emotional style, the encouragement given to men of little learning to "exercise their gifts" in preaching, and the preponderance of humble folk in the movement gave to the proud gentry their readiest defense—contempt and ridicule. The stereotype of the Baptists as "an ignorant . . . set . . . of . . . the contemptible class of the people," a "poor and illiterate sect" which "none of the rich or learned ever join," became generally established. References in the *Virginia Gazette* to "ignorant enthusiasts" were common, and there could appear in its columns without challenge a heartless satire detailing "A Receipt to make an Anabaptist Preacher": "Take the Herbes of Hypocrisy and Ambition, . . . of the Seed of Dissention and Discord one Ounce, . . . one Pint of the Spirit of Self-Conceitedness."

An encounter with some gentlemen at an inn in Goochland County is recorded by Morgan Edwards, a college-educated Pennsylvania Baptist minister. He noted the moderation of the gentry in this area, yet their arrogant scorn for dissenters in general, and for Baptists in particular, is unmistakable from the dialogue reported. Since Edwards had just come from Georgia, they began with ribald jests about "mr Whitefield's children . . . by the squaw" and continued as follows:

Esq[uire] U: Pray are you not a clergyman? . . .
Capt. L: Of the church of England I presume?
N[orthern] M[inister]: No, Sir; I am a clergyman of a better church than that; for she is a persecutor.

Omnes: Ha! Ha! Ha! . . .

Esq. U: Then you are one of the fleabitten clergy?

N.M.:   Are there fleas in this bed, Sir?

Esq. U: I ask, if you are a clergyman of the itchy true blue kirk of Scotland? . . .

Capt. L. (whispers):   He is ashamed to own her for fear you should scratch him 'Squire.' . . .

[When they have discovered that this educated man, who shows such address in fencing with words, is a Baptist minister, they discuss the subject bibulously among themselves.]

Esq. U: He is no baptist . . . I take him to be one of the Georgia law[ye]rs.

Mr. G: For my part I believe him to be a baptist minister. There are some clever fellows among them. . . .

Major W: I confess they have often confounded me with their arguments and texts of Scripture; and if any other people but the baptists professed their religion I would make it my religion before tomorrow.

The class of folk who filled the Baptist churches were a great obstacle to gentry participation. Behind the ridicule and contempt, of course, lay incomprehension, and behind that, fear of this menacing, unintelligible movement. The only firsthand account we have of a meeting broken up by the arrest of the preachers tells how they "were carried before the magistrate," who had them taken "one by one into a room and examined our pockets and wallets for firearms." He accused them of "carrying on a mutiny against the authority of the land." This sort of dark suspicion impelled David Thomas, in his printed defense of the Baptists, to reiterate several times that "We concern not ourselves with the government . . . we form no intrigues . . . nor make any attempts to alter the constitution of the kingdom to which as men we belong."

Fear breeds fantasy. So it was that alarmed observers put a very crude interpretation on the emotional and even physical intimacy of this intrusive new society. Its members were associated with German Anabaptists, and a "historical" account of the erotic indulgences of that sect was published on the front page of the *Virginia Gazette*.

Driven by uneasiness, although toughened by their instinctive contempt, some members of the establishment made direct moves to assert proper social authority and to outface the upstarts. Denunciations from parish pulpits were frequent. Debates were not uncommon, being sought on both sides. Ireland recalled vividly an encounter that reveals the pride and presumption of the gentlemen who came forward in defense of the Church of England. Captain M'Clanagan's place was thronged with people, some of whom had come forty miles to hear John Pickett, a Baptist preacher of Fauquier County. The rector of a neighboring parish attended with some leading parishioners "who were as much prejudiced . . . as he was." "The parson had a chair brought for himself, which he placed three or four yards in front of Mr. Pickett . . . taking out his pen, ink and paper, to take down notes of what he conceived to be false doctrine." When Pickett had finished, "the Parson called him a schismatick, a broacher of false doctrines . . . [who] held up damnable errors that day." Pickett answered adequately (it appeared to Ireland), but "when contradicted it would in a measure confuse him." So Ireland, who had been raised a gentleman, took it on himself to sustain the Baptist cause. The parson immediately "wheeled about on his chair . . . and let out a broadside of his eloquence, with an expectation, no doubt, that he would confound me with the first fire." However, Ireland "gently laid hold of a chair, and placed . . . it close by him, determined to argue." The contest was long, and "both gentlemen and ladies," who had evidently seated themselves near the parson, "would repeatedly help him to scripture, in order to support his arguments." When the debate ended (as the narrator recalled) in the refutation of the clergyman, Ireland "addressed one of the gentlemen who had been so officious in helping his teacher; he was a magistrate . . . 'Sir, as the dispute between the Parson and myself is ended, if you are disposed to argue the subject over again, I am willing to enter upon it with you.' He stretched out his arm straight before him, at that instant, and declared that I should not come nigher than that length." Ireland "concluded what the consequence would be, therefore made a peaceable retreat." Such scenes of action are the stuff of social structure, as of social conflict, and require no further comment.

Great popular movements are not quelled, however, by outfacing, nor are they stemmed by the ridicule, scorn, or scurrility of incomprehension. Moreover, they draw into themselves members of all sections of society. Although the social worlds most open to proselytizing by the Baptists were the neighborhoods and the slave quarters, there were converts from the great houses too. Some of the defectors, such as Samuel Harris, played a leading role in the movement. The squirearchy was disturbed by the realization that the contemptible sect was reaching among themselves. The exchanges between Morgan Edwards and the gentlemen in the Goochland inn were confused by the breakdown of the stereotype of ignorance and poverty. Edwards's cultured facility reminded the squires that "there are some clever fellows among [the Baptists]. I heard one Jery Walker support a petition of theirs at the assembly in such a manner as surprised us all, and

[made] our witts draw in their horns." The pride and assurance of the gentry could be engaged by awareness that their own members might withdraw from their ranks and choose the other way. The vigorous response of Ireland's patron to the challenge implicit in his defection provides a striking example.

The intensity of the conflict for allegiance among the people and, increasingly, among the gentry, makes intelligible the growing frequency of violent clashes of the kind illustrated at the beginning of this article. The violence was, however, one-sided and self-defeating. The episode of April 1771 in which the parson brutally interfered with the devotions of the preacher, who was then horsewhipped by the sheriff, must have produced a shock of revulsion in many quarters. Those who engaged in such actions were not typical of either the Anglican clergy or the country gentlemen. The extreme responses of some, however, show the anxieties to which all were subject, and the excesses in question could only heighten the tension.

Disquiet was further exacerbated by the fact that the law governing dissent, under which the repressive county benches were intent on acting, was of doubtful validity, and became the subject of public controversy in the fall of 1771. This controversy, combined with the appalling scenes of disorder and the growing numbers of Separate Baptists, led the House of Burgesses to attempt action in its spring 1772 session. The Separates had shown renewed tendencies to intransigence as recently as May 1771, when a move was strongly supported to deny fellowship to all ministers who submitted to the secular authority by applying for permission to preach. The fact that eight months later the House of Burgesses received a petition for easier licensing conditions was a sign that a compromise was at last being sought. Nevertheless, prejudices were so strong that the bill that the Burgesses approved was considerably more restrictive than the English act that had hitherto been deemed law in the colony.

The crisis of self-confidence which the evangelical challenges and the failure of forceful responses were inducing in the Virginia gentry was subtly revealed in March 1772 by the unprecedented decision of the House, ordinarily assertive of its authority, not to send the engrossed bill to the Council, but to have it printed and referred to the public for discussion. Nearly two years later, in January 1774, the young James Madison, exultant about the progress of the American cause in the aftermath of the Boston Tea Party, despaired of Virginia on account of religious intolerance. He wrote that he had "nothing to brag of as to the State and Liberty" of his "Country," where "Poverty and Luxury prevail among all sorts" and "that diabolical Hell conceived principle of persecution rages." In April of the same year he still had little hope that a bill would pass to ease the situation of dissenters. In the previous session "such incredible and extravagant stories" had been "told in the House of the monstrous effects of the Enthusiasm prevalent among the Sectaries and so greedily swallowed by their Enemies that . . . they lost footing by it." Burgesses "who pretend too much contempt to examine into their principles . . . and are too much devoted to the ecclesiastical establishment to hear of the Toleration of Dissentients" were likely to prevail once again. Madison's foreboding was correct inasmuch as the old regime in Virginia never accomplished a legal resolution of the toleration problem.

The Revolution ultimately enshrined religious pluralism as a fundamental principle in Virginia. It rendered illegitimate the assumptions concerning the nature of community religious corporateness that underlay aggressive defense against the Baptists. It legitimated new forms of conflict, so that by the end of the century the popular evangelists were able to counterattack and symbolize social revolution in many localities by having the Episcopal Church's lands and even communion plate sold at auction. But to seek the conclusion to this study in such political-constitutional developments would be a deflection, for it has focused on a brief period of intense, yet deadlocked conflict in order to search out the social-cultural configurations of the forces that confronted each other. The diametrical opposition of the swelling Baptist movement to traditional mores shows it to have been indeed a radical social revolt, indicative of real strains within society.

Challenging questions remain. Can some of the appeal of the Revolution's republican ideology be understood in terms of its capacity to command the allegiance of both self-humbled evangelicals and honor-upholding gentry? What different meanings did the republican ideology assume within the mutually opposed systems of values and belief? And, looking forward to the post-Revolutionary period, what was the configuration—what the balance between antagonistic cultural elements—when confrontation within a monistic framework had given way to accommodation in a more pluralist republican society? These questions are closely related to the subject that this study has endeavored to illuminate—the forms and sources of popular culture in Virginia, and the relationship of popular culture to that of the gentry elite.